PSYCHOLOGICAL
TECHNIQUES
FOR TEACHERS

PSYCHOLOGICAL TECHNIQUES FOR TEACHERS
Second Edition

Don C. Locke, Ed.D.

Professor and Director
North Carolina State University—
Doctoral Program in Adult and Community College Education
University of North Carolina Asheville Graduate Center
Asheville, North Carolina

Joseph C. Ciechalski, Ed.D.

Associate Professor
Department of Counselor and Adult Education
East Carolina University
Greenville, North Carolina

ACCELERATED DEVELOPMENT
A member of the Taylor & Francis Group

USA	Publishing Office:	ACCELERATED DEVELOPMENT
		A member of the Taylor & Francis Group
		1101 Vermont Avenue, N.W., Suite 200
		Washington, D.C. 20005-3521
		Tel: (202) 289-2174
		Fax: (202) 289-3665
	Distribution Center:	ACCELERATED DEVELOPMENT
		A member of the Taylor & Francis Group
		1900 Frost Road, Suite 101
		Bristol, PA 19007-1598
		Tel: (215) 785-5800
		Fax: (215) 785-5515
UK		Taylor & Francis, Ltd.
		4 John St.
		London WC1N 2ET
		Tel: 071 405 2237
		Fax: 071 831 2035

PSYCHOLOGICAL TECHNIQUES FOR TEACHERS, Second Edition

1 2 3 4 5 6 7 8 9 0   B R B R   0 9 8 7 6 5

This book was set in Times Roman by Sandra F. Watts. Technical development and editing by Cynthia Long; additional editing by Alice S. M. Rowan. Prepress supervisor was Miriam Gonzalez. Cover design by Michelle Fleitz. Printing and binding by Braun-Brumfield, Inc.

A CIP catalog record for this book is available from the British Library.
 ⊚ The paper in this publication meets the requirements of the ANSI Standard Z39.48-1984 (Permanence of Paper).

Library of Congress Cataloging-in-Publication Data

Locke, Don C.
    Psychological techniques for teachers / Don C. Locke, Joseph C.
Ciechalski.—2nd ed.
        p. cm.
    Includes bibliographical references and index.
    1. Educational psychology. 2. Teaching. I. Ciechalski, Joseph C. II. Title.
LB1051.L765 1995
370.15-dc20   95-10447
                                                                                    CIP

ISBN 1-56032-388-4 (case)
ISBN 1-56032-389-2 (paper)

To our parents:

Willie and Carlene
and
Charles and Olga

TABLE OF CONTENTS

UNIT I
BASIC MODELS AND TECHNIQUES
FOR TEACHERS

UNIT II
IMPROVING SELF-CONCEPT
AND RELATIONSHIPS

UNIT III
WORKING WITH GROUPS

UNIT IV
ENCOUNTERING PROBLEMS

UNIT V
GATHERING CAREER
AND EDUCATIONAL INFORMATION

CHAPTER 10
CAREER DEVELOPMENT   197

CHAPTER 11
OCCUPATIONAL, CAREER, AND EDUCATIONAL
INFORMATION   219

UNIT V I
OBTAINING AND USING
TEST AND NON-TEST DATA

CHAPTER 12
APPLYING STATISTICAL CONCEPTS TO TEST DATA   241

LIST OF FIGURES

LIST OF TABLES

PREFACE

The purpose of this book has not changed since the writing of the first edition: to emphasize the application of counseling, guidance, and counseling psychology principles in the classroom. The book is designed to enable teachers to become more aware of the academic and personal needs of their students. Techniques pertinent to teachers will be presented as thoroughly as is possible within a single book. Reading and understanding the material will provide teachers with a foundation on which to build effective teaching practices.

No book, including this one, is a panacea for all problems and situations that may arise in a classroom. This book also is not a substitute for seeking help and assistance from school counselors. School counselors are an excellent resource for teachers confronted with students' problems. Teachers are urged to consult with their school counselor when the need presents itself.

The authors wish to express their sincere gratitude to the many students and instructors who have used the first edition of the book. Many of the errors contained in the first edition have been eliminated. Additional exercises and activities have been included. In addition, readers of the first edition will note that this edition has been arranged into 6 units and that the 14 chapters in the first edition have been rearranged to enhance continuity.

The authors hope that you become the most meaningful and positive person in each of your students' lives.

Don C. Locke, Ed.D.
Joseph C. Ciechalski, Ed.D.
January 1995

PREFACE TO THE FIRST EDITION

The primary purpose of this book is to emphasize the application of counseling, guidance, and counseling psychology principles in the classroom. Whether a pre-service or in-service teacher, this book will help you to be a better teacher. Your background in education will be enriched through an exposure to a variety of problems and the application of counseling, guidance, and psychological principles to the solution of those problems. You will develop a greater appreciation and understanding of children while improving your ability to teach them. The material in the book has been arranged in fourteen chapters which can be adapted to either a semester or a quarter course. The material is organized so that a chapter may be used independently without having to read preliminary material.

The fundamental belief of the authors, elaborated in every chapter, is that teachers have a major role in the total psychological climate within a school. We have chosen to illustrate how teachers may be successful as human relations persons while incorporating psychological techniques into regular classroom activities. We begin from the assumption that every child is a spark or an ember and can become a flame. The teacher is the one who can and hopefully will kindle that spark. That is to say, the essence of the educative process is to involve students to the extent that they will change in desirable ways as they learn academic material. The curriculum must be conceived as the means by which students achieve social and emotional roles and adjustments.

A teacher must know each student individually, much more than their test scores, social class, or economic status. An empathic understanding will encourage maximum growth of every student. Students who perceive teachers as interested in them will likely respond by showing interest in classroom activities. This book will help you communicate to each student that he or she is important, special, and worthy. In doing so you may become the most meaningful and positive person in each of your student's lives.

Don C. Locke, Ed.D.
Joseph C. Ciechalski, Ed.D.
January 1985

ACKNOWLEDGMENTS

Many people have contributed either directly or indirectly to the development of this book. We received support from North Carolina State University Dean Carl J. Dolce and Counselor Education Department Head William Hopke for the initial idea and the writing of the first edition.

We wish to extend our appreciation to a number of individuals and organizations for support of the second edition. Both our deans, Joan J. Michael at North Carolina State University and Charles Coble at East Carolina University, have encouraged our professional efforts, and we are grateful for their support. A number of students and colleagues at both institutions have helped us sharpen our focus, and we are grateful for their assistance. Library personnel at North Carolina State University, East Carolina University, and The University of North Carolina at Asheville have been extremely helpful in locating information. Cindy Long and Joe Hollis at Accelerated Development have been most helpful as we moved this book through the publishing process. We acknowledge their contributions and express our appreciation for their efforts.

Our families, especially Marjorie and Olga, provided consistent moral support for this project. To each of you we say "thank you."

Don C. Locke
Joseph C. Ciechalski

Chapter 1

INTRODUCTION

Teachers are expected to teach the whole child. This means that in addition to teaching a subject, teachers need to have a basic understanding of the developmental, social, emotional, personal, and career concerns of their students. Students cannot learn while they are encountering problems. For example, the following situations may hinder learning:

A student appears tense and upset. After class the teacher asks the student if something is wrong. The student tells the teacher that something the student had said privately had been overheard, repeated, and misinterpreted. As a result, false rumors had been started. She is very upset.

A high school student approaches you during lunch and tells you that he would like to talk to you. He tells you that his girlfriend has just "dumped" him and that he does not know how to handle it or what, if anything, to do.

You have a student who has always obtained A's and B's on his tests and class work. However, during the past three weeks, you note that he has not handed in any assignments and has failed three tests. When you ask him if anything is wrong, he informs you he recently found out that his parents are getting a divorce. He doesn't know if he will be living with his mother or his father. In addition, he fears that he may be moving away.

A student is habitually absent from school. Her mother frequently comes to get her out early to run errands. She is dangerously close to failing because of the school's policy on absences.

A student is having problems choosing a college. His parents want him to attend the college they attended. He would rather attend another that specializes in engineering. He doesn't know what to do.

As the above situations illustrate, the problems that students encounter may be academic, social, or personal. Teachers usually do not have a problem dealing with the academic needs of their students. Skills for dealing with the academic needs of students are emphasized in teacher education programs. However, many teachers often lack the skills needed to address their students' personal and social problems. Unfortunately, these skills either were not included or were not emphasized in their teacher education programs. Within the last few years, a number of colleges and universities have initiated undergraduate, interpersonal relationship courses for teacher education candidates. In addition, some teacher education programs are requiring teacher candidates to complete at least one counseling skills course.

To deal with the personal and social needs of their students, teachers must be able to develop positive relationships. Relationships between students and teachers succeed in part because of positive interactions—interactions that can be strengthened by understanding and utilizing communication techniques. Therefore, communication techniques that teachers may easily use are included in Chapter 3.

WHAT IS GUIDANCE?

When one of the authors attended public school, the school did not have a counselor. His social studies teacher was also his homeroom teacher and his guidance instructor. Every Monday morning, the homeroom period was reserved for guidance. The teacher said that this period was designed to help us understand ourselves better. During the guidance period, we discussed health, rest, budgeting time, getting along with others, how to study, how to plan for our future, and what to do if we had a problem. We were expected to listen to the teacher, and no grade was given for guidance.

Although *guidance* is considered an outdated term, guidance and teaching are similar. For the most part, they are cognitively structured activities. Both a teacher in a math class and a counselor discussing study skills to a group of students are working toward stated outcomes and have clearly defined goals and objectives. The study skills could also be taught by the classroom teacher.

Teaching and guidance activities are group oriented and may involve some or all members of the group. In addition, teaching and guidance are demanding, because they require that a given amount of material be covered during the period.

Guidance activities do not provide answers, rather, they permit each student to resolve conflict by providing the necessary information and a climate for change. They place emphasis on the dignity and worth of each individual without any manipulation. To resolve a conflict, a student must first understand himself or herself. This self-discovery may involve understanding his or her strengths and weaknesses, likes and dislikes, and place in the real world.

Teachers can provide various guidance activities for their students; however, most teachers are not trained to counsel their students. School counselors are trained to counsel. While counseling is one of the functions of guidance, in-depth counseling is an area reserved for the certified or licensed school counselor.

WHAT IS COUNSELING?

In a statement entitled "What is Counseling?" published by the American Personnel and Guidance Association (1981)—currently the American Counseling Association (ACA)—counseling is defined as

> the art of helping people. Professional counselors are individuals trained to share knowledge and skills with those who need help. Counseling recognizes that all persons need help as they routinely pass through childhood, adolescence, and adulthood. Effective counseling is preventive. Counselors help persons with their personal, social, career, and educational development. Counselors serve people through schools, colleges, community agencies, and private practice. (p. 1)

Counseling is an interactive process between a helper and one or more helpees. As a process, counseling is less structured than guidance or teaching. Counselors have a master's degree which may include courses in counseling theories, assessment, career information, interaction skills, multicultural counseling, and practicums and internships. In addition, courses in psychology and sociology may be required. School counselors are certified by their state and/or other accrediting agency.

THE EFFECTIVE TEACHER

The teacher is one of the more important professionals in a school. A teacher has daily contact with all the students in his or her classes. Although a teacher's primary responsibility is to educate students, he or she is usually the first person to recognize students' problems and unique abilities. An effective teacher has many of the same characteristics as an effective counselor.

Characteristics of the Effective Teacher

An effective teacher is usually *friendly* and, consequently, popular with students. Students are more likely to accept a teacher who has a smile for everyone and appears to enjoy teaching. This friendly behavior often inspires students to seek out the teacher after class to discuss personal concerns and problems.

Another characteristic of an effective teacher is *patience*. A teacher who is patient usually understands that his or her classes include students who are at different learning levels. The patient teacher furnishes students with a positive learning environment. A positive environment provides students with an opportunity to inquire about and explore personal problems and concerns. *Answers to problems are not as important as the means of arriving at answers.*

The third characteristic of an effective teacher is *understanding*. Understanding means that a teacher is aware of his or her students' abilities, interests, and aptitudes. An effective teacher understands that students are not all alike. They come from different cultural and ethnic backgrounds. Because students are individuals with individual needs, an effective teacher knows that by understanding students' present needs, he or she can prepare them for tomorrow. An effective teacher knows what to expect from students and how to help them reach their maximum potential.

THE TEACHER'S ROLE

The teacher's primary role in counseling is a supportive one. A teacher supports a school's counseling program by taking on the following roles:

The Teacher's Role as Communicator

The key to developing harmonious relationships is learning to use communication techniques. Communication techniques include listening, reflection, clarification, questioning, interpretation, and reinforcement. A teacher who is aware of and uses these techniques effectively soon discovers that she or he has fewer discipline problems.

A teacher, for example, who listens attentively and is nonjudgmental may help a student resolve a problem by discussing various alternatives with the student. By exploring a variety of options, the teacher permits the student to work out a solution in an objective and nonjudgmental manner.

Communication techniques (listening, reflection, clarification, etc.) as well as the Rogerian terms *empathy, genuineness,* and *unconditional positive regard* are covered in more detail in Chapter 3.

The Teacher's Role with Groups

Working with groups is not new to teachers. A teacher spends a great deal of time teaching groups of students. It is not unusual, for example, for an elementary school teacher to have 20 or more students in class, or for a secondary school teacher to teach his or her subject to five or six classes each day.

During class, a teacher may observe that some students get along with others and some do not. A teacher soon discovers that in addition to teaching math, or science, or social studies, or some other subject, he or she needs to work with the personal interactions within the class.

A teacher who needs to develop personal interactions with students will find Chapter 5 on developing relationships especially helpful. Understanding group dynamics also will enable a teacher to recognize the roles acted out by each member of a group. Chapter 6 describes the essentials of group work and also includes a discussion on conducting parent-teacher conferences.

A teacher must be able to work with and understand the special groups of students in his or her class. Chapter 7 includes discussions on teaching African American students and other racial-ethnic groups. The chapter also contains lesson plans for developing self-esteem and diminishing prejudice among class members. Teachers also need to work with the exceptional students in their classes. Exceptional students include but are not limited to learning disabled, emotionally handicapped, mentally handicapped, and gifted/talented students.

The Teacher's Role in Testing

A teacher's role in testing depends in part on the school or school district in which he or she works. For example, one school may require a teacher to administer a standardized test, while in another school the counselor, school psychologist, or principal may administer the test. Because a teacher may be affected by a school's testing program, he or she should have at least a minimal understanding of testing terminology.

One of the authors was an elementary and middle school counselor. He discovered that more time was spent preparing for and administering standardized tests than using the results to improve learning. He also noted that many of the teachers had very little if any understanding of testing or test interpretation.

All teachers are necessarily very involved in their school's testing program. Because teachers will be exposed to school testing programs, they need to become familiar with testing terminology, the different kinds of tests available, and the appropriate and inappropriate uses of tests. Chapter 13 provides teachers with this information. The chapter describes standardized tests, performance tests, speed and power tests, norm and criterion referenced tests, and validity and reliability.

The use and interpretation of test results are described in Chapter 12, along with the basic statistical concepts necessary for analyzing test results. Although school counselors are responsible for interpreting tests results, teachers need to understand the interpretation as well. Teachers who understand the concepts in Unit VI, Obtaining and Using Data, will be better able to analyze and use test results.

The Teacher's Role in Providing Information

The teacher's role includes providing information to students and parents in the areas of educational, personal, and career concerns through the use of both test and non-test data. Used together, test and non-test information will equip a teacher with information that may help a student achieve his/her maximum potential.

Test information was described in the preceding section; this discussion begins, therefore, with non-test information. Non-test information includes information that can be obtained by reviewing cumulative folders, anecdotal records, and rating scales, and by using sociometric techniques. A brief description of cumulative records follows. (Chapter 14 presents the cumulative folder and other non-test information in more detail.)

The cumulative folder contains important information about students. A teacher who wants to know about a student's family, previous grades, standardized test scores, and attendance and health records, and to read comments by a student's former teachers, will find the cumulative folder very helpful. The information contained in students' folders can be used by a teacher to help the students reach their maximum level of development.

The Teacher's Role as Career Educator

In addition to academic and personal support, a teacher may be required to provide students with information about careers. A teacher may need to become familiar with sources of such information, as well as with the factors that may interrupt career development.

Chapters 10 and 11 were written for teachers interested in helping students with their career aspirations. Chapter 10, for example, examines some of the factors that may have an impact on a student's career development. These factors include dropping out, pregnancy, drug and alcohol abuse, delinquency, and minority status.

A description of four career-development theories is also presented in Chapter 10. The selected theories focus on matching people to jobs; the effect of child rearing on career selection; and the roles that personality, self-concept, life stages, career maturity, and other factors play in influencing career decision making.

Chapter 11 provides teachers with sources of occupational and career information. For example, the *Dictionary of Occupational Titles* (DOT), *Occupational Outlook Handbook* (OOH), and *Exploring Careers* may provide teachers and students with answers to their occupational and career questions.

Other sources of occupational and career information may be found in the community. For a listing of local industries and businesses, teachers may find their telephone book helpful. Teachers may find additional information about employment opportunities in the local community from their state employment service. This agency may even send employment counselors to the schools to help students with their career concerns.

Many students will continue their education after graduating from high school. Teachers may find that their students will seek out their help in choosing a college or other training school. Chapter 11 describes several books that contain information on colleges, careers, and trade schools. With the help of these books, teachers will be able to answer such questions as, "Where can I get a degree in mortuary science?" or "I am moving to Missouri; where can I obtain a degree in pharmacy?" or "What school can I attend to become a radiologist?"

Finally, teachers may help their students by using software packages on their school's computers. These software packages may help the user to reduce the time required in locating career, occupational or educational information.

The Teacher's Role as Advisor

The teacher's role as advisor includes all of the roles described above. An advisor-advisee program is a planned approach to providing routine and systematic contact between a teacher and his/her advisees (students). As the students' advisor, a teacher may incorporate counseling techniques into his or her routine. In the advisor role, a teacher may assist students with improving grades, interpreting test results, and presenting career information. In addition, a teacher may need to discuss study skills techniques, health concerns, or how to make decisions. A teacher may administer a needs assessment to determine what areas or topics to include in an advising program he or she is developing, or the teacher may purchase an existing advisor-advisee program. Published advisor-advisee programs focus on developing positive self-awareness and growth. In addition, published programs have the advantage of having been field tested.

As an advisor, a teacher is assigned a group of students. To be an effective advisor, a teacher should have no more than 30 students. In some schools, these students may constitute a teacher's homeroom class. In other schools, a teacher may be required to advise students on an individual basis throughout the school year.

The overall goal of an academic advising program is to assure that every student has a significant adult in the school with whom he or she can develop a personal and caring relationship. In their role as advisors, teachers may serve as student advocates, assist students in decision making, and serve as links between students and other teachers, administrators, or parents.

It is important to note that advisor-advisee relationships are designed to supplement, not replace, the role of school counselor. A counselor cannot know all 300 to 1,000 students to whom he or she is assigned. When the need arises, an advisor may facilitate a student and counselor's involvement with each other by referring the student to the counselor. The activities included in advisor-advisee programs will benefit even the most novice teacher. Chapter 5 describes advisor-advisee programs. It also describes programs that may be purchased by schools that do not have an advisor-advisee program of their own.

With enthusiasm and sensitivity, the teacher as advisor may be more responsive than the counselor, not only to the academic and career needs of each student but also to students' personal needs. Implementing an advisor-advisee program may enhance positive relationships between students and teachers which in turn may foster the development of more positive educational experiences.

The Teacher's Role in Counseling

As stated earlier, the teacher's role in a counseling program is a supportive one. The school counselor is the primary person responsible for counseling students. However, the role descriptions provided earlier illustrate how a teacher may assist and support the school counselor.

A counselor may also help teachers understand their counseling roles by providing in-service training. Such training may include using and interpreting test results, improving and developing effective communication techniques, and enhancing classroom management skills. If additional skills are needed, a teacher may list the areas in which training is desired and seek the counselor's assistance.

The purpose of this book is to provide prospective teachers and those presently teaching with a basic understanding of the problems that may occur in their classrooms and a means of resolving them. No attempt will be made to solve problems per se; however, practical alternatives using counseling techniques will be emphasized.

REFERENCES

American Personnel and Guidance Association (1981). *What is counseling?* Alexandria, VA: Author.

UNIT I
BASIC MODELS
AND TECHNIQUES
FOR TEACHERS

Chapter 2

BASIC THEORETICAL MODELS APPLICABLE TO TEACHING

Each teacher has a primary responsibility to help students learn. Selection of materials, goals, objectives, and desired outcomes is based on the needs of learners and the learning process. The teacher coordinates the components of the learning process—*theory* and *practice*. Developmental theorists have concluded that children proceed through separate, identifiable, age-related stages of intellectual, social, and cognitive development. Reviewing several of these theories of development contributes to a holistic approach to knowledge about students and about how to teach them.

Teachers frequently ask, What is the nature of the students I teach? To answer such a question would require one to explore numerous avenues and a variety of concepts. A more focused question might be, What is the nature of *each individual* student I teach? Differences between students are numerous and complex. Consider the range of differences that might be observed in a single classroom: ages, ability levels, social levels, emotional levels—enough variety to make it difficult to determine what the students have in common.

The goal of studying theory is to determine scientific techniques useful in evaluating the behavior of students in a classroom. The four theories presented in this chapter are relatively simple and straightforward in their attempts to explain the behavior of children. Each theory makes certain speculations about children which can be translated into observable, measurable behaviors. The four theories are examined in relation to the underlying assumptions. The assumptions serve as a basis for much of the material that follows in this book.

JEAN PIAGET

Jean Piaget (1896–1980), a Swiss psychologist, is considered a pioneer in the area of developmental psychology. Wadsworth (1984) has provided an excellent summary of Piaget's work. Piaget, who studied with Alfred Binet ([1857–1911] the developer of the first scales for measuring intelligence), developed his system in an attempt to uncover developmental changes in individual cognitive functioning from birth through adolescence. He sought to answer two basic questions: How are children able to adapt to their environments? How can development be classified in a simple, accurate way?

Piaget borrowed much from the biological sciences. He found the answer to his first question by observing how organisms adapt to their environments. Piaget concluded that children adapt to their environments through either *assimilation* or *accommodation.*

Assimilation occurs when individuals incorporate new information into existing knowledge. The concept suggests that to react to a new stimulus, the child employs a response already learned. For example, a child identifies a collie dog as an animal with four legs, a long bushy tail, a wet nose, and so forth. On the first occasion of seeing a horse, the child is quite likely to identify the new animal as a large collie dog. The child has reviewed his or her repertoire of animals and has concluded that these two animals have similar characteristics. The horse was assimilated into the framework of the definition of collie dog. Thus, assimilation is the process by which new environmental stimuli are placed into existing frameworks. The child is always increasing the number (quantity) of existing frameworks into which new experience can be placed.

Accommodation is the process by which a child adjusts to new information or internalizes a stimuli that does not fit any of the frameworks already possessed. When a child is presented with a situation for which no reference exists, the child must create a completely new framework in which to place the new material. Sometimes the child can modify extensively an existing framework. In both cases, accommodation is the result.

Suppose that the same child who had internalized the meaning of collie dog is confronted by an opossum. The child sees enough difference between this animal and the dog that the opossum does not fit into the dog framework. A young child may create a completely new framework into which the opossum may be placed. An older child may see the similarity between the two and place the opossum into the "animal framework." Both of these approaches are examples of accommodation. Accommodation is a qualitative change in the existing frameworks into which new experiences are placed. Once the child has developed the new framework, the child can assimilate the new experience. Assimilation is always the final stage of the process.

Piaget suggested that children seek to maintain equilibrium by balancing the amount of assimilation and accommodation. When equilibrium is not maintained, the child is motivated to seek a balance. The level of cognitive development will determine the means by which the child will maintain this desired state.

PIAGET'S COGNITIVE DEVELOPMENT STAGES

Piaget developed four stages of cognitive development through which the child progresses. Through this developmental-stage theory, Piaget was able to answer his second question: How can development be classified in a simple, accurate way?

Piaget (1963) divided cognitive development into four major stages and approximate corresponding ages. These are presented in Table 2.1. A brief description of Piaget's four stages are provided based upon Berzonsky (1978).

Sensorimotor Stages

Piaget did not discount the notion that learning may begin before birth; however, he chose to begin his study of the child at birth. He labeled the first stage

TABLE 2.1
**Piaget's Four Major Cognitive Development Stages
and Approximate Corresponding Ages**

Stage	Age
1. Sensorimotor stage	Birth–2 years
2. Preoperational stage	2–7 years
a. preconceptual stage	2–4 years
b. intuitive stage	4–7 years
3. Concrete operational stage	8–11 years
4. Formal operational stage	11–15 years

Note. Table based on information in *The Psychology of Intelligence* (p. 123) by J. Piaget, 1963, Patterson, NJ: Littlefield Adams. Copyright 1963 by Littlefield Adams.

of development the *sensorimotor* stage, because the child seems unaware of any difference between his or her own body and the environment. All experiences seem restricted to those to which the child can respond with one of the five senses. The child is intrigued with all objects encountered and attempts to interact with them through sensory exploration. Thus the very young child explores most objects by taking them into his or her mouth, probably because the earliest reflex actions involve sucking with the mouth and grasping with the hands. Gradually, the other senses are put into play. Noises become important, particularly if the infant can discover a relationship between some behavior and the resulting sound. In general, the first two years of life are characterized by motoric responses to the environment. By the end of this stage, children have developed complex sensorimotor patterns and are beginning to use primitive symbols.

Preoperational Stage

Toward the end of the second year, the child develops an ability to use symbols to represent various aspects of the environment. The child is no longer restricted to the sensorimotor environment. Piaget divided this preoperational stage into two substages. A brief discussion of the preconceptual and intuitive stages follows.

Preconceptual Stage.   During this stage, the child does not realize that objects with similar characteristics are members of the same class but have unique identities. For example, a child at this stage may think only one Santa Claus exists even though he or she may have seen a dozen Santas in different shopping malls. Language is acquired quite rapidly during this stage. The average two-year-old possesses a vocabulary of 250 words; by age four his or her vocabulary will have grown to 4000 words.

Intuitive Stage.   At about four years of age the child's thinking becomes more logical, although reason does not yet dominate. This stage is called *intuitive* because it lacks operational characteristics. For example, a coin is shown to a child in one hand, then both hands are placed behind one's back. The child will say the coin is in the hand in which it was shown because he or she has not yet developed the level of reasoning that considers that the person showing the coin has the ability to switch it to the other hand.

Obstacles of Preoperational Stages

Phillips (1975) summarized the obstacles to logical thought that are characteristic of the operational stage as follows: irreversibility, egocentrism, centering, states versus transformations, and transductive reasoning (pp. 59-67).

Irreversibility.   This thought pattern is the opposite of reversibility, which means that a thought can follow a line of reasoning back to where it originated. For example, a child is shown two rows of coins with 10 pennies in each row, but the rows are different lengths. The child will say that more coins are in the longer row. By the same token, a child shown two test tubes filled with liquid will say they are the same. However, when the liquid from one test tube is poured into a larger glass, the child will say the test tube has more liquid, primarily because the liquid in the test tube will be higher. These are illustrations of the child's inability to reverse an operation. The child is unable to maintain the concept of the equal number of coins or the equal amount of liquid when faced with perceptual change.

Egocentrism.   This term suggests that the preoperational child is unable to take another person's point of view. Because social order is built on the ability of individuals to take into consideration the viewpoints of others (empathy or role taking), the communication of the preoperational child suffers. The child gradually becomes socialized, near age six or seven, when he or she is able to seek verification of thoughts by comparing them with the thoughts of others.

Centering.   This concept suggests that the preoperational child is able to focus on only one aspect or detail of an event. In the example of the 10 pennies used earlier, the child was able to focus only on the concept of length and not on the concept of number. Also, with the test-tube-and-liquid example, the child "centered" only on the height of the liquid in the containers. If the child could avoid this centering, he or she could take both height and width into account, or shift from one factor to the other and thus correctly solve the problem.

States versus Transformations.   The preoperational child is unable to perceive events in action sequences. Using the test tube example again, the preoperational child can watch the actual pouring of the liquid and still be unable to determine that the quantities were the same. This inability is the result of focusing only on the static event and not observing the process—the transformation—involved.

Transductive Reasoning.   Instead of proceeding from the general to the specific (deductive reasoning) or from the specific to the general (inductive reasoning), the preoperational child proceeds from the specific to the specific (transductive reasoning). The child who is unaware that the succession of Santa

Clauses seen in shopping malls are different persons, but instead thinks all are the same person, is thinking transductively.

Concrete Operational Stage

During the concrete operational stage, children begin to engage in logical reasoning, though still at a concrete level. Piaget used the term "concrete" because this stage includes concrete elements, operations, and rules. In other words, children at this stage are quite likely to interpret events in a literal manner.

Concrete operational children are capable of classifying objects or events into a hierarchy. This permits them to form a variety of class relationships as well as to understand that some relationships are included in other classes; for example, A B and B C, therefore A C.

The child at this stage also can rank objects in order according to size, a behavior that Piaget called *serializing*. The principle of conservation also is developed during this stage. The concrete operational child confronted with the liquid from one test tube being poured into a glass is able to understand that identical amounts of water are included in both. Finally, the concrete operational child is capable of reversibility, the process of following a line of reasoning back to where it originated, for instance, 2 plus 3 equals 5 and 5 minus 2 equals 3.

Note that a child at this stage also becomes less egocentric and is capable of taking the point of view of another person. Taking another person's point of view enables a child to develop a sense of cooperation. Children at this stage are quite interested in the rules of games they play. All these developments prepare the child for the kind of thinking that is characteristic of the final period of intellectual development, formal operations.

Formal Operational Stage

This final stage of intellectual development continues for the remainder of a person's life. Piaget identified this stage as parallel with the period of adolescence. However, because this concept is a theory of intellectual development, limited intellectual ability and other cultural factors may slow the development of the operations characteristics of this stage.

The primary characteristic of this stage is development of ability to think in abstract terms. Adolescents at this stage are able to solve problems mentally.

They are capable of both inductive and deductive reasoning. In other words, they can plan systematic investigations, routinely and accurately implement them, and draw logical conclusions from results. This process permits the adolescent to be creative, inventive, imaginative, and original in thinking.

Piaget's theory of intellectual development offers several useful principles for teaching. Teachers cognizant of the stages remain aware of the difficulty of tasks presented to students and remember that some tasks are too difficult for children at certain ages. Once a teacher is able to determine what a student knows, an appropriate level can be established for new learning. Finally, teachers can recognize individual differences between learners, even those who are within the same stage.

LAWRENCE KOHLBERG

Kohlberg (1975) studied Piaget's work on the theory of cognitive development, which also included work on the development of moral judgment. Piaget's work formed a basis for Kohlberg's research on moral development. Like Piaget, Kohlberg saw moral development as progressing through a universal set of stages. Kohlberg stated that these stages are characterized by (1) organized systems of thought, (2) forward movement, and (3) higher-stage thinking, which includes lower-stage thinking (1975, p. 670). Table 2.2 outlines Kohlberg's six stages of moral judgment. He did not associate specific ages with each stage because individuals in the same age group may be at different levels of moral thinking.

Kohlberg used stories of moral dilemmas to investigate the level of moral reasoning being used by a respondent. Perhaps the most familiar dilemma is one involving a man named Heinz. This dilemma and subsequent questions asked about the dilemma are reported by Hersh, Paolitto, and Reimer (1979):

> In Europe, a woman is near death from a special kind of cancer. There is one drug that the doctors think might save her. It is a form of radium that a druggist in the same town has recently discovered. The drug is expensive to make, but the druggist is charging ten times what the drug cost him to make. He paid $200 for radium and is charging $2000 for a small dose of the drug. The sick woman's husband, Heinz, goes to everyone he knows to borrow the money, but he can get together only about $1000, which is half of what it costs. He tells the druggist that his wife is dying and asks him to sell the drug cheaper or let him pay later. The druggist says, "No, I discovered the drug and I'm going to make money from it." Heinz

is desperate and considers breaking into the man's store to steal the drug for his wife.

1. Should Heinz steal the drug? Why or why not?
2. If Heinz doesn't love his wife, should he steal the drug for her?
3. Suppose the person is not his wife but a stranger. Should Heinz steal the drug for a stranger? Why or why not?
4. (If you favor stealing the drug for a stranger): Suppose it's a pet animal he loves. Should Heinz steal to save the pet animal ? Why or why not?
5. Why should people do everything they can to save another's life anyhow?
6. It is against the law for Heinz to steal. Does that make it morally wrong? Why or why not?
7. Why should people generally do everything they can to avoid breaking the law, anyhow?
7a. How does this relate to Heinz's case? (pp. 54–55)

Teachers can write their own dilemmas or use actual real-life situations as a basis for helping children cope with delicate situations in their environments. The following dilemma (Locke & Hardaway, 1980) was written as an example to be used in a multicultural classroom to foster a discussion of race and racial relations.

Beulah and Amy are two 12-year-olds who grew up together and were best of friends since growing up together. Though Beulah was Black and Amy was white, their racial difference has seemed unimportant in the past.

However, Beulah's father was recently fired from his job at the local industry after having worked there for 22 years. He has filed charges of discrimination against the company for what he described as "racist" treatment. His firing has put the community in a turmoil, with Blacks marching to protest his firing, and the local Ku Klux Klan marching to protect the community from violence. The local police were trying to maintain order in a community that had considered itself a model of racial cooperation. Most recently, the company was fire bombed, and more violence was expected.

Amy's parents insisted that Amy avoid any further contacts with Beulah, because Amy's father was also an employee of the company and he did not wish to arouse suspicion.

One night, Amy heard a knock at the door and when she opened it she found Beulah standing there crying and out of breath. Beulah

TABLE 2.2
Kohlberg's Six Stages of Moral Judgment

Level and Stage	What Is Right	Reasons for Doing Right	Social Perspective of Stage
Level I: Preconventional Stage 1: Heteronomous Morality	Sticking to rules backed by punishment; obedience for its own sake; avoiding physical damage to persons and property	To avoid punishment; fear of superior power of authorities	*Egocentric:* Doesn't consider the interests of others or recognize that they differ from one's own; doesn't relate two differing points of view. Actions considered physically rather than in terms of psychological interests of others. Confusion of authority's perspective with one's own.
Stage 2: Individualism, Instrumental Purpose, and Exchange	Following rules only when in one's immediate interest; acting to meet one's own interests and needs and letting others do the same. Doing what is fair or what is an equal exchange, deal, agreement.	To serve one's own needs or interests in a world where one has to recognize that other people also have interests.	*Concrete individualistic:* Is aware that everybody has interests to pursue and that these can conflict; right is relative.

TABLE 2.2 (*Continued*)
Kohlberg's Six Stages of Moral Judgment

Level and Stage	What Is Right	Reasons for Doing Right	Social Perspective of Stage
Level II: Conventional Stage 3: Mutual Interpersonal Expectations, Relationships, and Conformity	Living up to what people close to one expect, or to what people generally expect of a good son, sister, friend, etc. "Being good" is important and means having good motives, showing concern for others, and keeping trust, loyalty, respect, gratitude, etc. in mutual relationships.	To be a good person in one's own eyes and the eyes of others; to care for others; believing in the Golden Rule; desiring to maintain rules and authority that support stereo-typical behavior.	*The individual in relationships with other individuals:* Is aware of shared feelings, agreements, and expectations, which take primacy over individual interests; relates points of view through the Golden Rule, putting oneself in the other person's shoes. Does not yet consider generalized system perspective.
Stage 4: Social System and Conscience	Fulfilling duties to which one has agreed; upholding laws except in extreme cases in which they connect with other fixed social duties; contributing to one's society, group, or institution.	To keep the institution as a whole going, avoiding a breakdown in the system "if everyone did it"; to meet one's defined obligations as an imperative of one's conscience. (Easily confused with Stage 3 belief in rules and authority.)	*Differentiation of societal point of view from interpersonal agreement or motives:* Views the system as defining roles and rules; considers individual relations in terms of place in the system.

Level III: Postconventional, or Principled	Being aware that people hold a variety of values and opinions, and that most of one's values and rules are relative to one's group; relative rules usually upheld in the interest of impartiality and because they are the social contract; some nonrelative values and rights (e.g., life and liberty) must be upheld in any society regardless of majority opinion.	To obey the law because of one's social contract to make and abide by laws for the welfare of all and for the protection of all people's rights, out of a feeling of commitment freely made, to family, friendship, trust, and work obligations; being concerned that laws and duties be based on rational calculations of overall utility, "the greatest good for the greatest number."	*Prior to society:* Is aware, as a rational individual, of values and rights prior to social attachments and contracts. Integrates perspectives by formal mechanisms of agreement, contract, objective impartiality, and due process. Considers moral and legal points of view; recognizes that they sometimes conflict and finds it difficult to integrate them.
Stage 5: Social Contract or Utility and Individual Rights			
Stage 6: Universal Ethical Principles	Following self-chosen ethical principles of justice, equality of human rights, and respect for the dignity of human beings as individuals; particular laws or social agreements are seen as valid because they rest on such principles, and when laws violate these principles, one acts in accordance with principle.	As a rational person, one believes in the validity of universal moral principles and is personally committed to them.	*Moral point of view from which social arrangements derive:* Recognizes, as a rational individual, the nature of morality—that persons are ends in themselves and must be treated as such.

Note. From "Moral Stages and Moralization: The Cognitive Developmental Approach," by L. L. Kohlberg, 1976, *Moral Development and Behavior: Theory, Research, and Social Issues,* pp. 34 35. Copyright 1976 by Holt, Rinehart & Winston. Reprinted by permission.

told Amy that when she had returned home from playing with another friend, she had found her house in flames and surrounded by lots of people in sheets. Not knowing what to do, she ran to Amy's house.

The following questions identify relevant dimensions of the dilemma and serve to stimulate discussions: What should Amy do? Should she turn Beulah away? Should she invite her inside? From Beulah's point of view, what should Amy do? From the point of view of Amy's parents, what should Amy do? Suppose they were only class-mates and did not know each other well, would that make any difference? What would be Amy's responsibility if Beulah were white? What would be Amy's responsibility if Amy were black? What is the obligation of one friend to another? Should a friend risk scorn for the welfare of another? Should a friend risk life or limb for the welfare of another? Is the obligation of a friend altered if the friend is of a different race? What is Amy's responsibility in keeping her promise to her parents and being obedient? (pp. 279–280)

Kolhberg presents a consistent way of viewing moral development. His theory also offers teachers a chance to use his material in making determinations about what types of strategies may be appropriate for teaching children at the different stages of moral reasoning. Further, if educational programs can be developed that are geared to the different levels of development, teachers can foster moral growth by teaching students at the level immediately beyond their current individual levels of functioning.

ERIK ERIKSON

Erikson (1963) has formulated a system of psychosocial development that focuses on specific developmental tasks unique to each stage. He was influenced by the work of Freud (1961), and Erickson's "ages of man" can be seen to parallel the psychosexual stages presented by Freud. Erikson, however, has gone well beyond Freud's presentation to offer stages of development that correspond to crises of both positive and negative factors. Not only is Erikson's theory more optimistic than Freud's, but it also seems more useful to teachers who wish to understand the development of students. Table 2.3 presents the developmental stages as viewed by Erikson and parallel's them with Freud's stages. Freud's theory and his psychosexual stages will not be discussed; Erikson's system provides a review of adult development, whereas Freud's theory stops at the end of adolescence.

TABLE 2.3
Erikson's Stages of Psychosocial Development

Stage	Developmental Task	Age	Freud's Stage
I	Basic Trust vs. Basic Mistrust	0–1	Oral
II	Autonomy vs. Shame and Doubt	1–4	Anal
III	Initiative vs. Guilt	4–6	Phallic
IV	Industry vs. Inferiority	6–12	Latency
V	Identify vs. Role Confusion	12–20	Genital
VI	Intimacy vs. Isolation	20–30	
VII	Generativity vs. Stagnation	30–65	
VIII	Ego Integrity vs. Despair	65–	

Note. Table based on information in *Childhood and Society* (pp. 247–269) by E. H. Erikson, 1963, New York: W. W. Norton, copyright 1963 by W. W. Norton; and *The Standard Edition of the Complete Psychological Works of Sigmund Freud* (pp. 56–121) by S. Freud, 1961, London: Hogarth Press, copyright 1961 by Hogarth Press.

The process of socialization can best be understood through a brief review of the distinctive features of each of Erikson's eight stages—trust, autonomy, initiative, industry, identity, intimacy, generativity, and ego integrating.

Basic Trust Versus Basic Mistrust

At birth, an infant is dependent totally on other people for survival. The infant learns to *trust* these people to provide for his or her needs for food, warmth, physical comfort, and human contact. An infant who is denied these basic needs begins to learn to *mistrust.* Erikson characterized this stage as quite significant because it provides a foundation on which later tasks are built.

Autonomy Versus Shame and Doubt

The development of basic trust enables the child to begin developing both autonomy and self-control. During this stage the child learns to talk and walk, becoming less dependent on other people. During this stage children also are expected to begin taking care of their bodily functions (e.g., toilet training). The positive aspect of this stage is seen in the child who is given appropriate responsibility and freedom to do for self. Overprotection of children will often lead them to doubt their abilities and to have feelings of helplessness. Subsequently, children feel ashamed when unable to perform a task expected of them.

Initiative Versus Guilt

This stage often is characterized by imagination and pretense. The child is extending his or her level of independence, and this independence opens up a whole new world for exploration. The child begins to spend more time away from parents and with playmates. Children at this stage become quite inquisitive and curious. The initiative stressed in this stage is fostered by allowing children the opportunity to complete many tasks on their own. Guilt is the result of overcontrol and restriction of behavior.

Industry Versus Inferiority

The child is probably in school by the beginning of this stage and begins learning skills necessary for survival: reading, writing, and problem solving. The industry of this stage is learning how things are made and how they work. The child learns some skills necessary for survival, and equally important, learns to feel competent in interpersonal relations. The inferiority possible at this stage results from failure to accomplish the tasks that are expected. Children whose parents expect too much, who are unable to compete successfully with their peers, or who discover that factors such as race or gender or socioeconomic factors determine success, are likely to develop feelings of inferiority.

Identity Versus Role Confusion

The period of adolescence is the transition between childhood and adulthood. During this stage the individual is confronted with major developments that are necessary for successful movement into adulthood. Primarily, the individual must develop an identity, that is, an integration of all his or her roles and self-images into a unique person who is socially and emotionally capable of assuming the responsibilities of adulthood. Role confusion exists when an individual is unable to develop this unique identity and remains confused and uncertain about who he or she is. This confusion often manifests itself in the individual's inability to pursue further education beyond high school, or failure to select a career.

Intimacy Versus Isolation

Love and work are the major activities of the early adult years. Traditionally, the individual "settles down" to a career and develops sexual intimacy with another person. In other words, the individual is capable of merging his or her identity with the identity of another person. This intimacy extends not only to marriage but also to friends, family, and other persons. The inability to enter into rewarding interpersonal relations results in isolation.

Generativity Versus Stagnation

Generativity involves a person's need to guide those who will replace this generation. For most people, this need is satisfied through the rearing of offspring. Others satisfy this need through being creative and/or being productive. For example, some people write books dedicated to their children. Others might leave items accumulated over a lifetime to a local library or college/university. The person who does not develop a sense of contribution is likely to feel uselessness and apathy, what Erikson termed stagnation.

Ego Integrity Versus Despair

Erikson's eighth stage of life is characterized by the need to place trust in others to maintain the future. The individual is able to review his or her life with a feeling of satisfaction or ego integrity, and know that his or her existence will continue either through offspring or contributions to society. Despair is characteristic of the individual who has feelings of failure and realizes that it is too late to do anything about the last dream.

Erikson provides the educator with a lifelong view of the person and the important qualities to be developed at each stage of growth. Teachers can use this theory to assess the developmental needs of specific children and to provide academic and social experiences consistent with these needs.

An appreciation of the theory presented by Erikson helps the teacher to understand that human beings develop according to a predetermined psychosocial plan. Successful accomplishment of tasks at each stage should lead to relative happiness—both intrapersonal and interpersonal. Progression through the eight stages is based on a number of factors in the social environment. The skillful teacher will recognize tasks at each stage and will develop experiences and design the classroom environment to facilitate smooth positive movement from one stage to the next. Such facilitation can be accomplished by organizing school activities that permit and encourage students to gain a variety of new experiences.

ROBERT J. HAVIGHURST

In *Developmental Tasks and Education,* Robert J. Havighurst (1972) delineates the specific developmental tasks unique to specific age levels. He defines a developmental task as "midway between an individual need and a societal demand which assumes an active learner interacting with an active social environment" (p. iv). Thus a developmental task includes knowledge, skills, attitudes, and functions the individual must acquire at various stages through personal effort, social expectations, and physical maturity. Havighurst outlined the major developmental tasks significant at each of six age periods. Each stage is characterized by specific needs for affection, approval, independence, and self-competence. At the early childhood level (ages 5–9), one of the major tasks is to learn to accept rules and procedures while understanding the rights of others. In middle childhood (ages 10–11), major tasks include learning to get along with age-mates and accepting group codes of behavior while learning to compete within the code. The adolescent period (ages 12–20) includes the tasks of gaining emotional independence, acquiring sex roles, and finding a vocational direction.

Havighurst argued that a teachable moment, an ideal time for teaching a new task, exists. Each developmental task is built upon a prior developmental stage. Teachers need to recognize that this process of learning is based on social, physical, and personal factors. In his book, Havighurst identified specific educational implications at each developmental stage. The value of his contribution to understanding development is significant when viewed in perspective with the other theories presented previously.

The school, as a major social institution responsible for meeting a major part of youngsters' needs, must evaluate its total program for relevance to the tasks of each age level. The school staff must recognize the need for unique experiences appropriate for each stage.

A first step is to evaluate how effectively the school program is presently meeting these needs. On the basis of this assessment, changes can be made to correct perceived inadequacies. While this effort focuses on the general age category, teachers must know where each student ranks in his or her achievement of developmental tasks. Where a student is found to be below expected developmental level, the teacher can discuss the child's needs with the parents, other teachers, and school support personnel.

Where deemed necessary, resources outside the school system may be consulted for support. From this consultation, appropriate strategies may be developed to assist the student where needed. Much of the remainder of this book focuses on teacher activities that attempt to correct a particular developmental task difficulty.

APPLICATION OF THEORY

The purpose of this chapter has been to introduce the reader to four formal theories important to the total education process. The theories have been presented so that the teacher might use them as a foundation in the classroom. By understanding several theories, the reader should be able to check views held about students in general and about specific students in particular. Such knowledge should be useful as one works with students with a variety of needs. The following points should be recalled as one develops lessons:

1. Select objectives and goals for each lesson, keeping in mind the developmental needs of all students. Knowledge about the developmental levels of students should be useful in implementing strategies to carry out objectives. *Both content and process should be considered while objectives are being established.*
2. Select classroom materials and content that are appropriate and suitable to the unique developmental needs of all students. This necessitates the inclusion of varied materials, because developmental levels in each classroom will be varied. Learning tasks should be analyzed in terms of the developmental components involved. Lessons should build on previous learning experiences. Diversity in teaching materials and resources should take into consideration the mode by which students learn best. Learners vary in their modes among the following types: visual, auditory, or tactical (manipulative).
3. Knowledge of various theories of development help teachers determine the "readiness" of each student for attempts at new tasks. It is important to avoid tasks that are far beyond a student's developmental level. Obviously, students must be presented with challenges appropriate to levels attainable by the students.
4. Determine appropriate levels of "telling" students things versus allowing them to "discover" things themselves (process). For example, lecturing, an abstract method of instruction, may prove frustrating to concrete learners. As a general rule, verbal abstractions should follow some concrete (direct) experience.
5. Knowledge of developmental theories provides a foundation for teachers who wish to use group situations or peer instruction in their classrooms. Different developmental levels require teachers to make different methodical decisions in order to maximize teaching effectiveness.
6. Teachers need to focus on the total person in the learning environment. Such a focus would include attention to sensorimotor, linguistic, cognitive, and moral development.

7. Finally, it is important to remember the principle of individual differences. Chronological age and developmental levels are not consistent. Each student learns in his or her own way at his or her own rate and in his or her own time.

CONCLUDING COMMENTS

A teacher should know many things about children in general and many things about his or her own students in particular. This review of four theories of development provides a brief survey of some fundamental notions about child development and individual differences. A successful teacher enters into the classroom informed about human nature.

In addition to the cognitive developmental theories, there are behavioral, social learning, and ecological theories. Behaviorism advocates an examination of only those things that can be directly observed and measured. The name most frequently associated with behaviorism is B. F. Skinner.

Social learning theory, developed by Albert Bandura and Walter Michel, emphasizes a combination of behavior, environment, and cognition as the primary factors in development. These psychologists argue that individuals are neither robots responding mechanically to the environment nor weather vanes directed by the wind.

Ecological theories emphasize the role of social context in development. The most prominent ecological theorist is Urie Bronfenbrenner. He emphasized a focus on the setting in which the individual lives, and on the relation of family experiences to school experiences, peer experiences, and the culture in which the individual lives.

A grasp of theoretical knowledge serves as a foundation for providing specific unique learning experiences for each student. This knowledge base also serves to help the teacher avoid mistakes. The teacher seeks to learn about individual traits, physical limitations, habits, and so forth, so that subject matter may be adapted and methods varied to lead the student toward the desired learning. An understanding of the works of Piaget, Kohlberg, Erikson, and Havighurst can serve in meeting these desired goals.

REFERENCES

Berzonsky, M. D. (1978). Formal reasoning in adolescence: An alternative view. *Adolescence, 13,* 279–290.

Erikson, E. H. (1963). *Childhood and society.* New York: W. W. Norton.

Freud, S. (1961). *The standard edition of the complete psychological works of Sigmund Freud.* London: Hogarth Press.

Havighurst, R. J. (1972). *Developmental tasks and education.* New York: David McKay.

Hersh, R. H., Paolitto, D. P., & Reimer, J. (1979). *Promoting moral growth: From Piaget to Kohlberg.* New York: Longman.

Kohlberg, L. (1975). The cognitive–developmental approach to moral education. *Phi Delta Kappan, 56,* 670–677.

Kohlberg, L. (1976). Moral stages and moralization: The cognitive–developmental approach. In T. Lickona (Ed.), *Moral development and behavior: Theory, research and social issues* (pp. 34–35). New York: Holt, Rinehart and Winston.

Locke, D. C., & Hardaway, Y. V. (1980). Moral perspectives in the interracial classroom. In D. Cochrane & M. Manley-Casimir (Eds.), *Development of moral reasoning: Practical approaches* (pp. 269–285). New York: Praeger.

Phillips, J. L., Jr. (1975). *The origins of intellect: Piaget's theory.* San Francisco: W. H. Freeman.

Piaget, J. (1963). *The psychology of intelligence.* Patterson, NJ: Littlefield, Adams.

Wadsworth, B. J. (1984). *Piaget's theory of cognitive development.* New York: Longman.

Chapter 3

COMMUNICATION TECHNIQUES FOR TEACHERS

Personal relationships between teachers and students are the core of the learning process. Learning is facilitated by an environment in which students are encouraged to believe that their contributions and value as individuals are appreciated and respected. The effective teacher encourages self-disclosure and recognizes ambiguity as an avenue for exploring alternatives. The learning environment is enhanced by the teacher's acceptance of confrontation and differences of opinions as potentially constructive forces. Through the use of effective communication skills, the teacher can create an environment conducive to academic achievement.

In the past, educators have often expressed the opinion that "humaneness and promotion of cognitive growth are antithetical" (Aspy & Roebuck, 1972, p. 365). The use of effective communication, however, intensifies the humane aspects of the teaching/learning spectrum and concurrently facilitates cognitive growth.

Hawes (1989) concluded that teachers are not taught how to communicate effectively with children. Effective communication provides teachers with more time to teach and students with more time to learn. Effective communication conveys acceptance of the child. Good communication is based on mutual respect. Teachers must strive to accentuate the positive in communicating acceptance, confidence, appreciation, and recognition of students' efforts.

FACILITATIVE CONDITIONS

More than two decades ago, Rogers (1961) reasoned that three skills determine conditions within the interpersonal process—empathy, genuineness, and unconditional positive regard—and that these skills are related directly to learning outcomes. "To the extent that the teacher creates such a relationship with his class, the student will become a self-initiated learner, more original, more self-disciplined, less anxious and other directed" (p. 37). This statement focuses attention on the fact that education is a process, and all factors that have bearing on that process ought to be considered.

The purpose of this chapter is to study facilitative conditions, which are germane to the counseling profession, that will enhance the process of learning. Techniques for accomplishing these conditions will also be examined.

Empathy

Empathy is often viewed both as an attitude and as a technique in interpersonal relations. Empathy is the process of reacting to another's feelings with an emotional response that is similar to the other person's feelings (Damon, 1988). Rogers (1962) defined empathy as

> understanding the [student's] private world, and [being] able to communicate some of the significant fragments of that understanding. To sense the [student's] inner world of private, personal meanings as if they were your own, but without ever losing the "as if" quality. To sense his confusion or his timidity as his anger, or his feeling of being treated unfairly as if it were your own. (p. 419)

This understanding of the student implies much more than simply having knowledge of what the student is feeling. It means understanding those feelings as a basis for implementing change in the relationship. When the world of the student becomes clear to the teacher, and the student senses this understanding, the student is likely to allow the teacher to enter more of his or her world of experience. The teacher may be able to aid the student in exploring feelings of which the student may not yet be aware. This type of relationship serves as a basis for the student to learn, to change, and to develop.

Rogers (1969) illustrated how teacher empathy works when a student believes that he or she really is understood:

> This attitude of standing in the other's shoes, of viewing the world through the student's eyes, is almost unheard of in the classroom.

One could listen to thousands of ordinary classroom interactions without coming across one instance of clearly communicated, sensitively accurate, empathic understanding. But it has a tremendously releasing effect when it occurs. (p. 112)

To illustrate his point, Rogers went on to describe a classroom situation he borrowed from Virginia Axline, a pioneer in the use of play therapy with children:

A seven year old boy had been classified as a slow learner, difficult to manage, acting out, and one who used profanity. Eventually, the boy received a paddling by the school principal for his use of profanity. In a play session with the therapist, the boy constructed a clay model of a man who closely resembled the school principal. When the therapist inquired as to whom the boy had built, he replied that he did not know. When the therapist told the boy that the model resembled the principal, the boy agreed and began tearing the head off, an experience that seemed to produce satisfaction. The therapist responded empathically by saying "Sometimes you get so mad at him you feel like tearing his head off, don't you?" At which point the boy tore off the arms and then beat the model to a pulp. The therapist allowed the boy to do this and when it appeared that he had finished, she said to him, "You must feel much better now." The boy smiled and began to rebuild the model.

This example demonstrates that the therapist really understood the boy's feelings. The therapist demonstrated this understanding without being judgmental or evaluative. She may not have liked what she saw or approved of the behavior, yet she demonstrated that she fully understood the boy's feelings, and she verbalized the understanding in an empathic way. One word of caution: A teacher should not pretend to understand the student when he or she does not. An inauthentic expression of empathy is likely to confuse the student and produce distrust of the teacher.

Genuineness

Genuineness means that the teacher is "real" in his or her relationships with students. This means that the teacher is basically being himself or herself, not playing a role in particular situations, but being authentic in all interactions. The teacher does not present a facade, does not deny self, and is able to communicate this self-awareness to others.

An example of realness was reported by Rogers (1969) when he described the behavior of a sixth grade art teacher:

This teacher gave students a great deal of liberty in her classroom and in the process of doing so shared her realness with them. She not only shared her feelings of happiness and pleasure but also her feelings of anger and disappointment as well. Because she gave these students freedom in the classroom it meant that students could select art supplies on their own. The result was that the room was frequently messy. The teacher confronted the students with her real feelings of wanting to allow them freedom and wanting to have the room neat and orderly. She first asked if they had a solution. Their recommended solution was to allow those who volunteered to clean the room. She explained that the solution seemed unfair but she would accept it. She had shared her realness in a manner that allowed the students to understand the importance of the issue. She had expressed directly what she was experiencing and the message was communicated with the motivation clear. There was also an element of the "here-and-now" included in the message.

The classroom is an excellent setting for students to learn to label their emotions and to express them appropriately. By being genuine in communicating with students, the teacher provides a model from which students can learn an honest means of expressing anger, anxiety, hostility, and fear, as well as the more pleasant emotions.

Unconditional Positive Regard

The third condition, unconditional positive regard, exists when the teacher accepts students totally and without conditions, judgment, or evaluation. Unconditional positive regard involves an affirming response to each student as a person of worth without regard to the student's behavior or other characteristics that may be unacceptable or unlikeable. The teacher accomplishes this unconditional positive regard by actively listening and by showing nonpossessive warmth through sincerity and caring. The teacher accepts the student's imperfections in the context that faults are a part of the student's individual human condition.

Rogers (1977) stated that the feeling of having been given unconditional positive regard facilitates the development of feelings, reason, emotions, and intellect. Role expectations tend to be diminished and replaced by the student's choosing his/her own way of behaving. When students are trusted to make responsible decisions, they may begin to change their world.

Some people overreact to unconditional positive regard as acceptance of all that the student does. While the emphasis is on the positive aspects of interpersonal relationships between teachers and students, it is important to point out that unconditional positive regard does not include acceptance of "inappropriate" behaviors. The teacher first convinces the student of the unconditional prizing and then shares with the student dislike of the behavior. Logically, students will act quite differently in interactions with teachers they believe care genuinely about them and accept them without evaluation. Quite simply, this unconditional positive regard involves separating the person from the acts of that person. Indeed, this seems to represent the optimal level toward which the teacher should strive.

Some examples of good teacher comments that communicate empathy, genuineness, and unconditional caring are as follows:

1. I am angry when I find the classroom messy.
2. I am concerned that you have been late to class three times this week. I am distracted when you enter late.
3. I am pleased that you requested my assistance with your problem. You've become frustrated looking for an answer, haven't you?
4. Do you have a suggestion for how we can resolve our difference so we will both feel good about the decision?

The same statements can be made negatively, as illustrated in the following examples:

1. You kids make me so mad with such a messy room.
2. How do you expect me to be able to teach with you coming into class late. You have been late three times already this week.
3. I don't like to get involved in the personal problems of students. I'm sure time will solve your problem.
4. This is my classroom and I make the rules here. Your role is to obey the rules.

FACILITATIVE TECHNIQUES

Basic techniques used to facilitate the three conditions discussed previously will be presented. The purpose is to help teachers become familiar with techniques that seem useful in classes or in out-of-class interactions involving students.

Listening

Listening skills often are divided into two categories: active listening and analytical listening. *Active listening* involves communicating to the student that the teacher is interested in understanding what is being said and that the student is cared for as a person. This listening requires that the receiver of the message maintain an "active" role in the communication process. Some simple techniques are helpful in conveying this active role. Mehrabian (1971) has suggested that active listening can be demonstrated by maintaining good eye contact, facing the student squarely, and listening without interrupting. Other behaviors such as nodding the head, maintaining a close proximity to the student, leaning toward the student (if seated), and pausing following a student's statement, all tend to communicate an interest in what the student is saying.

Gordon (1974) has identified seven attitudes necessary for accurate active listening. These attitudes are as follows:

1. The foundation of the attitude system is trust in students' abilities to resolve any difficulties they face. Active listening encourages students to seek solutions themselves. Teachers need only remember that such a process will take time, much more than if the teacher provided the solution.
2. The use of unconditional positive regard exemplifies the teachers' willingness to accept all feelings expressed by students. The statement "you shouldn't feel that way" is not representative of the teacher who genuinely accepts all feelings.
3. Teachers must remember that feelings are extremely changeable. Most feelings occur as a momentary state. Active listening is the connecting link between these momentary states.
4. There must be a genuine desire on the part of the teacher to help students with their problems. Sometimes teachers feel that too much has already been included in job descriptions to allow additional time to help. The reality is that teachers already handle difficult situations. Active listening is a means of helping by using alternative strategies.
5. Accurate empathy involves being "with" each student and yet, at the same time, maintaining one's own identity. This implies that a fine line exists between optional involvement with a student and too much involvement with a student. Too much involvement tends to communicate a lack of faith in the students' ability to solve his or her own problem.
6. Teachers must understand that the first problem presented is usually not the real problem. Through active listening the teacher is able to encourage the student to explore additional areas of possible concern.
7. Students must believe that what they say to teachers will be treated confidentially. Private conversations must remain as such and not be shared with other school personnel. Where necessary, have the student

himself or herself share the information. In some instances, it is appropriate for a teacher to share information at the request of the student.

In summary, active listening communicates the following: a trust in the student; that responsibility to solve problems rests with the student; a belief in the student's ability to solve problems; and a commitment from teachers to be involved in close meaningful relationships with students.

Analytical listening involves assessing ideas presented in a message and making choices, decisions, or judgments about that message. Clearly, analytical listening relates to much of the cognitive discussion that takes place in the classroom. More important is the way teachers respond to ideas presented by students. Teachers need to communicate to students that their ideas are valid, important, and relevant to a discussion. This process involves giving the student feedback on the message sent. Effective feedback is characterized according to Bostrom (1990) by (1) response to the student, (2) responding at an appropriate level and context, (3) clarifying the meaning in the feedback, and (4) making sure that the feedback is received and understood.

Silence also is treated sometimes as a form of listening. The student is uninterrupted and the teachers exhibits nonverbal active listening behaviors. For many students this opportunity to "think aloud" without interruption is appreciated and may serve to help think through a situation. The timing of a teacher's silence is extremely significant. Silence may be used to allow the student time to think about (process) what has been said or to reduce the intensity of the conversation. The latter use allows the student an opportunity to focus the conversation and accept responsibility for what is being said.

Reflection

Reflection means simply to mirror what the student has said, to attempt to restate and thus clarify essential attitudes expressed by the student. Reflection can be of two types: reflection of *content* or reflection of *feeling*. The former is a mirroring of what the student has said; the latter mirrors the implied underlying feelings.

The teacher must be sensitive to students' feelings and capable of clarifying, simplifying, and mirroring them back to the students as expressed. The expression of feelings is encouraged by the teacher's reflection, and this encourages self-confrontation—with the result that the student more fully understands his or her own ideas, experiences, and thought processes, which underlie and influence feelings and actions. Note the emphasis on reflection as the paraphrasing of subjective attitudes, not the objective content of statements. The technique also may take the form of interpreting nonverbal behavior (i.e., voice tone, gestures, and mannerisms), and reflecting the teacher's own perceptions of the influence this behavior may have on statements made by students.

Reflection of content involves acting as a mirror by restating what the student has said. For example:

> **Student:** *I don't want to stand up in front of the class and give an oral report.*

> **Teacher:** You *don't want to give an oral report in front of the class.*

In this example, the teacher responds to the content of what the student said. The teacher who desires to respond to the underlying feeling might react to the same student statement as follows:

> **Teacher:** *Perhaps you are afraid that you will not do well in front of your friends.*

The attempt in reflection is basically to confront an apparent contradiction of what the student is saying with what the teacher hears the student expressing. Any reflection, however, requires that the teacher choose from verbalizations and actions of students those elements that have the greatest quality of feeling and are in the greatest need of clarification. Damage could be done by failing to reflect accurately or by reflecting accurately and then not working through the feelings properly (Brammer & Shostrum, 1989).

Gendlin (1974) has stated that too often inaccuracies occur in reflection, obscuring rather than clarifying meaning. The student then tries to deal with the teacher's inaccurate response, and the teacher, not realizing the first inaccuracy, reflects the student's comeback. The result is that both people are so far from the student's original feeling that they never return. The teacher must be very aware of the task of accuracy. Without the ability "to listen, to hear, to respond exactly, to help the person share what is felt, the . . . [teacher] is actually leaving the . . . [student] basically alone. . . . Without making real touch with what there is in another, one cannot relate to that other" (p. 217).

Furthermore, the teacher must avoid what Porter (1950) has identified as four pitfalls of reflection:

1. Reflecting content, or blind repetition of the statement of the client, without any attempt at introspection
2. Lack of depth, or inappropriate level of response
3. Altering of meaning, or inaccurate restatement of the client's words
4. Inappropriate language, or rephrasing in lofty or overly simplified terms

Table 3.1, taken from Hammond, Hepworth, and Smith (1977), provides a vocabulary of feelings that may be encountered by teachers. The suggestion, as a first step in responding to feelings, is for teachers to develop an awareness of feeling words as well as awareness of feeling intensity. Once this awareness has been developed, teachers can develop the ability to communicate to the student this awareness of exact feelings perceived. Such skill requires a broad vocabulary of words and expressions.

Hammond, Hepworth, and Smith (1977) also suggested some empathic response leads or introductory phrases (Table 3.2) that should be helpful as one learns skills in reflection of both content and feelings. They called their list one of "empathically communicative lead-in phrases" designed to help teachers respond more naturally.

Other Techniques

Many additional techniques from the counseling profession have proven helpful to the teacher. Among these techniques are clarification, questioning, interpretation, modeling, positive reinforcement, and gestalt language.

Clarification. Clarification seeks to check out or verify the meaning of a student's statement. When the teacher fails to understand accurately either content or feeling inherent in a student's statement, seeking clarification to avoid misperception is necessary. An example of clarification follows:

Student: *You never call on me when I raise my hand.*

Teacher: *You think that I deliberately ignore you?*

Questioning. Questioning is a technique that allows the teacher to obtain additional information necessary to understand fully the meaning intended by the student. Questioning also serves to help the student focus on areas of concern the teacher perceives as significant. This involves asking who, what, when, and how questions of the student. A good rule of thumb for encouraging verbalization is to avoid questions the student can answer with a simple yes or no.

TABLE 3.1
The Vocabulary of Feelings

Levels of Intensity	Happy	Caring	Depressed	Inadequate	Fearful
Strong	thrilled	tenderness	desolate	worthless	terrified
	on cloud nine	toward	dejected	good for	frightened
	ecstatic	affection for	hopeless	nothing	intimidated
	overjoyed	captivated by	alienated	washed up	horrified
	excited	attached to	depressed	powerless	desperate
	elated	devoted to	gloomy	helpless	panicky
	sensational	adoration	dismal	impotent	terror-
	exhilerated	loving	bleak	crippled	stricken
	fantastic	infatuated	in despair	inferior	stage fright
	terrific	enamored	empty	emasculated	dread
	on top of	cherish	barren	useless	vulnerable
	the world	idolize	grieved	finished	paralyzed
	turned on	worshop	grief	like a failure	
	euphoric		despair		
	enthusiastic		grim		
	delighted				
	marvelous				
	great				
Moderate	cheerful	caring	distressed	inadequate	afraid
	light-hearted	fond of	upset	whipped	scared
	happy	regard	downcast	defeated	fearful
	serene	respectful	sorrowful	incompetent	apprehensive
	wonderful	admiration	demoralized	inept	jumpy
	up	concern for	discouraged	overwhelmed	shaky
	aglow	hold dear	miserable	ineffective	threatened
	glowing	prize	pessimistic	lacking	distrustful
	in high spirits	taken with	tearful	deficient	risky
	jovial	turned on	weepy	unable	alarmed
	riding high	trust	rotten	incapable	butterflies
	elevated	close	awful	small	ackward
	neat		horrible	insignificant	defensive
			blue	like Caspar	
			lost	Milquetoast	
			melancholy	unfit	
				unimportant	
				incomplete	
				no good	
				immobilized	
Mild	glad	warm toward	unhappy	lacking	nervous
	good	friendly	down	confidence	anxious
	contented	like	low	unsure of	unsure
	satisfied	positive	bad	yourself	hesitant
	gratified	toward	blah	uncertain	timid
	pleasant		disappointed	weak	shy
	pleased		sad	inefficient	worried
	fine		glum		uneasy
					bashful
					embarrassed
					ill-at-ease
					doubtful
					jittery
					on edge
					uncomfortable
					self-conscious

Note. From *Improving Therapeutic Communication* (pp. 86–87) by D. C. Hammond, D. H. Hepworth, and permission.

Confused	Hurt	Angry	Lonely	Guilt-Shame
bewildered	crushed	furious	isolated	sick at heart
puzzled	destroyed	enraged	abandoned	unforgivable
baffled	ruined	seething	all alone	humiliated
perplexed	degraded	outraged	forsaken	disgraced
trapped	pain(ed)	infuriated	cut off	degraded
confounded	wounded	burned up		horrible
in a dilemma	devastated	pissed off		mortified
befuddled	tortured	fighting mad		exposed
in a quandry	disgraced	nauseated		
full of	humiliated	violent		
questions	anguished	indignant		
confused	at the mercy of	hatred		
	cast off	bitter		
	forsaken	galled		
	rejected	vengeful		
	discarded	hateful		
		viciuos		
mixed-up	hurt	resentful	lonely	ashamed
disorganized	belittled	irritated	alienated	guilty
foggy	shot down	hostile	estranged	remorseful
troubled	overlooked	annoyed	remote	crummy
adrift	abused	upset with	alone	to blame
lost	depreciated	agitated	apart from	lost face
at loose ends	criticized	mad	others	demeaned
going around	defamed	aggravated	insulated	
in circles	censured	offended	from others	
disconcerted	discredited	antagonistic		
frustrated	disparaged	exasperated		
flustered	laughed at	belligerent		
in a bind	maligned	mean		
ambivalent	mistreated	vexed		
disturbed	ridiculed	spiteful		
helpless	devalued	vindictive		
embroiled	scorned			
	mocked			
	scoffed at			
	used			
	exploited			
	debased			
	slammed			
	slandered			
	impugned			
	cheapened			
uncertain	put down	uptight	left out	regretful
unsure	neglected	disgusted	excluded	wrong
bothered	overlooked	bugged	lonesome	embarrassed
uncomfortable	minimized	turned off	distant	at fault
undecided	let down	put out	aloof	in error
	unappreciated	miffed		responsible for
	taken for	irked		blew it
	granted	perturbed		goofed
		ticked off		lament
		teed off		
		chagrined		
		cross		
		dismayed		
		impatient		

TABLE 3.2
Empathic Response Lead-ins

Kind of feeling . . .
Sort of saying . . .
As I get it, you felt that . . .
I'm picking up that you . . .
If I'm hearing you correctly . . .
To me, it's almost like you are saying, "I . . ."
Sort of hear you saying that maybe you . . .
Kind of made (makes) you feel . . .
What I hear you saying is . . .
So, as you see it . . .
As I get it, you're saying . . .
What I guess I'm hearing is . . .
I'm not sure I'm with you, but . . .
I somehow sense that maybe you feel . . .
You feel . . .
I really hear you saying that. . .
I wonder if you're expressing a concern that . . .
It sounds as if you're indicating you . . .
I wonder if you're saying . . .
You place a high value on . . .
It seems to you . . .
Like right now . . .
You often feel . . .
You feel, perhaps . . .
You appear to be feeling . . .
It appears to you . . .
As I hear it, you . . .
So, from where you sit . . .
Your feeling now is that . . .
I read you as . . .
Sometimes you . . .
You must have felt . . .
I sense that you're feeling . . .
Very much feeling . . .
Your message seems to be, "I . . ."
You appear . . .
Listening to you it seems as if . . .
I gather . . .
So your world is a place where you . . .
You communicate (convey) a sense of . . .

Furthermore, the questioning should not be of such a nature as might be perceived as prying or interrogating. A tendency exists for "why" questions to lead into intellectualization and excuse giving and therefore should be avoided. A "why" question usually can be rephrased as a "what" or "how" question.

Interpretation. Interpretation is a technique that serves to help the student understand the underlying motivation behind a statement. Ideally, the student, assumed to be capable of understanding motivations behind statements, should be encouraged to interpret his or her own statements. This process not only relieves the teacher of the responsibility, but helps the student learn how to deal with feelings in other situations. Furthermore, by encouraging the student to seek self-meaning, the teacher is communicating a trust or faith in the student's ability to assume major responsibility in the process of problem solving. The following example illustrates the technique of interpretation:

> **Student:** *If only I could get a part-time job, my problems would be over.*

> **Teacher:** *But you'd feel you were missing out on participating in extracurricular activities, which also are important to you.*

Modeling. Modeling is mentioned as a technique because it has long been recognized by sociologists and anthropologists as important in shaping learned behaviors. To use the technique most effectively, the teacher should first determine the precise behavior to be modeled. Then follows a tailoring of a specific modeling experience for the student. Peer modeling is useful, because students seem to identify readily with the model. This technique has utility with career planning, speech training, and teaching students acceptable behaviors.

Reinforcement Techniques. Reinforcement techniques often are used in connection with other techniques. Positive reinforcement seems to be useful in instilling useful habits in students. Generally the technique is aimed at developing a new behavior, or changing an existing problem behavior. The reinforcement may take the form of verbal reinforcement, in which the teacher reinforces the student with positive statements when a desired behavior is exhibited.

Gestalt Language. Gestalt language techniques are useful in promoting self-awareness for many students. The teacher works to help the student achieve awareness by putting him or her in touch with what is being said and the possible meanings of these statements. Passons (1975) described what a teacher might say to a student about voice to enhance awareness, for example:

> Listen to yourself in a conversation. Do you usually listen to what you say as you are talking? What do you hear? Listen to the range of your vocabulary. When was the last time you learned and used some new words to express yourself? Do you tend to speak slowly or rapidly? Listen to the volume of your voice. . . . From the viewpoint of others, would you say your voice is settling? Unnerving? What do you feel are the most distinguishing qualities of your voice? (p. 58)

Other gestalt language techniques involve personalizing pronouns (changing the impersonal referent pronouns of "it," "you," and "we" to the self-referent pronoun "I"), changing questions to statements, using body expressions, and sharing hunches.

These skills are basic to good interpersonal relations, and thus they are basic to good teaching. Regardless of the level of knowledge a teacher possesses, the effect of the interpersonal relationship will determine how much of that knowledge will be learned by students.

CONCLUDING COMMENTS

The development of skills in effective communication is necessary for good interaction with students and should lead to a better general classroom environment. The saying that "children are people, too" should serve as a basis for teacher-student interactions. Empathy, genuineness, and unconditional positive regard help communicate to students that they are accepted as persons. Teachers must communicate not only an interest in their students' academic achievement but also in their personal and social development as well. To do this teachers must be available and willing to interact with students in discussing matters important to them. The effective teacher listens to students, respects students, and genuinely cares about them. He or she is nondefensive and honest in helping students explore their thoughts and feelings. This is not an easy role to fulfill, yet it is so critical to the total development of students. Using and teaching students to use effective facilitative techniques will assist the teacher in fulfilling the role.

REFERENCES

Aspy, D. N., & Roebuck, F. N. (1972). An investigation of the relationship between student levels of cognitive functioning and the teacher's classroom behavior. *Journal of Educational Research, 65, 365–368.*

Bostrom, R. N. (1990). *Listening behavior: Measurement and application.* New York: Guilford.

Brammer, L. M., & Shostrum, E. L. (1989). *Therapeutic psychology: Fundamentals of counseling and psychotherapy.* Englewood Cliffs, NJ: Prentice–Hall.

Damon, W. (1988). *The moral child.* New York: Free Press.

Gendlin, E. T. (1974). Client-centered and experiential psychotherapy. In D. A. Wexler & L. N. North (Eds.), *Innovations in client-centered therapy.* New York: Wiley.

Gordon, T. (1974). *Teacher effectiveness training.* New York: P. H. Wyden.

Hammond, D. C., Hepworth, D. H., & Smith, V. G. (1977). *Improving therapeutic communication.* San Francisco: Jossey-Bass.

Hawes, D. J. (1989). Communication between teachers and children: a counselor consultant/trainer model. *Elementary School Guidance and Counseling, 24,* 58–67.

Mehrabian (1971). *Silent Messages.* Belmont, CA: Wadsworth.

Mortensen, B. F. (1978). *If you're mad, spit!* Provo, UT: Brigham Young University Press.

Passons, W. R. (1975). *Gestalt approaches in counseling.* New York: Holt, Rinehart, and Winston.

Porter, E. H., Jr. (1950). *An introduction to therapeutic counseling.* Boston: Houghton Mifflin .

Rogers, C. R. (1957). The necessary and sufficient conditions of therapeutic personality change. *Journal of Consulting Psychology, 21,* 95–103.

Rogers, C. R. (1961). *On becoming a person.* Boston: Houghton Mifflin.

Rogers, C. R. (1962). The interpersonal relationship: The core of guidance. *Harvard Educational Review, 32,* 416–429.

Rogers, C. R. (1969). *Freedom to learn.* Columbus, OH: Charles E. Merrill.

Rogers, C. R. (1977). *Carl Rogers on personal power.* New York: Delacorte Press.

UNIT II
IMPROVING
SELF-CONCEPT
AND RELATIONSHIPS

Chapter 4

SELF-CONCEPT
AND DISCIPLINE

This chapter focuses on two elements of student-teacher interactions—self-concept and discipline—and discusses the close relationship between these two concepts. The chapter also includes a brief discussion of "processes" in the classroom and the importance of recognizing, developing, and communicating understanding of these various processes in student-teacher interactions.

Self-concept is one of those global terms that is sometimes difficult to grasp in all its broad interpretations. *Self-concept is defined as the total of all qualities that an individual attributes to self.* It is an individual's way of saying, "This is I." It represents an individual's physical, social, and emotional worlds and his or her ways of responding to challenges and feedback, which help shape the view of self. The self-concept is determined by answers to such questions as: Who am I? What will significant persons in my life think if I do such and such? Why don't I feel like other persons my age? What is the purpose of my life? *Teacher effectiveness with students depends on how self-concepts are developed and maintained.*

Questions such as "Who are you?" lead to other questions. But which "you" is the student using in responding? Should an individual describe the private picture of what he or she is really like? What he or she fears he or she is like? The ideal self? The bad self? The self pictured by others? If so, which others? What about the different ways the individual thinks of self at different times? These questions illustrate the necessity of distinguishing among the selves, because the selves seem to have independent meanings, to be elicited in different situations, and to have different responses to feedback from significant others.

Snygg and Combs (1959) identified three parts of the self: the self as object, the self as doer, and the self as observer. It is on the basis of these classifications that some authors use the term *self-concept* to mean the self as "object," or the perceptions an individual holds of self. The term *self-esteem* is then used to mean the "observer" part of the individual, which places a value or judgment on self. McCandless (1961) described six qualities of the self-concept: accuracy, clarity, complexity, consistency, flexibility, and self-acceptance.

Fitts (1965) presented eight subidentities as part of the self-concept:

1. **Identity.** This is how the individual views self. It is the individual's way of saying, "This is what I am."
2. **Self-satisfaction.** This might also be called self-acceptance because it includes the individual's feelings about the way self is viewed.
3. **Behavior.** Here the individual reflects on feelings about the way he or she acts.
4. **Physical self.** This subidentity presents feelings about "body, state of health, physical appearance, skills, and sexuality" (p. 3).
5. **Moral-ethical self.** This part of the self-concept reflects one's feelings about being a "bad" or "good" person.
6. **Personal self.** This component of the self-concept involves the individual's feelings of personal worth and adequacy, appraising personal worth apart from the individual's relationships with others.
7. **Family self.** This self conveys how the individual feels about self in relationships with family members or other significant persons.
8. **Social self.** This self is concerned with one's perceptions of worth as related to other persons in general.

Another significant part of self-concept is *self-disclosure,* or the degree to which an individual reveals self to others. There is some degree of freedom, openness, and trusting involved in self-disclosure. It involves all of the eight subidentities previously discussed, because it is concerned with awareness of human behavior as well as with perceptions of self and feedback from others in interpersonal relations.

JOHARI WINDOW

The Johari Window (Luft, 1984) is one way of examining the concept of self-disclosure. The Johari Window (Table 4.1) takes its name from the first names of the two men who developed the model: Joseph Luft and Harry Ingram.

TABLE 4.1
Johari Window

SELF

		KNOWN	UNKNOWN
OTHERS	**KNOWN**	PUBLIC (open and free discussion, no threat, appropriate topics of discussion with most anyone.)	BLIND (others see things about which we are unaware, areas of vulnerability.)
	UNKNOWN	HIDDEN (private person, requires self-disclosure, requires risk to share.)	UNCONSCIOUS (the unknown, presumed to exist, revealed in dreams, untapped resources.)

Note. From *Group Processes: An Introduction to Group Dynamics* (p. 13) by J. Luft, 1984, Palo Alto, CA: Mayfield. Copyright 1984 by Mayfield Publishing. Reprinted by permission.

The window is actually a series of different windows or panes, and is read as a matrix

The four panes in the window in Table 4.1 represent significant characteristics of an individual in relationship with another individual or with a group of individuals. These characteristics fall into four areas: public, blind, hidden, and unconscious.

1. **Public.** This is the area known both to self and to others. It is limited only by what one is willing to reveal within a given period of time and under a given set of circumstances.
2. **Blind.** This area is known to others but unknown to self. The individual is unaware of certain characteristics about self that are fairly obvious to others. The individual remains unaware until he or she is capable of receiving objective feedback concerning such characteristics.
3. **Hidden.** Information in this area is known to self but unknown to others. This pane in the window includes personal information that one generally does not reveal to others. Such information remains private until the individual is willing to self-disclose.

   4. Unconscious. This area is unknown to self and to others. Information
   in this area may be revealed under stress, through dreams, or by hypno-
   sis. This is the area in which much of an individual's potential can be
   said to exist.

The Johari window can be applied to any individual. However, the relationship of the size of each pane will vary from individual to individual. The
public and blind areas will be larger than the hidden and unconscious areas for
a person who is open and quick to self-disclose. For one who is closed and
keeps feelings to self, the public and blind areas will be small and the hidden
and unconscious areas will be large.

Teachers who establish a climate for open and honest discussions will find
their students more apt to self-disclose thoughts, feelings, values, and opinions.
In situations where students feel threatened, they will probably not feel free to
reveal themselves. We emphasize the need for feedback in the process. Unless
persons are willing to provide feedback, and unless the feedback is heard, behaviors or attitudes will not change.

MASLOW'S HIERARCHY OF NEEDS

Maslow (1970) placed self-concept needs, including the need for self-esteem,
among other needs of the individual. His concept of *self-actualization* also includes much of what has been discussed under the heading of self-concept. In
looking at self-actualization, one can divide the total identity into actual, potential, aspired, and ideal selves. The *actual self* is the total pattern of characteristics
in terms of which one perceives self at a given moment in time. The *potential self*
is the total pattern that might be attained if all capabilities were developed to their
fullest. The *aspired self* is the total pattern of attributes one perceives oneself as
attempting to attain. The *ideal self* is the total pattern of characteristics one would
credit to self if one were able to realize an ultimate standard of perfection.

Maslow took the position that needs can be placed in a hierarchy from the
most basic needs to the higher order needs. Figure 4.1 presents Maslow's hierarchy.

The most basic needs are those characterized as *physiological.* These needs
must be satisfied to maintain life. The next level involves physical and psychological *safety* needs. Meeting these needs requires living in a nonthreatening
environment in which one is free from fear. The third level in the hierarchy

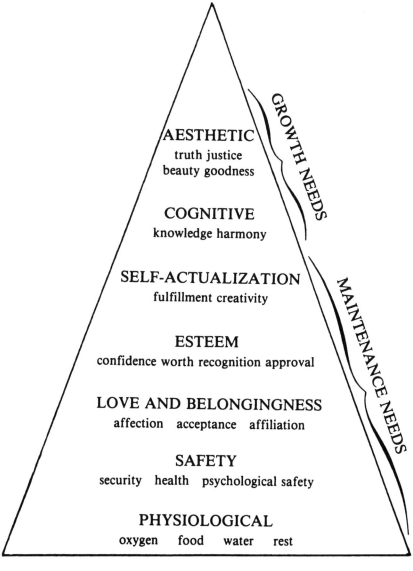

Figure 4.1. Hierarchy of needs data from *Motivation and Personality*, 2nd ed. by Abraham H. Maslow. Copyright © 1954 by Harper & Row Publishers, Inc. Copyright © 1970 by Abraham H. Maslow. Reprinted by permission of Harper Collins Publishers, Inc.

involves *reciprocal affection*—having family and friends and belonging to a group. This level is followed by the need for *esteem,* or to hold a high opinion of oneself and have the respect, admiration, and confidence of others.

Once these four basic maintenance needs are satisfied, the motivation of the individual is then toward *self-actualization.* Maslow (1970) identified the following attributes as characteristic of self-actualizing persons: having a clear perception and an acceptance of reality; being able to recognize and accept personal limitations as well as the limitations of others; being interested in improving discrepancies between what is and what ought to be; having the ability to be spontaneous spontaneous; being problem oriented; being detached, reserved, dignified, calm, and independent of the environment; having the ability to gain satisfaction from within themselves; being able to experience wonder, awe, and an appreciation of the mysteries of life; identifying with human beings in general, and having few deep, profound interpersonal relationships; having a democratic character structure; focusing equally on ends and means; possessing an unhostile, philosophical sense of humor; and being creative and resisting conformity. Maslow felt that perhaps less than one percent of the population might attain self-actualization.

The next level in the hierarchy is the *cognitive* need, or the desire to know and understand. The final level is an *aesthetic* need, or a need for order, symmetry, and closure. It is not clear if these final three needs are actually a part of the hierarchy or if they are interactive. It appears that some persons achieve self-actualization and develop themselves in the cognitive or aesthetic realms while others actually use their cognitive and/or aesthetic interests as a part of their self-actualizing tendencies.

This hierarchy of needs has important implications for teachers. Teachers must understand the importance of fulfilling basic needs, for both themselves and their students, before the teaching-learning process can be expected to be effective. Teachers also must understand the important role they play in the lives of all students, who need attention, affection, belonging, and a sense of achievement. In fact, *an instructional goal of teachers should be to promote the self-actualization of each student.*

POSITIVE SELF-CONCEPT DEVELOPMENT

Coopersmith (1967) provided the following description of persons with a high self-concept:

Persons high in their own estimation approach tasks and persons with the expectation that they will be well received and successful. They have confidence in their perceptions and judgments and believe that they can bring their efforts to a favorable resolution. Their favorable self-attitudes lead them to accept their own opinions and place credence and trust in their reactions and conclusions. This permits them to follow their own judgments when there is a difference of opinion and also permits them to consider novel ideas. The trust in self that accompanies feelings of worthiness is likely to provide the conviction that one is correct and the courage to express those convictions. The attitudes and expectations that lead the individual with high self-esteem to greater social independence and creativity also lead him to more assertive and vigorous social actions. They are more likely to be participants than listeners in group discussions, they report less difficulty in forming friendships, and they will express opinions even when they know these opinions may meet with a hostile reception. Among the factors that underlie and contribute to these actions are their lack of self-consciousness and their lack of preoccupation with personal problems. Lack of self-consciousness permits them to present their ideas in a full and forthright fashion; lack of self-preoccupation permits them to consider and examine external issues. (pp. 70–71)

In contrast, Coopersmith (1967) described a person with a low self-concept thusly:

The picture of the individual with low self-esteem that emerges from these results is markedly different. These persons lack trust in themselves and are apprehensive about expressing unpopular or unusual ideas. They do not wish to expose themselves, anger others, or perform deeds that would attract attention. They are likely to live in the shadows of a social group, listening rather than participating, and preferring the solitude of withdrawal above the interchange of participation. Among the factors that contribute to the withdrawal of those low in self-esteem are their marked self-consciousness and preoccupation with inner problems. This great awareness of themselves distracts them from attending to other persons and issues and is likely to result in a morbid preoccupation with their difficulties. The effect is to limit their social intercourse and thus decrease the possibilities of friendly and supportive relationships. (p. 71)

Swayze (1980) described three causes of low or negative self-concepts: overprotection, domination, and neglect. The adult who is overprotective communicates to the child that he or she is incapable of completing a task without help from the adult. The adult who dominates communicates to the child that he or she is untrustworthy in addition to being incapable. The child who is neglected must resort to negative behavior to get attention from adults. In all three cases, the child feels humiliated and is likely to strike back with aggressive behavior.

Readers are cautioned not to use these descriptions to the disadvantage of students. The self-fulfilling prophecy (see Chapter 7) operates on the self-concept just as it operates on achievement. Children probably will behave as they are expected to behave. With this in mind, teachers must be aware of what their expectations will do to students' feelings about themselves. Teachers therefore must understand that the child with characteristics of a low self-concept is vulnerable to teacher behaviors that further decrease self-concept. Teachers must communicate to such students, both verbally and nonverbally, that they are persons of worth and importance, both as individuals and as a part of the class. Next to the home, the school is probably the most important determinant of self-concept. School personnel have the responsibility for working to build the child's feelings of self worth, feelings of autonomy, and skills in dealing with expectations of self, parents, and teachers. The teacher should think of self-concept as a subject for study throughout the school year.

Phillips and Zigler (1980) described how children develop positive self-concepts through curiosity, independence, pride in their accomplishments, and the ability to recover from failure and frustrating situations. They presented some guidelines for teachers who wish to contribute to children's positive self-concepts:

1. Positive self-concept is expressed differently at various stages of development. This expression should be kept in mind when planning interventions so that children are reassured of their capabilities and self-worth and are not challenged to attain unreasonable goals. Teachers are reminded that unrealistically high aspirations lead to frequent failure and to a low self-concept. Aspirations that are so low that they are guaranteed to avoid failure also lead to a low self-concept because accomplishments are unimpressive and so far below potential that the student is depressed.
2. Teachers must transmit feelings of acceptance and unconditional positive regard to children. This is accomplished by communicating these feelings verbally and physically. The teacher works to create a climate in which all children feel special and useful. The teacher who fosters a positive environment responds to the needs of each child. Teaching material is matched to each child's ability and interest. Comparisons between children are not made, because the teacher recognizes the uniqueness of each child.

3. The environment should be predictable and responsive so that the child learns how to attain personal goals. This includes not only the physical environment but the social environment as well. Such an environment contains clearly defined standards and rules.

4. The child is given support in an attempt to rid him or her of unacceptable behaviors. Positive behaviors are rewarded while restraint, denial of participation in desirable activities, and separation from instigating incidents or situations are used to address undesirable behaviors. Teachers avoid corporal punishment, degrading remarks, or withdrawal of love as consequences for undesirable behaviors.

5. Children are provided an opportunity to help plan activities and to establish class rules, in a manner appropriate to their ability to make decisions. This can be accomplished in a classroom discussion in which all children feel free to voice their opinions and express their beliefs.

6. Challenges are provided that are difficult for children but within their potential to grasp. Children benefit by seeing themselves do something they doubted they could do. Ample time is allowed to insure some degree of success. *Efforts are praised as well as accomplishments.*

7. Constructive coping skills for dealing with failure and frustration are taught to children. The teacher can provide a constructive, supportive explanation about why the child failed and can help children accept the inevitability of some failures and mistakes. Teachers should be encouraged to help children learn how to cope with both their successes and their failures.

8. Opportunities are provided for the development of self-reliance and self-initiative. The procedure to accomplish this goal is, first, to help students develop reasonable, realistic goals; second, to help students select those concrete actions necessary to reach the goals; third, to divide a goal into subgoals and develop an appropriate timetable so that each student can see progress toward the goal; and fourth, the goal must be defined clearly enough for each student to know when it is met. This process encourages students to rely on their own perceptions.

The preceding list substantially covers the necessary components for teachers who desire to have positive influence on the self-concept of students. Several helpful suggestions may be added. Readers might conclude that the following suggestions are more informal and indirect. In all cases, teachers should adjust expectations to the developmental levels of students.

Students need to be taught both verbal and nonverbal communication skills. These skills involve communicating their thoughts and feelings to others while also learning to interpret behaviors of others. Too often students interpret nonverbal behaviors as indicators of something negative about themselves when those behaviors had nothing to do with them. Assertiveness training can be helpful to students who are learning how to communicate with and provide feedback to others.

Students need to be helped to learn differences between thoughts and actions. Many people interpret what someone thinks about them with the same intensity as they interpret what someone actually does to them. While we believe that what one thinks determines how one acts, we should also recognize that the receiver decides how to respond to thoughts and actions of others.

Students need to learn that complicated questions do not have simple answers. Questions students raise are complicated, difficult to answer, and involve much more than appears on the surface. Students who experience acceptance and positive regard come to believe a teacher is genuinely interested in providing answers. Teachers who do not communicate caring will be perceived as evasive and perhaps even dishonest.

Most literature on self-concept describes independence and trust in self as characteristics of a positive self-concept. Students need to learn when to trust others, especially adults, and when to seek adult support. Both the ability to recognize limitations and the ability to request assistance are manifestations of a positive self-concept.

TEACHER'S SELF-CONCEPT

Teachers' feelings toward themselves have a tremendous bearing on their acceptance of students. A warm, supportive, empathic environment is directly related to high self-concepts among students in such an environment. Purkey (1978) concluded that teachers who understand and accept themselves have greater capacity to understand and to accept their students. This self-acceptance seems to transcend teaching methods, skills, or techniques. Spaulding (1964) found a positive relationship between teacher self-concept and student academic achievement. Students in classrooms where teachers were calm, supportive, and accepting had higher self-concepts, while students who had dominating, threatening, or sarcastic teachers had more negative self-concepts. Other studies also have found strong relationships between students' self-concepts and their academic achievement (Brookover, Thomas, & Paterson, 1964; Epps, 1969; Rosenberg & Simmons, 1971). In addition, Reckless, Dinitz, and Kay (1957) found a significant relationship between low self-concept and an inclination toward juvenile delinquency as well as low school achievement.

Despite these findings, Scheirer and Kraut (1979), in a review of the literature linking self-concept and achievement, concluded that such a relationship is not causal. They went on to caution educators against focusing too much attention on enhancement of self-concept if the goal is toward improving academic achievement.

The self-concept of students is affected by many factors, but none probably as significantly as the self-concept of the teacher. Because teachers spend more time with students than even their parents, teachers provide models of self-acceptance and self-worth. Teachers who demonstrate positive self-concepts also provide encouragement and support to students who are developing expressions of their uniqueness. A teacher with a good self-concept will not be threatened by a student who is uniquely different. Because teacher self-concept is so important, teachers need opportunities to focus on their own mental health. Chapter 9 is devoted to special problems of teachers.

At this point, one noteworthy proposal is presented for use in helping teachers who desire to develop a more positive self-concept. This proposal was presented by Wrenn (1980), who identified three elements.

The first element is to recognize one's own personal qualities. This recognition may be accomplished by learning to admit successes and to accept compliments from others. Too often persons dismiss a real personal strength or a real compliment because they do not know how to respond to one who offers praise. A simple "thank you" or "I'm glad you noticed" is sufficient. Another essential component for maintaining positive self-concept is to have a "significant other" in whom one can confide, with whom one can share, and from whom one can receive support.

The second element identified by Wrenn is to develop a positive outlook about life and positive beliefs about the nature of people and of the universe. Such beliefs provide the foundation for forming beliefs about a specific student. Explore beliefs and values with other persons and learn how these beliefs and values determine behaviors. Christenson (1977) identified some values he believed all persons can accept (Table 4.2). His list may be useful as one examines personal values and beliefs in the process of developing a personal philosophy of life.

Not only are these values significant for teachers to accept, they seem to be among the things students should understand and accept. To accomplish

TABLE 4.2
Values We Can All Accept

1. The most important thing in life is the kind of persons we are becoming, the qualities of character and moral behavior we are developing.
2. Self-discipline, defined as the strength to do what we know we ought to do even when we would rather not, is important in our lives.
3. Being trustworthy, so that when we say we will or will not do something we can be believed, is important.
4. Telling the truth, especially when it hurts to do so, is essential to trust, to self-respect, and to social health. Unless we can tell the truth when it is painful to us and seemingly injurious to our short-run interests, we are not truthful persons.
5. Being honest in all aspects of life, including our business practices and our relations with government, is important.
6. Doing work well, whatever it may be, and the satisfactions that come from this attitude, are important.
7. Personal courage and personal responsibility in the face of group pressures to do what, deep down, one disbelieves in, are important.
8. Using honorable means, those that respect the rights of others, in seeking our individual and collective ends is important.
9. Can it survive the sunlight?" is one of the most reliable tests of dubious conduct in private as well as in public life.
10. It is important to have the courage to say, "I'm sorry, I was wrong."
11. Recognizing inconspicuous, unsung people who have admirable qualitites and live worthwhile lives is important.
12. Good sportsmanship should be understood and celebrated. Winning is *not* all-important.
13. It is necessary to get facts straight and to hear both sides before drawing conclusions adverse to a person, group, or institution.
14. It is important to listen, really listen, to persons with whom we are having disputes or difficulties.
15. Treating others as we would wish to be treated is one of the best guides to human conduct. This principle applies to persons of every class, race, nationality, and religion.
16. Another good guide is this: If everyone in comparable circumstances acted as you propose to act, would it be for the best?
17. No man is an island; behavior that may seem to be of purely private concern often affects those about us and society itself.
18. Adversity is the best test of our maturity and of our mettle.
19. Respect for law is essential to a healthy society, but responsible, nonviolent civil disobedience can be compatible with our ethical heritage.
20. It is important to acquire respect for the democratic values of free speech, a free press, freedom of assembly, freedom of religion, and due process of law. We should recognize that this principle applies to speech we abhor, groups we dislike, persons we despise.

Note. From "McGuffrey's Ghost and Moral Education Today" by R. M. Christenson, 1977, *Phi Delta Kappan, 58*, p. 738. Copyright 1977 by Phi Delta Kappa. Reprinted by permission.

this goal, teachers should incorporate value lessons into the regular subject matter.

The third element in Wrenn's presentation involves demonstrating a sense of caring for others. A person who has developed a sense of self-worth may share it with others so that they too may rapidly move toward feelings of self-worth. The communication techniques discussed in Chapter 3 will be helpful in this area. The ability to communicate positive feelings to students may indeed be the single most important function in teaching.

This caring and communication have been discussed by Frey and Young (1979) in their presentation of ideas that have proven effective in helping students meet their psychological needs. (See Table 4.3.)

The importance of self-concept development should not be underestimated. The way a student feels about self will affect every area of school life. Students will behave in a manner consistent with how they feel about themselves. Certainly, the self-concept is a central factor in student discipline.

BEHAVIOR AND DISCIPLINE

Glasser (1969) distinguished between punishment and discipline by, on the one hand, characterizing punishment as imposed by someone, expressive of authority, based on retribution or revenge, and essentially negative and short-term without sustained personal involvement. Discipline, on the other hand, is based on natural or logical consequences expressive of rules which must be learned in order to function adequately. In discipline, the responsibility for behavior is assumed by the individual and emphasizes teaching ways to act that will result in more successful behavior. Furthermore, punishment is easy and expedient, while discipline is difficult and time consuming.

Adler (Dreikurs, 1982; Grunwald & McAbee, 1985) suggested that children have four goals of misbehavior: attention, power, revenge, or feelings of inadequacy. The approach recommended for dealing with these problems is, first, to help the student understand the goal of misbehavior. Second, the teacher should stop making misbehavior worthwhile to the student. Third, the teacher should look for ways to "encourage" the student to succeed in positive activities.

Lasley (1981) observed two junior high schools for six weeks in an attempt to determine the nature of student misbehavior, the teacher's response to the

TABLE 4.3
Helping Students Meet Psychological Needs

Caring

1. Greet students at the door, in the hallway, or in the cafeteria.
2. Listen to students by focusing, clarifying, and accepting.
3. Speak to the shy person with a friendly smile.
4. Touch students on the arm or shoulder while listening; this shows concern and caring.
5. Know and use student's preferred name.
6. Learn something personal about each student.
7. Send "I care-o-grams" to students.
8. Have teachers write positive comments on papers in addition to grades.
9. Maintain more personal contact after school hours in non-curriculum areas.

Understanding

1. Notice nonverbal indicators that the student is happy, sad, glad, tired, etc., and communicate these observations.
2. Have students develop autobiographies around five important events in their lives.
3. Place success within reasonable reach for every student. Know what the student can do and what is necessary to learn before giving more difficult tasks.
4. Give students the opportunity to air their views or share their hidden agendas.
5. Make positive personal contact with the home.
6. Be willing to listen and *hear* students.
7. Have students interview each other.
8. Allow students to interview you.
9. Allow more sharing of feeling words: "Right now I feel . . ."
10. Use caring and feeling words in the classroom and office.
11. Talk personally with each student during the year and get to know at least one thing special about each person.
12. Eat lunch or share lunch with a student.
13. Reverse roles with students.
14. Show that mistakes are legitimate.

Identifying

1. Have lower ability students tutor lower grade childen.
2. Encourage students to write special goals for themselves for the next day, and follow through on these goals.
3. Provide for student self-evaluation of their work and plans for future growth.
4. Encourage students to keep journals of ideas, successes, etc.
5. Provide space for students to display their work.
6. Have students create values crests and share with others.

TABLE 4.3 (*Continued*)
Helping Students Meet Psychological Needs

Identifying (*Cont.*)

7. Make pictures or profiles of students and have other students write positive comments about them.
8. Announce student achievements on the school public address system.

Recognizing

1. Let students choose someone to work with, and have them share their partner's success with the teacher.
2. Send notes home to parents when students do something well. Do this especially with "problem" students.
3. Find one positive strength or interest in a "problem" student, and give recognition for this, as well as providing opportunities to extend it.
4. Help older students plan learning experiences, make books, etc., for younger children.
5. Have a "teach-in" where students can teach other students things they are especially interested in or skillful at.
6. Try to build on positive ideas you find in a student's work and relate this to previous work when possible.
7. Have teachers identify students on their birthdays.
8. Allow students with birthdays during the summer to pick a date during the school year for personal recognition.
9. Give recognition to individuals as well as the whole class using behavior modification rewards identified and selected by the students.
10. Use teacher assistants.
11. Praise student efforts.
12. Recognize the "Aha" moments and help the student get "in touch" with feelings at that moment.

Note. From "Self-concept Continuum for Understanding Student Behavior" by D. Frey and J. A. Young, 1979, *NASSP Bulletin, 63,* pp. 31–32. Copyright 1979 by National Association of Secondary School Principals. Reprinted by permission.

misbehavior, and the reaction of the student to the teacher. His observations led him to conclude that student misbehavior falls into two categories: coping behaviors and challenging behaviors. *Coping behaviors* appeared to be reactions to boredom (talking, writing notes, or pounding desk)or designed to achieve peer acceptance (smoking, fighting, or indicating willingness to fight). *Challenging behaviors* were either smarting (confronting the teacher verbally or making satirical remarks) or ignoring (disregard for the teacher). Effective teacher management techniques fell into two categories: *nonresponding* and *faceworking*. By ignoring, or not responding to, the misbehavior, the teacher appeared to indicate a willingness to forgive. This action also allowed students an opportunity to develop self-discipline. The behaviors that were ignored were all minor violations of rules of good conduct. Faceworking helped students save face by treating the misbehavior as appropriate rather than as inappropriate. Such a response helps protect the student's self-concept. Ignoring and faceworking can be effective only when the teacher is extremely aware of the difference between real and perceived discipline problems (Thompson, 1976). A *real discipline problem* is one student infringing on the rights of the teacher or other students. In a *perceived discipline problem* no rights are violated and only the teacher perceives the behavior to be a problem. For the teacher, perceived discipline problems are not less significant than real problems. However, the teacher needs to have this distinction clear and be able to avoid confrontations with students where no real problem exists.

The most important point relating to student discipline is to have few rules and to enforce those rules consistently. The personal characteristics of teachers are more important than their theoretical orientation, and personality is more important than subject matter. We recall that discipline is not something isolated from everything else that takes place in the classroom but is an extension of an adult's concern for a child's welfare. Discipline should be a part of the total educational program. The best discipline is that which provides "guidance without domination and freedom without laxity" (Wheeler, 1989, p. 8).

RELATING SELF-CONCEPT TO DISCIPLINE

If one accepts the proposition that self-concept is directly related to discipline, it follows that the better the self-concept, the fewer the discipline problems. A better self-concept is indicated in students whose teachers have close, caring relations with them. Close caring relations are characterized by honesty, acceptance, empathy, respect, and trust. These concepts were discussed in Chapter 3. The teacher who demonstrates these qualities should have a positive self-concept, which leads to better attitudes *about* students, which in turn leads to better self-concepts *in* students.

Goldsmith (1981) identified some significant components of an effective school or classroom discipline code. When rules are developed, they should be written to avoid ambiguity or arbitrariness and the individual rights of students should be respected. Effective rules are based on fair procedures that are flexible enough to provide for the individuality of students. Yet while rules need to be flexible, they also should be administered in a firm, consistent, evenhanded, and uniform manner. The consequences of misbehavior should fit the offense and the lesser consequence should be used.

Other guidelines consistent with a recognition of the relationship between self-concept and discipline, which are important for a pleasant learning environment, are listed here. They are not listed in order of significance.

1. Be the central figure in the classroom. The teacher lays the foundation for successful educational experiences void of discipline problems. The teacher should be enthusiastic about teaching, use student-centered instruction, and emphasize self-respect in the classroom. Lessons should be designed to avoid boredom. The teacher should involve parents and students in decision making while recognizing that the teacher is ultimately responsible for the classroom climate. The practice of allowing students an opportunity to air "gripes" should prove helpful in meeting students' needs to have a voice in classroom management.
2. Set a good example. One of the ways to teach self-discipline is through example. Students, especially in the lower grades, imitate their teachers. Teachers should endeavor to demonstrate honesty, acceptance, empathy, respect, and trust so that students will have an opportunity to imitate these qualities.
3. Make the school experiences interesting, challenging, and exciting. Teachers should arrange for successes for all students. Successful students are most likely to have incentive to attempt new tasks, to feel capable, and to have better self-concepts.
4. Make students feel important, unique, worthwhile and invited (Purkey, 1978). This guideline is directly related to guideline 3. Important to the accomplishment of this goal is correcting students privately and individually. This prevents students from losing face in the presence of their peers. While it may be necessary to delay talking with a student, teachers also should remember that any correcting is to be done as close as possible to the incidence of misbehavior.
5. Deal with improvement of student behavior from a positive basis. Instead of reminding a student of misbehavior, teachers remind the student of preferred behavior. Teachers can help shape behaviors by regularly reinforcing positive behaviors.
6. Be aware of nonverbal messages communicated to students. Mehrabian (1981) concluded that of the total liking behavior communicated, 7% is verbal, 38% is vocal (tone, rate, volume and pitch) and 55% is nonverbal (facial and body language). With this recognition of the impact

of nonverbal messages, teachers should concentrate on congruence between verbal and nonverbal messages and focus on what they may be communicating nonverbally.

7. Establish parameters for expected behavior in the classroom. Teachers are to be firm, yet fair and honest in dealing with students. Students are to know and understand the limits of appropriate behavior in the classroom.

8. Give attention to the behavior, the symptom, and the possible cause(s). Teachers should be aware of symptoms of lowered self-concept such as unhappiness, aggression, withdrawal, insecurity, short attention span, quickness to anger, lack of motivation, reading considerably below grade level, and being easily upset over failures. If these behaviors are observed, they not only may be symptoms of a lowered self-concept but also causes of misbehavior.

9. When inappropriate behavior occurs, isolate the situation and define the problem. Ask the following questions: What is the problem? What is the cause? Who is involved? What strategies might be useful to improve the behavior? Make an attempt to see each situation individually without generalizing the behavior to other situations.

10. Be clear in directions and expectations. Make efforts to have students take responsibility for their behavior. If the expectations are clear, little room is left for students to make excuses.

11. Separate the person from the behavior. Communicate to students your unconditional respect and acceptance of them as persons even when their behavior may be inappropriate. Respond to the specific behavior rather than to the person when unacceptable behavior occurs.

12. Communicate with parents about their children. Involve parents in significant school decisions about their children. Communicate to parents that you want and need their support and that you welcome their contributions.

13. Read about effective discipline practices and classroom management techniques. Plan to attend professional meetings, conferences, or workshops where interaction with colleagues can take place. Develop a list of personal practices and techniques. Develop a personal support system among friends both within and outside of school.

14. Remember that some students will be discipline problems despite your best efforts. Learn about referral sources in the school where students might be sent when all available classroom resources and techniques have been exhausted.

Wheeler (1989) provided a slightly different list of criteria to be used in establishing discipline standards. Her recommendations included the following:

1. Set standards early.
2. Teach a varied, interesting lesson.
3. Let students know that you respect them as students.
4. Be poised, firm, and fair.
5. Teach to the positive.
6. Make discipline quick, consistent, just, and inevitable.
7. Do not group punish.
8. Do not argue or humiliate students.
9. Do not threaten the pupil with their grades.
10. Know the background of each child.
11. Document any proplems thoroughly.
12. Cultivate your own techniques or discipline.
13. Do not assign extra homework as a punishment. (pp. 10–11)

Finally, Gartrell (1987) summarized his discipline principles with the suggestion that teachers strive to build a personal relationship with each child. In these relationships, teachers get to know each student very well in terms of the student's strengths and weaknesses. This knowledge will permit teachers to recognize who will need extra orientation or encouragement. Many discipline problems arise when students become bored. The best solution to student boredom is to change activities and reduce the transition time between activities.

SUCCESSFUL CLASSROOM MANAGEMENT

The six-step problem-solving method proposed by Gordon (1974) is consistent with the fourteen guidelines for creating a pleasant learning environment presented previously. Gordon's method permits teachers and students to plan, organize, implement, and participate in shared classroom activities. The teacher serves as leader/facilitator and encourages leadership among students. Such a system trains students in responsible decision making, a skill needed in adult life. The problem-solving method involves the student at each level of the process. Gordon's (1974) six steps are as follows:

1. **Definition of the Problem.** Raise the following questions at the initial level: What is the student actually doing? Is the behavior a problem? What does the student think about the behavior? Does the student have control over the behavior? Getting down to the real problem may be difficult unless both teacher and student are willing to explore the situation. The teacher can help by emphasizing a willingness to find a solution acceptable to the student. Make sure the student recognizes the behavior as a problem and as a behavior that he or she feels a need to

change. Otherwise, the process loses its mutuality. Remember to look beyond symptoms to the cause(s).

2. **Generation of Possible Solutions.** Both teacher and student should present suggestions for what might be done to solve the problem. At this stage all alternatives are noted without evaluating or judging their relative usefulness. Spend enough time at this stage so that all possible solutions are listed. Keep working until apparently no additional alternatives exist.

3. **Evaluation of Alternatives.** The first step in this stage is to decide which alternatives are totally unacceptable to either teacher or student. This sometimes results in the combining of two or more of the possible solutions generated in step 2. An alternative should be judged on how well it satisfies the teacher, how well it satisfies the student, its effects on others, how practical it is, and the probability of being a lasting solution.

4. **Decision on Best Alternative.** At this stage the teacher and student agree on the best alternative. The best alternative may be a compromise from several of the alternatives presented in step 2. Definitely both teacher and student need to understand fully the alternative chosen. Making a written copy of the alternative chosen and seeing that both parties receive a copy are wise procedures.

5. **Implementation of Decision.** Are preliminary steps necessary before the plan can be implemented? A timetable should be established that includes plans for evaluation of the alternative.

6. **Evaluation.** The success of the alternative selected must be determined. Because not all alternatives will be good ones, the evaluation stage will allow modifications to be made. Questions to ask include: Is the problem solved? What makes this alternative effective? Were both teacher and student satisfied with the results? How can this particular alternative be useful in future situations?

The system just described involves a "process" as much as it involves an "outcome." The process-focused approach is one in which the teacher examines the dynamics of the interaction between teacher and student. Because such an approach requires effective process skills, we believe it will be operative when conditions are established in which students recognize the classroom as a caring environment. A caring environment will result in fewer discipline problems. An effective teacher will demonstrate the value of processes by recognizing the importance of the learning that takes place during each stage in the development of a classroom management system. Also, rather than just meeting students' demands for attention, an effective teacher will communicate the importance of students' learning to solve problems.

The essence of positive discipline is to address behavior that needs addressing but to respect the felings of the child. The more the consequence is logical from the child's point of view, the closer we are to child guidance and the farther we are from a form of discipline that has the effect of punishment.

Group-focus behaviors are those which maintain attention on the group even when one student is receiving individual attention. Such a focus involves group alerting, the extent to which the teacher holds students responsible for completing tasks in the group. Group-focus behaviors are significantly related to effective classroom management.

Teacher behaviors have been found to be related to successful classroom management. Behaviors focus primarily on the process involved in the classroom group and secondarily on individual students.

Regardless of the technique, strategy, or teacher behavior involved, the goal should be student *internalization of group norms* of appropriate behavior. Internalization results from extending one's concept of self to include attributes which were parts of other people. A student can extend conception of self to include many roles and this internalization can vary in degree. In any case, the internalizations become values for the student.

Once values have been internalized, the student reacts to them as he or she reacts to the rest of self. If some behavior violates a value, the student is more likely to react in such a way as to alter the value, or to simply employ self-discipline. The entire process is very important to our society today. Youngsters need to learn responsibility and cooperation, responsibility for solving problems, and a willingness to work with others.

In a relationship with a teacher, a student is constantly exposed to the evaluation of his or her actions. Teachers are proud or ashamed, approving or disapproving, rewarding or punishing, soothing or irritating. Before long, a student applies the implications of these actions to what it means to be a person, and becomes keenly aware of the valued or devalued attributes of these roles and identities.

So pleasant are the consequences that follow from a teacher's approval of one or more attributes that the student becomes proficient at displaying them as a means of earning an even higher self-concept. So unpleasant are the consequences of teacher disapproval of attributes that the student becomes equally proficient at hiding them or playing them down to avoid a lowering of self-concept. The student learns the rules of the game. Then after a period of playing the required roles, those rules are finally internalized. The student then applies them to self and suffers a lowered self-concept when he or she violates them, whether or not anyone else knows about the violation. At that point the student is self-disciplined and has the potential for a higher self-concept.

REFERENCES

Brookover, W. B., Thomas, S., & Paterson, A. (1964). Self-concept of ability and school environment. *Sociology of Education, 37,* 271–278.

Christenson, R. M. (1977). McGuffey's ghost and moral education today. *Phi Delta Kappan, 58,* 737–742.

Coopersmith, S. (1967). *The antecedents of self-esteem.* San Francisco: W. H. Freeman.

Dreikurs, R. (1982). *Maintaining sanity in the classroom.* New York: Harper & Row.

Epps, E. G. (1969). Correlates of academic achievement among northern and southern urban Negro students. *Journal of Social Issues, 25,* 55–70.

Felker, D. W. (1974). *Building positive self-concepts.* Minneapolis, MN: Burgess.

Fitts, W. H. (1965). *Tennessee Self-Concept Scale Manual.* Nashville, TN: Counselor Recording and Tests.

Frey, D., & Young, J. A. (1979). Self-concept continuum for understanding student behavior. *NASSP Bulletin, 63,* 27–33.

Gartrell, D. (1987). Punishment or guidance. *Young Children, 42,* 55–61.

Glasser, W. (1969). *Schools without failure.* New York: Harper & Row.

Goldsmith, A. H. (1981). Legal requirements of student discipline codes. *The Education Digest, 47,* 17–20.

Gordon, T. (1974). *Teacher effectiveness training.* New York: David McKay Co.

Grunwald, B. B., & McAbee, H. V. (1985). *Guiding the family: Practical counseling techniques.* Muncie, IN: Accelerated Development.

Lasley, T. J. (1981). Classroom misbehavior: Some field observations. *The High School Journal, 64,* 142–149.

Luft, J. (1984). *Group processes: An introduction to group dynamics* (3rd Ed.). Palo Alto, CA: Mayfield.

Maslow, A. H. (1970). *Motivation and personality.* New York: Harper & Row.

McCandless, B. R. (1961). *Children and adolescents.* New York: Holt, Rinehart & Winston.

Mehrabian, A. (1981). *Silent messages.* Belmont, CA: Wadsworth.

Phillips, D. A., & Zigler, E. (1980). Self-concept theory and its practical implications. In Yawkey, T. D. (Ed.), *The self-concept of the young child* (pp. 111–112). Provo, UT: Brigham Young University.

Purkey, W. W. (1978). *Inviting school success: A self-concept approach to teaching and learning.* Belmont, CA: Wadsworth.

Reckless, W. C., Dinitz, S., & Kay, B. (1957). The self component in potential delinquency and potential nondelinquency. *American Sociological Review, 22,* 566–570.

Rosenberg, M., & Simmons, R. G. (1971). *Black and white self-esteem: The urban school child.* Washington, DC: American Sociological Association.

Scheirer, M. A., & Kraut, R. E. (1979). Increasing educational achievement via self-concept change. *Review of Educational Research, 49,* 131–149.

Snygg, D., & Combs, A. W. (1959). *Individual behavior: A new frame of reference for psychology.* New York: Harper and Row.

Spaulding, R. L. (1964). Achievement, creativity, and self-concept correlates of teacher pupil transactions in elementary schools. In C. B. Stendler (Ed.), *Readings in child behavior and development.* New York: Harcourt, Brace, and World.

Swayze, M. C. (1980). Self-concept development in young children. In Yawkey,

T. D. (Ed.), *The self-concept of the young child* (pp. 33–48). Provo, UT: Brigham Young University.

Thompson, G. (1976). Discipline and the high school teacher. *The Clearing House, 49,* 408–413.

Wheeler, Nedra (1989). A motivational behavioral approach to violence in school. Paper presented at the National Conference of the Council for Exceptional Children, Charlotte, NC, September 24–26. 12 pages.

Wrenn, C. G. (1980). The importance of believing in yourself, or, building a more positive self-image. *The School Counselor, 27,* 159–167.

Chapter **5**

DEVELOPING RELATIONSHIPS

The purpose of this chapter is to incorporate the interpersonal processes and facilitative techniques presented in Chapters 3 and 4 into practical strategies for developing relationships.

TEACHER-STUDENT RELATIONSHIPS

Teachers' attitudes and beliefs affect their relationships with students. Sometimes teachers develop faulty beliefs about students which result in negative effects. Dinkmeyer and Dinkmeyer (1979) listed several faulty beliefs that may impede learning. For example, "(1) students must cooperate with me, as the teacher, (2) my plans must succeed at all costs, and (3) children are the product of their heredity and environment and thus cannot be changed" (p. 5).

Negative beliefs come from within the person. They are learned and can be changed. For example, a teacher was upset over the fact that her lesson was ruined because of an unruly student. She had been having difficulty with this student for months. The teacher disciplined the student, but this did not help the situation. She held the faulty belief that all of her students must cooperate at all times. One day, the teacher decided to talk with the student. During the discussion, she discovered that the student's father had a terminal illness. Understanding the situation, the teacher was able to change her negative feelings toward the student. She was able to recognize that the behavior manifested by the student was meaningful. The relationship between them improved.

Developing An Awareness of Needs

Positive teacher-student relationships can be developed. Teachers may begin by becoming aware of their students' needs. Effective teachers understand that before any learning can take place, students' needs must be satisfied. Teachers can facilitate learning by becoming familiar with Maslow's (1970) hierarchy of needs (see Chapter 4). Once again, listed from lower to higher order, those needs are:

1. Physiological or Biological
2. Safety
3. Belongingness and Love
4. Esteem
5. Self-Actualization
6. Knowing and Understanding
7. Aesthetic

Lower order needs must be satisfied before higher order needs can be met. At each level, students will require different degrees of satisfaction. For example, one student may require 40% satisfaction at level one, 60% satisfaction at level two, and 80% satisfaction at level three. Another student may require 80% satisfaction at level one, 50% satisfactions at level two, and 95% satisfaction at level three before proceeding to level four.

The first three levels in the hierarchy are particularly important for teachers to understand. When the first three needs are satisfied, self-esteem (level four), positive relationships, and learning may take place. The following examples illustrate this point.

If, on the one hand, a student does not eat breakfast and attends school hungry, then the level one need is not satisfied. On the other hand, another student may eat junk food instead of a well-balanced breakfast. The first student may not be able to concentrate in class and may fall asleep. The second student may become hyperactive, which may result in disruptive classroom behavior. To resolve these problems, a teacher may decide to meet with the parents and their children to discuss the importance of eating a well-balanced breakfast.

A student who comes from a single parent family may have satisfied the level one need but not the safety need of level two. For example, a second-grade student returns from school to an empty house. The father left home a few years ago and the mother works. This student may develop a fear that the mother will decide to leave also. This fear may affect the student's ability to concentrate and learn. A teacher who identifies this need may talk to the student and listen to the student's concerns.

A student whose parents have divorced may have levels one and two satisfied but not level three, love and belongingness. This student may have a father who rarely, if ever, visits. The student may believe that the father doesn't care about him or her. These beliefs in turn may affect the student in class. A caring and understanding teacher may be able to help the student by listening to the student's needs.

If a student has failed continuously in school, he or she may believe that there is no use in trying. This student believes that he or she is incapable of learning and feels worthless. Level four, esteem, has not been satisfied. A teacher may need to investigate the situation further to determine which of the previous levels, if any, have not been satisfied. This student may need special or additional help. In addition, to help satisfy this need, a teacher may decide to assign the student activities that he or she can accomplish.

Activity

Think of a situation in your life in which one of the listed needs was not satisfied. Describe the situation. What need was not satisfied? How did you feel? How was the need satisfied? How do you feel about the situation in retrospect?

Creating a Positive Atmosphere

Creating an atmosphere or environment of mutual understanding and respect is another means by which teachers can develop positive teacher-student relationships. Classes in which positive teacher-student relationships have developed are easy to identify. These classes are usually well organized and when you visit them you can feel the warmth. Students are busy and appear to enjoy the tasks that are assigned. Teachers listen to their students and are aware of their feelings.

Conversely, teachers who have not developed positive working relationships with their students are also easy to identify. These teachers focus their attention exclusively on the cognitive abilities of their students. They subscribe to the faulty belief that their plans must succeed at all costs. Often, these teachers praise their "good" students and are negative in their dealings with their "poorer" students. One frequently hears negative comments about the "poorer" students in the teachers' lounge. Such comments center around descriptions of students who cannot learn, do not do their class work, appear to be in a trance, or are just a plain nuisance in class.

Preventing Discipline Problems

Most discipline problems occur in classes where teachers have not developed positive relationships with their students. Disciple problems may be avoided by establishing rules during the first few days of class. Positive teacher-student relationships can be initiated by having students help in formulating the rules. While school policies and procedures must be included, other rules can be established through the cooperation of students. During this time, teachers and students may discuss the consequences for breaking rules. When students participate in making rules, teachers find that students break the rules less frequently.

The following list of fifteen discipline suggestions for teachers, developed by Stoops and King-Stoops (1981), may serve as a guide for developing your own classroom rules.

1. On the first day, cooperatively develop classroom standards.
2. Incorporate school and district policies in the classroom list.
3. Establish consequences for good and poor behavior.
4. Expect good behavior from your students, and they will try to live up to your expectations.
5. Plan motivational, interesting, and meaningful lessons. Show your own enthusiasm for lesson activities.
6. Prevent negative behavior by continuous emphasis upon positive achievement.
7. Develop student discipline as rapidly as possible. Lead each student to make his/her own decision rather than rely on yours.
8. If behavior problems cannot be solved in the classroom, seek the help of counselors and administrators.
9. Reinforce good behavior by rewarding students in public. Correct or punish in private.
10. Work closely with parents. Encourage them to send students to you with positive attitudes toward classroom learning.
11. Avoid useless rules, snap judgments, and loss of composure.
12. Be consistent, fair, and firm.
13. Refrain from threats or promises that you may not be able to implement.
14. Recognize that children have limited attention spans and assign alternate activities.

15. Discipline yourself in manners, voice, disposition, honesty, punctuality, consistency, fairness, and love for your students so that your own example inspires behavior at its best. (p. 58)

In formulating classroom rules, it is important that the number of rules be kept to a minimum. Five essential rules that lead to the development of a positive atmosphere are better than ten that don't.

Activity

Working in groups of four or five, develop a list of five rules that may enhance classroom discipline. Then share your results with the other groups. Which rules, if any, were common among the groups? Which rules were different?

The Advisor-Advisee Program

An advisor-advisee or teacher advisor program (TAP) is a means by which schools can become more responsive to the needs of every student. This program is a planned approach to providing routine and systematic contact between teachers and students in which the primary goal is positive self-awareness and growth. With enthusiasm and sensitivity, teachers can be more involved not only in the academic and career needs of their students but also in the affective areas. Implementing a teacher advisor program may enhance teacher-student relationships, which may ultimately enhance the educational experiences of the students.

The overall goal of a teacher advisor program is to guarantee that every student will have a significant adult in the school with whom he or she may establish a personal caring relationship. The goal is similar to the purpose of the homeroom period. Myrick and Myrick (1990) included eight goals of the teacher advisor program. The first three deal with understanding the school environment, self and others, and attitudes and behavior. The remaining goals deal with decision making and problem solving; interpersonal, communication, and school success skills; career awareness and educational planning; and pride and involvement in the community.

When necessary and appropriate, teachers may serve as advocates for students and as links between the school and the home. Activities designed to supplement, not replace, the work of the school counselor are included in the program. A counselor who is responsible for 300 to 1000 students simply cannot develop the relationships that a teacher-advisor can develop with 15 to 20 students.

The Advisory Program

The National Resource Center for Middle Grades Education publishes products and materials on affective and teacher-as-advisor products, classroom teaching materials, workshops, and consultative services. Teachers and schools will find their products useful. One of their advisor/advisee programs for the middle grades, *Advisory,* will be described.

Advisory contains a set of three books at three grade levels: Level 1 (grades five and six), Level 2 (grade seven), and Level 3 (grade eight). Each book includes four major themes: school culture and academic survival; communication; self-concept and relationships; and problem solving and decision making. Each thematic unit contains nine separate lesson plans with sets of advisory tasks for extension or follow-up. Each lesson plan has a title, objective, points to ponder (discussion questions), and projects to pursue (extended activities). The *Advisory* program contains a teaching guide with a scope and sequence chart, scheduling options, instructions for use of core materials, do's and don'ts for advisors, evaluative criteria, a letter to parents, and information to initiate the program. It also includes more than 300 supplementary activities and reproducible masters.

Information about the *Advisory* program and other materials and services may be obtained by writing to:

The National Resource Center for Middle Grades Education
University of South Florida
College of Education-EDU-118
Tampa, Florida 33620-5650

A Human Relations Model

A model of teacher-student relations was developed by Moracco (1981). Moracco and Higgins (1985) expanded the concepts in their book entitled *Comprehensive Approach to Human Relations Development.* It is designed to be useful for teachers who desire a model that can be adapted for a number of teacher-student problem-solving situations.

The model includes six stages, each of which includes goals for the teacher (helper) and student (helpee). *Expressing* is the first stage. The goal of this stage is to identify and explore the feelings and emotions of the student. Using the skills developed in Chapter 3, a teacher is able to assist a student by developing the relationship.

The second stage is *defining.* In this stage, a student needs to identify his or her concerns. To be able to help the student, a teacher must be able to talk with the student about and understand his or her concerns or problems. Once the problems have been defined, a teacher and student are ready to progress into the third stage.

In the third stage, *committing,* the student must be ready to make any changes necessary. The student recognizes that he or she owns the problem and makes a commitment to solving it.

Next, solutions to the problem must be generated. In the *generating alternatives* stage, the teacher can assist the student by using brainstorming techniques. Through brainstorming, a list of possible solutions to the problem may be generated.

Once a list of possible solutions have been generated, the student, with the teacher's help, *selects an alternative.* A teacher can help facilitate the process by suggesting strategies to the student.

Evaluating the alternative is the last stage of the model. In this stage, the student must assess whether the alternative is effective. To facilitate this process, the teacher may decide to role-play the situation with the student using the alternative generated from the previous stage. If the role-playing situation proves positive, then the teacher may suggest that the student try it out.

Activity

Obtain a copy of Comprehensive Approach to Human Relations Development, *or write to the National Resource Center, or contact your local school district office and review the materials. Which materials are suitable for your grade level? Why?*

PARENT-TEACHER RELATIONSHIPS

Parent-Teacher Conferences

Parent-teacher relationships must be developed. Teachers need to communicate with parents about their children. When an academic or behavior problem occurs, the teacher should contact the child's parents either in writing or by phone to explain his or her concerns. The teacher may invite the parents to school to discuss the problem. A parent-teacher conference can be a positive experience where solutions to the problem can be generated. Suggestions for conducting a parent-teacher conference follow:

1. **Plan the conference.** Before meeting with the parents, the teacher needs to prepare. The teacher should know what he she wants to discuss and gather as much information as possible.
2. **Welcome the parent.** Parents may be nervous when they have to discuss their children. The teacher needs to create an atmosphere that is warm and caring. In addition, the teacher should select a meeting location that is comfortable. Planning the conference and welcoming the parents helps to set the stage for ultimately helping the student.
3. **Say something positive.** The teacher must be able to say something positive about the student. Parents will be more receptive to concerns if the conference begins on a positive note.
4. **Communicate Concerns.** The parent-teacher conference is an excellent vehicle for communicating concerns. During the conference, teachers and parents may obtain information about the student that may be used to help him or her. For example, during the conference, a parent may indicate that a divorce is pending. The child was informed of the divorce two weeks ago. The teacher notes that the behavior problem began about two weeks ago.
5. **Take Action.** After the concerns have been discussed, some action needs to be taken. What can the teacher and parents do to help the student? For example, a student who is having academic difficulty in class has indicated to his or her parents that no homework is assigned. The teacher, however, informs the parents that homework is indeed assigned every day. The teacher promises to send the parents a weekly report. If the report is not received, the parents are urged to contact either the school counselor or any of the child's teachers. It is a good idea to have the student present during this stage of the discussion, so that the teacher and parents can indicate to the child what was discussed and what was decided.
6. **End the conference on a positive note.** The teacher should thank the parents for taking the time and effort to attend the conference. In addition, the teacher should indicate that he or she looks forward to hearing from the parents whenever the need arises.

Activity

Have you ever attended a parent-teacher conference? If yes, what positive and/or negative feelings did you experience? Why?

PARENT-CHILD RELATIONSHIPS

Communication Is the Key

Teachers can help parents in their role of parenting. A major source of family problems is ineffective communication. According to Framo (1981):

> Parents tend to do to children what was done to them, or in their efforts to undo what was done to them, will commit other wrongs to their children. Consequently one sees children exploited, parentified, shamed, overindulged, infantilized, teased, humiliated, seduced, neglected, persecuted, and sometimes murdered. (p. 212)

Parenting, then, may be looked upon as a learning experience. During parent-teacher conferences, for example, we often find that parents are confused about dealing with their child's problem. Some parents may not be aware that their child has a problem or concern. Parental lack of adequate self-understanding and their ineffective communication skills seem to be the primary sources of this confusion.

Most parents came from homes in which both parents were present; however, today only one parent may be rearing the child. The other parent may fail to pay child support or may not visit the child. Conversely, even when both parents are home, there may be a lack of effective communication among the family members. In communicating with their children, parents must understand the importance of enhancing individual self-worth, and remember that one communicates not only by words but also by actions.

Parents must be aware of their communication patterns. Satir (1972) described four patterns of communication that cause difficulty:

1. *Placate:* Placating often occurs when one constantly agrees with the other person so that the other person doesn't get angry. This person believes that harmony will be maintained by communicating to the other person that whatever they say or want is all that matters.
2. *Blame:* The blamer always finds fault in others' actions. A blamer conveys to the other that no matter what they are doing it is not good. They are always putting the other person down.
3. *Compute:* This person responds to situations like a computer. No feelings are indicated in the responses made by this person. They deal with any threats as though they were harmless.

4. *Distract:* The distractor never makes a point. They do not answer the questions. It is a way to ignore the threat, behaving as though it were not there. (pp. 63–71)

Activity: How Well Do You Listen?

The most important communication technique that a teacher can develop with students is listening. In this activity, the class is divided into dyads. The objective is to learn as much as possible about the other member of the dyad. Each member of the group alternately questions the other person. However, before asking your question, you must tell the other person what they said. At the conclusion of the activity, summarize what you learned about the person. How did you feel about repeating what the other person said before asking your question?

PARENT EFFECTIVENESS PROGRAMS

A number of published parent effectiveness programs are available. A sampling of these programs and books are described in this section.

STEP Program

The *Systematic Training for Effective Parenting* (STEP) program was developed by Don Dinkmeyer and Gary D. McKay (1976) and is published by the American Guidance Services, Publisher's Building, Circle Pine, Minnesota 55014.

The STEP program consists of a leader's manual, parent handbook, audio and video cassettes, discussion guide cards, posters, and charts. The program is divided into sessions lasting from one and a half to two hours. During each session, participants discuss the assigned reading, listen to audiocassettes or view videotapes, work on activities, role-play, and discuss problem situations. Each participant is encouraged to practice those concepts learned during the session.

The following topics are included in the STEP program:

Understanding Children's Behavior and Misbehavior
Understanding How Children Use Emotions to Involve Parents and the "Good Parent"
Encouragement

Communication: Listening
Communication: Exploring Alternatives and Expressing Your Ideas and Feelings to Children
Developing Responsibility
Decision Making for Parents
Family Meeting
Developing Confidence and Using Your Potential

How To Talk So Kids Will Listen

How To Talk So Kids Will Listen was written and developed by Adele Faber and Elaine Mazlish (1981) and is published by the Negotiation Institute, Inc., 230 Park Avenue, New York, N.Y. 10069.

This program consists of a chairperson's guide which includes a workbook, pocket cards, and puzzles and materials, plus six audiocassettes and reading materials (*How to Talk So Kids Will Listen and Listen So Kids Will Talk* and *Liberated Parents/Liberated Children*).

The following topics are included in the program:

Helping Children Cope with Their Feelings
Engaging Cooperation
Alternatives to Punishment
Praise
Freeing Children from Playing Roles
Final Review

Parent Effectiveness Training (PET)

Parent Effectiveness Training (PET) was developed by Thomas Gordon (1978). His book, based on the course, is published by Peter H. Wyden, 750 Third Avenue, New York, N.Y. 10017. The following topics are included in the book and course:

Parents are Blamed But Not Trained
Parents are Persons, Not Gods
How to Listen So Kids Will Talk to You
Putting Your Active Listening Skills to Work
How to Listen to Kids Too Young to Talk Much
How to Talk So Kids Will Listen to You

Putting "I-Messages" to Work
Changing Unacceptable Behavior
Inevitable Parent-Child Conflicts
Parental Power: Necessary and Justified
The "No-Lose" Method for Resolving Conflicts
Parents' Fears and Concerns
Putting the "No-Lose" Methods to Work
How to Avoid Being Fired as a Parent
How Parents Can Prevent Conflicts by Modifying Themselves
The Other Parents of Your Children

Transactional Analysis (TA)

Transactional Analysis (TA) was developed by Eric Berne. Centers for Transactional Analysis have conducted training sessions and workshops throughout the United States. TA assumes that three states exist in all people: *parent, child,* and *adult* (P.A.C.). Berne proposes four life positions that are important for understanding relationships:

I'm not OK, you're OK.
I'm not OK, you're not OK.
I'm OK, you're not OK.
I'm OK, you're OK. (p. 43)

The book *I'm OK, You're OK* by Thomas A. Harris (1969) is based on the TA course. It is published by HarperCollins, and is widely available in bookstores. Parents and teachers may wish to read the book for a more detailed understanding of the TA concepts and how they apply to relationships. *I'm OK, You're OK* includes the following topics:

Parents, Adult, and Child
Four Life Positions
We Can Change
Analyzing the Transaction
How We Differ
How We Use Time
P.A.C. and Marriage.
P.A.C. and Adolescents
When Is Treatment Necessary?
P.A.C. and Moral Values.
Social Implications of P.A.C.

A Field Guide to Human Relations

Bundy (1979) described a field guide to a human relations week for students. This program was developed by the Tennessee Personnel and Guidance Association (TPGA) and the Tennessee Educational Association (TEA). The program utilized the concepts from Harris' book, *I'm OK, You're OK*. Activities that parents may use to relate to their children are included. For example:

1   Sending a letter from students to parents explaining the week and making suggestions for parent-child O.K. activities. Some examples include:
   a   Encouraging eye contact, i.e., demonstrate good listening skills by looking at the person with whom you are talking.
   b   Sharing O.K. feelings with family members.
   c   Giving a "warm fuzzy" to someone in the family at a certain time each day. (The term "warm fuzzy" refers to such concepts as giving compliments, expressing gratitude, giving praise, and offering special recognition.) "Warm fuzzies" may be expressed to other people as a way to help them feel good toward themselves. It is hoped that these good feelings will generate positive feelings toward others.
   d   Conducting a family meeting to discuss good things about the family and its members.
2   Holding O.K. parent meetings (P.T.A., etc.). (p. 174)

STUDENT-STUDENT RELATIONSHIPS

Cooperative Learning

Cooperative learning enables students to work together to achieve a common goal (Slavin, 1990). Studies have indicated that cooperative learning strategies enhance the academic achievement and social interactions of students (Lyman & Foyle, 1990). Although research on cooperation dates back to the 1920s, applications of cooperative learning methods did not begin until the 1970s (Slavin, 1990). A team approach is one of the keys to cooperative learning.

Most students are familiar with and enjoy being a part of a team. They play on baseball, basketball, or football teams. As a member of a team, students work for a common goal. For any team to succeed, each member must contribute something and cooperate with the other team members. These concepts also apply to cooperative learning.

Slavin (1988) describes three student learning techniques: (1) Student Teams-Achievement Divisions (STAD), (2) Teams-Games-Tournament (TGT), (3) Jigsaw II, and (4) Team Accelerated Instruction (TAI). Each technique includes heterogeneous groups of four to five members; rewards; and recognition. A brief description of each technique follows:

Student Teams-Achievement Divisions (STAD).   The STAD model begins with the teaching of a lesson. Next, teams of four or five students may study worksheets on the material and discuss or quiz each other. After the material is learned, a test is administered to each member of the group. Members are not permitted to help each other on the test. The tests scores are converted to team scores. In the last step (team recognition), a one-page class newsletter recognizes the teams with the highest scores.

Teams-Games-Tournament (TGT).   The first two steps of TGT are identical to STAD, but then instead of administering a test, team members play academic games in weekly tournaments. Team scores are determined and a newsletter recognizes teams with the highest team scores.

Jigsaw II.   Instead of having a lesson taught to them as in STAD or TGT, students are assigned a specific topic. Students with the same topic are assigned to groups to discuss their topic. After mastering the topic, the students return to their original teams and teach the other members what they have learned. Students are then tested and team scores are determined. Highest scoring teams are then recognized in the newsletter.

Team Accelerated Instruction (TAI).   In TAI, students work in heterogeneous teams as in the above examples. TAI combines individualized and team learning. Unlike STAD, TGT, and Jigsaw II, TAI team members are given individualized materials based on the results of a placement test. Using the individualized materials, each team member works at their own level and rate. After the materials are completed, each team member checks the other members' work. Scores are based on the accuracy and average number of units completed by each team. Teams that have achieved the preset criterion receive rewards or certificates.

Teachers who would like further information about these programs or other cooperative learning materials and training may write to:

The Johns Hopkins Team Learning Project
Johns Hopkins University
3505 N. Charles Street
Baltimore, MD 21218
(301) 338-8249.

Additional Resources

Cooperative Learning: Theory, Research, and Practice, by Robert E. Slavin, is published by Prentice-Hall, Englewood Cliffs, NJ 07632. It is an excellent resource for teachers wishing to further their understanding of cooperative learning. It contains the following chapters: (1) An Introduction to Cooperative Learning; (2) Cooperative Learning and Student Achievement; (3) Cooperative Learning and Outcomes Other Than Achievement; (4) STAD and TGT; (5) TAI and CIRC; (6) Task Specialization Methods; and (7) Other Cooperative Learning Methods and Resources.

Student Team Learning: An Overview and Practical Guide (2nd ed.), by Robert E. Slavin, is published by the NEA Professional Library, National Education Association, 1201 16th St., NW, Washington, D.C. 20036. It contains an overview of the following team techniques: (1) Student Teams-Achievement Divisions (STAD); Teams-Games-Tournaments (TGT); Jigsaw II; Original Jigsaw; Team Accelerated Instruction (TAI); and Cooperative Integrated Reading and Composition (CIRC). In addition, it contains a practical guide that presents an overview, and instructions for preparing, starting, and scheduling activities for the above team techniques.

Cooperative Grouping for Interactive Learning: Students, Teachers, and Administrators, by Lawrence Lyman and Harvey C. Foyle, is also published by the NEA Professional Library. The book is an excellent resource for anyone interested in developing positive group interactions. Separate chapters deal with developing positive interactions between administrators and teachers, among teachers, and among students. The final chapter presents practical suggestions for assessing outcomes.

Activity

Obtain and review one or more of the resources described in this chapter. Is the resource(s) suitable for your particular group? What are some advantages and disadvantages of the resource(s)?

CONSULTATION

The relationships discussed thus far involve teachers' direct interaction with students. However, teachers may become involved in enhancing the development of positive relationships among individuals by becoming a consultant. The consultant role involves the other person (the student) indirectly.

Teachers are in a unique position to become consultants in their schools because they have more contact hours with students than any other school staff member. Classroom teachers may be trained by their school counselor to observe, teach, test, and interact with others.

Consultation is based upon communication and human interaction processes and techniques included in this book. As a process, consultation involves two or more individuals (administrators, teachers, school psychologists, and parents) who are concerned with helping another person (the student).

The consultation model described below was developed by Kurpius (1978). It contains nine stages: pre-entry, entry, gathering information, defining the problem, determination of a problem solution, stating objectives, implementation of the plan, evaluation, and termination. The model will be described and applied to a hypothetical example of a teacher who believes that a student may require placement to a special education class.

Stage 1: Pre-entry. The school counselor may be instrumental in establishing this stage. The stage may be initiated by having a counselor conduct a workshop for teachers on the role of a consultant. During the workshop, the definition of the consultant's role and the skills needed to become an effective consultant may be addressed.

Stage 2: Entry. In this stage, a teacher and counselor may develop an effective working relationship and an understanding of the ground rules and the teacher's roles in serving as a consultant.

A classroom teacher may meet with the counselor to discuss a problem that has developed regarding a student. During this meeting, the teacher will indicate the nature of the problem and any steps taken to alleviate it. The teacher and the counselor may determine that additional information needs to be gathered before referring the student for placement in a special education class.

Stage 3: Gathering Information. The teacher collects as much information as possible about the student, including observations, anecdotal records, grades, test scores, and any information gathered from parent-teacher conferences as well as from conferences with the student.

In addition, with the permission of the student's parents, the school psychologist may be requested to evaluate the student utilizing psychological instruments.

Stage 4: Defining the Problem. Once the information has been gathered, the teacher, counselor, administrator, school psychologist, and parent will schedule a meeting to discuss the results of the information gathered. The nature of the problem as well as goals for change will be determined at this time.

Stage 5: Determination of the Solution. During this stage, alternatives will be generated and discussed by the teacher, counselor, administrator, school psychologist, and parents. For example, the problem may be resolved by, on the one hand, simply having the teacher and parents work together. In this case, the student may remain in his or her regular classroom. On the other hand, the solution may be to have the student remain in the regular classroom and receive services from a resource teacher, or to refer the student for placement in a special education class.

Stage 6: Stating Objectives. If the committee (teacher, counselor, administrator, school psychologist, special education teacher, and parent) determines that the student needs to be placed in a special class, then an individualized education plan (IEP) must be developed. The committee usually writes the IEP. The IEP contains objectives and procedures for achieving them.

Stage 7: Implementation of the Plan. When the IEP is completed, the student is referred to a special education class and the IEP is processed by the school-based committee.

Stage 8: Evaluation. Evaluation is an ongoing process. The student is observed continuously. The special education teacher determines whether the student is meeting the objectives stated in the IEP. If the student is having difficulty in meeting any of the objectives, then the special education teacher may consult with the counselor, parents, and administrator to determine whether another course of action may be necessary. The special education teacher may also consult with the counselor, parents, and administrator when the student is satisfactorily achieving the objectives.

Stage 9: Termination. The goal is to return the special education student to a regular class. Therefore, the special education teacher may determine that the student has met the objectives and is ready to return to the regular class. A committee consisting of administrator, special education teacher, classroom teachers, parents, counselor, and school psychologist meet to determine whether the student is eligible to be mainstreamed. If the committee decides to mainstream the student, then the consulting process continues by monitoring the student's success.

Identifying a student with special needs is only one of the teacher's consultation functions. Teachers also may function as consultants in any of the following ways:

1. Identifying their students' academic deficiencies and abilities.
2. Attending parent-teacher conferences.
3. Identifying strengths and weaknesses in classroom management (with the other teachers' permission).
4. Interpreting grades and standardized tests results to students and their parents.
5. Helping students make decisions about their goals both in and out of school.

REFERENCES

Bundy, M. L. (1979). Field guide to a human relations week. *The School Counselor, 26,* 172–177.

Dinkmeyer, D., Sr., & Dinkmeyer, D., Jr. (1979). Working with teachers: In-service and C groups. *Counseling and Human Development, 11,* 5.

Dinkmeyer, D., & McKay, G. D. (1976). *Systematic training for effective parenting* (STEP). Circle Pines, MN: American Guidance Services.

Faber, A., & Mazlish, E. (1981). *How to talk so kids will listen.* New York: Negotiations Institute.

Framo, J. L. (1981). Family theory and therapy. *Elementary School Guidance and Counseling, 15,* 205–213.

Gordon, T. (1978). *Parent effectiveness training.* New York: Peter H. Wyden.

Harris, T. A. (1969). *I'm ok, you're ok: Guide to transactional analysis.* New York: Harper & Row.

Kurpius, D. (1978). Consulting theory and process: An integrated model. *The Personnel and Guidance Journal, 56,* 335–338.

Lyman, L., & Foyle, H. C. (1990). *Comparative grouping for interactive learning: Students, teachers, and administrators.* Washington, DC: National Education Association.

Maslow, A. H. (1970). *A theory of human motivation and personality* (2nd ed.). New York: Harper & Row.

Moracco, J. (1981). A comprehensive approach to human relations for teachers. *Counselor Education and Supervision, 21,* 129.

Moracco, J., & Higgins, E. (1985). *Comprehensive approach to human development.* Muncie, IN: Accelerated Development.

Myrick, R. D., & Myrick, L. S. (1990). *The teacher advisor program.* Ann Arbor, MI: ERIC/CAPS.

Satir, V. (1972). *Peoplemaking.* Palo Alto, CA: Science and Behavior Books.

Slavin, R. E. (1988). *Student team learning: An overview and practical guide.* (2nd ed.). Washington, DC: National Educational Association.

Slavin, R. E. (1990). *Cooperative learning: Theory, research, and practice.* Englewood Cliffs, NJ: Prentice-Hall.

Stoops, E., & King-Stoops, J. (1981). Discipline suggestions for classroom teachers. *Phi Delta Kappa, 63,* 68.

UNIT III
WORKING
WITH GROUPS

Chapter 6

THE TEACHER
AND GROUP SITUATIONS

One of the unique characteristics of the teaching profession is that teachers spend most of their time working with students in groups. While teachers are encouraged to recognize and teach toward individual difference, the effort often must be made in the context of a group with 20 to 30 students. Teachers frequently comment that a student does well when alone yet becomes a discipline problem in a group. Sometimes it is even obvious that the same student behaves quite differently when with another group. These realizations suggest a need for the classroom teacher to have some basic knowledge and skills in group dynamics.

Group experiences can contribute to the development of the individual. Every student has a need to belong, a need that can be fulfilled by participation in school groups. Through such participation the student is likely to experience feelings of recognition, acceptance, and approval. The student also may try some technique and, if successful, thereby gain self-confidence. The student is able to experience the satisfaction that comes from successful group effort. The teacher is responsible primarily for providing the kind of social climate and the kind of experiences that lead to social adjustment. In order to meet this recognized responsibility the teacher needs to understand the operation of group dynamics in a regular classroom.

The purpose of understanding group dynamics is not to make group counselors out of all teachers, but to provide enough background information so that teacher, assisted by the school counselor and other school personnel, can create the kind of classroom climate believed to be conducive to social adjustment.

Shaw (1981) has defined a "group" as "two or more persons who are inter-acting with one another in such a manner that each person influences and is influenced by each other person" (p. 11). This definition seems sufficient to describe a typical classroom in which teacher and students are interacting with one another and in which teacher and students are influencing each other. The classroom group fulfills this definition as it progresses through a series of stages.

One typical way in which the classroom group becomes mutually interac-tive and influential is when a given task or goal is established which everyone in the classroom, including the teacher, has decided is desirable. If the teacher chooses the task or sets the goal for the class without understanding his or her own goals, chances for success are minimal. In order to help the class establish realistic and desirable goals, the teacher needs to understand those wishes and desires that seem most important to students. When teachers ask students about goals, they are likely to receive a variety of responses, with some tendency that a large number will be related to both interpersonal relations and academic success. These responses are likely to be those which have produced some kind of reward in the past, a reward that was satisfying. These include items such as good grades, being first to complete some work, being called on to answer a question, and gaining teacher or peer approval. With some knowledge of groups, the teacher should be better able to facilitate the occurrence of these satisfac-tions more frequently and more deeply.

The suggestion is not that academic goals should become of secondary importance to personal-social goals, but that goals related to worthy group mem-bership should be recognized and given some importance when goals are being established. These two sets of goals are not inconsistent with each other. The teacher can help students see this relationship between educational and personal-social goals. The teacher also can help students discover which goals are easily attainable, which are long-range goals, which are probably unattainable, which are worthy to strive toward, and how to evaluate progress toward these goals.

All of this effort leads to what Schmuck and Schmuck (1988) summarized as ingredients for a healthy or positive classroom environment. They described a positive classroom environment as

> one in which the students share high amounts of potential influ-ence—both with one another and with the teacher; where high lev-els of attraction exist for the group as a whole and between class-mates; where norms are supportive for getting academic work done, as well as for maximizing individual differences; where communi-cation is open and featured by dialogue; and where the processes of

working and developing together as a group are considered relevant in themselves. (p. 18)

GROUP DYNAMICS

Knowledge of group dynamics enhances teacher understanding of individuals. The network of interactions in the classroom is complex and holds different significance for each student. The information that follows should not be seen as absolute answers or reasons for a student's behavior, but only as a source of possibilities. In fact, Shaw (1981) even presented his statements about groups as hypotheses, suggesting that the statements are tentative and may be proven or disproven with some additional research. His general hypotheses were as follows:

1. The mere presence of others increases the motivation level of a performing individual when the individual expects to be evaluated.
2. Group judgments are superior to individual judgments on tasks that involve random error.
3. Groups usually produce more and better solutions to problems than do individuals working alone.
4. Groups usually require more time to complete a task than do individuals working alone, especially when time is measured in man-minutes.
5. Members of sociometrically cohesive groups learn more than members of less cohesive groups when they want to learn.
6. More new and radical ideas are produced by both individuals and groups when critical evaluation of ideas is suspended during the production period.
7. Decisions made after group discussion are usually more risky than decisions made by the average individual prior to group discussion. (pp. 78–80)

These seven hypotheses about groups suggest that some differences exist between individuals working alone and individuals working in groups. They suggest that a group has advantages over individuals working alone. They also seem to have significant implications for classroom groups. Shaw (1981) reviewed these hypotheses and research with children's groups to arrive at another set of hypotheses specifically related to children. These hypotheses are as follows:

1. Children learn socially approved ways of behaving in groups via the socialization process.

2. Heterogeneous ability grouping facilitates academic achievements to a greater extent than homogeneous ability grouping.
3. Teachers react more favorably to teaching homogeneous ability groups than to teaching heterogeneous groups.
4. Homogeneous ability grouping tends to raise the self-esteem of the less capable group members; whereas, heterogeneous grouping tends to raise the self-esteem of the more capable individuals.
5. Team-teaching facilitates academic achievements in the lower grades but impedes academic achievement in higher elementary grades.
6. Children are more creative in groups than when alone.
7. Children are more creative in small groups than in large groups.
8. Creativity may be fostered in children by permitting them to manipulate and ask questions about things in their environment.
9. Children are more creative in homogeneous groups than in heterogeneous groups.
10. Cooperative behavior can be developed and maintained by either direct or vicarious reinforcement, although maintenance depends upon the continued presence of reinforcement.
11. Certain types of structuring of children's groups encourage the development of cooperative behavior. (pp. 380–382)

In many respects, classroom groups, in which the teacher finds himself/herself, are similar to any other group in a number of ways. These hypotheses reveal to the teacher a framework against which to organize and view the interactions in the class. They may not provide absolute answers, but they should give some clues as to where to look for sources of successful classroom organization patterns or for patterns that seem to be responsible for some problem behaviors. The answers to these questions cannot be certain or final. They must be tentative. Group relationships are extremely complicated, and adding to this complexity is the teacher, who contributes to the interaction patterns that develop in the classroom.

Schmuck and Schmuck (1988) suggested that, in understanding classroom group dynamics, teachers consider both the formal and informal relationships students have with each other. These relationships are important because students develop both emotionally and intellectually in contact with each other. Teachers have some degree of control over the formal interactions, and they have less influence over informal peer interactions. Regardless of the degree of teacher influence, both formal and informal relationships share near equal importance in determination of self-concepts. In fact, informal peer relationships influence formal relations, thus influencing the actual learning experience.

CLASSROOM SEATING ARRANGEMENTS

The physical environment of the classroom has much to do with the general atmosphere for learning. We assume that a classroom will have sufficient lighting, adequate ventilation, and a comfortable temperature. Another item in the physical environment is seating arrangements. The seating pattern used in a classroom will have major influences on the degree of acquaintance, friendliness, talkativeness, and productivity. Teachers must be aware that cultural influences also affect seating patterns. Factors such as personal space (the space needed between oneself and another to remain comfortable) and leadership preferences are but two areas in which children may have been subjected to cultural influences. Teachers must become aware of children who find it difficult to work in close proximity with other children. Teachers also must be aware of children who seem to take positions in groups (such as the "head of the table") because they perceive themselves in the leadership position. Likewise, an awareness of those children who seem reluctant to participate can often be identified by observing the seating position they take in a group.

Sommer (1967) studied seating arrangements in classrooms and concluded that classroom participation is related to seating arrangement. Four basic patterns of seating can be observed in classrooms. These four patterns are shown in Figure 6.1.

Arrangement A seems to be a typical row arrangement in which the teacher is the identified leader (authority). Students in this arrangement are unable to have eye contact with each other. Sommer (1967) concluded that in such an arrangement students in the front will participate more than students in the rear and students in the center will participate more than students on the sides.

Arrangement B has the advantage of the teacher being on an equal level with the students (democratic) and students can maintain eye contact with each other. This arrangement seems appropriate for any classroom activity in which all students are expected to participate and in which the role of the teacher as the leader is minimized. Hearn (1957) found that when groups are seated at a square table, communication is more likely to occur between persons sitting opposite each other rather than between persons sitting next to each other.

Arrangement C seems to combine the advantages of student-to-student eye contact with the identified leadership of the teacher. This arrangement seems ideal for a smaller classroom where a full circle is not possible or where a large table is unavailable. This arrangement can be modified to have two semi-circle rows when the numbers of students will not allow a single row.

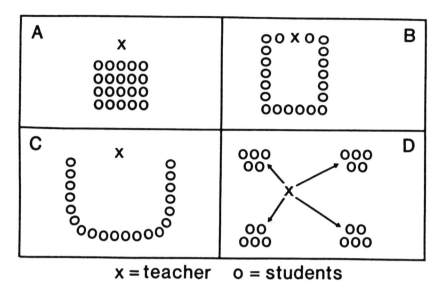

Figure 6.1. Four illustrative classroom seating arrangements. *Note.* Figure based on information in "Classroom Ecology" by R. Sommer, 1967, *Journal of Applied Behavioral Science, 3,* pp. 489–503. Copyright 1967 by the Journal of Applied Behavioral Science. Reprinted by permission.

Arrangement D is designed for instruction in which students will work independently with several other students. The small groups should be placed far enough apart to avoid distractions and they should each be easily accessible to the teacher, who can move from one group to another.

These arrangements offer possibilities for a variety of classroom situations. No one classroom seating arrangement is better than another. Whenever possible, classroom seating arrangements are to be adapted according to the particular task or the specific need that can be accomplished best by using that particular arrangement.

Hypotheses presented earlier must be taken into consideration when deciding on a classroom seating arrangement. These observations are especially important when making decisions about ability grouping in the classroom for instructional purposes. They are also important because the physical environment of the classroom serves to convey a message to the children about goals of learning and about how they should work.

ROLES OF GROUP MEMBERS

If the teacher is to use some principles of group dynamics in the classroom, there also must be an understanding of students' roles in a group setting. Perhaps the most thorough classification of group roles was made by Benne and Scheats (1948) who, observing small group behavior, found that role enactment could be divided into three categories: group task roles, group building and maintenance roles, and individual roles.

When a group must accomplish a task, members perform *task roles.* A task role may be composed of one or more of the following task functions:

1. **Initiating** suggestions and ideas, offering alternatives solutions, methods or procedures.
2. **Seeking information,** asking for ideas and suggestions, identifying areas where additional information is needed.
3. **Seeking opinions,** requesting clarification of feelings or opinions.
4. **Giving information,** giving relevant data and suggestions to the group.
5. **Giving opinions,** offering personal feelings about an idea, or acceptability of a proposed solution.
6. **Elaborating,** building on ideas of others, anticipating results of solutions offered by group, suggesting a rationale for some suggestion.
7. **Coordinating,** showing relationship between ideas expressed by pulling them together.
8. **Orienting,** summarizing what has happened, developing a theme of what has taken place.
9. **Clarifying,** questioning proposals, restating ideas, interpreting behavior in terms of some standard.
10. **Energizing,** stimulating, prodding group to higher level of achievement.
11. **Maintaining procedures,** performing routine tasks necessary for smooth and effective operation of group.
12. **Recording,** writing conclusions, taking votes, asking for concerns and commitment from group. (Benne & Sheats, 1948)

Task roles are concerned primarily with attainment of some goal, purpose, or task. This role does not occur in isolation from social needs or demands that individuals bring to the group meeting. To facilitate accomplishment of a given task, the group leader must be aware of these social needs. Needs that emerge in specific behaviors are called group building or maintenance functions and combine to make *maintenance roles*. The following list identifies maintenance roles of group members:

1. **Supporting,** offering praise, agreement, commendation and recognition of other points of view, suggestions or ideas.
2. **Harmonizing,** mediating disagreements, reducing tensions, helping explore each other's personal meaning operating from outside.
3. **Compromising,** from inside conflict, admitting personal errors, yielding to preserve group cohesion.
4. **Gatekeeping,** working to insure that lines of communication are open, encouraging interaction and full participation of all group members.
5. **Standard setting,** setting up ideal goal which group should strive to attain.
6. **Interpreting,** serving as commentator for group, observing group behavior and offering proposed interpretations of interactions.
7. **Following,** passively going along with group, accepting ideas and serving as an audience. (Benne & Sheats, 1948)

Group members who perform these maintenance roles are interested in the welfare of the group, in group cohesion, and in the social relationships within the group. Not all participants in the group have these interests. Some are in a group to fulfill a personal goal and may only be interested in themselves. These persons use the group only as a vehicle to solve personal needs, and at the expense of other group members. These *individual roles* are as follows:

1. **Disapproving,** refusing to accept any values, feelings, or behaviors of others, using sarcasm, acting aggressively.
2. **Blocking,** refusing to cooperate regardless of the issue or topic involved, point picking, serving as devil's advocate.
3. **Dominating,** calling attention to self, dictating to group, boasting, interrupting group members.
4. **Confessing,** using the group as an audience for personal, unrelated, irrelevant confession.
5. **Playboying,** joking about everything, refusing to take anything seriously, being cynical, engaging in horseplay.
6. **Help-seeking,** expressing need for group support, expressing insecurity or personal confusion.
7. **Special-interest pleading,** serving as a representative for another group, thereby hiding personal biases or prejudices. (Benne & Sheats, 1948)

Ringwald, Mann, Rosenwein, and McKeachie (1971) observed classrooms and isolated eight clusters of students and six teacher roles. The following are identifiable student roles adapted from the research:

1. **The Complaint Student:** typical, average student who is trusting, contented, and wants to absorb what the teacher offers, is likely to be found in most traditional classrooms.
2. **The Anxious-Dependent Student:** has low self-esteem, is very concerned about what the teacher thinks, and doubtful about his or her own abilities, rarely participates in class.
3. **The Discouraged Student:** depressed and personally distant, intelligent and hard-working.
4. **The Independent Student:** self-confident, involved, and interested, tends to identify with authority figures.
5. **The Hero:** intelligent, creative, involved, introspective, is ambivalent toward authority and erratic in classroom performance.
6. **The Sniper:** rebellious, indifferent, withdrawn, but not creative, has low self-esteem; typically waits for the classroom discussion to focus on the one subject the student knows something about, and then asks a question designed to trap the teacher, withdrawing after the attack.
7. **The Attention-Seeker:** feels vulnerable, helpless, and threatened by authority, speaks only when sure to get the teacher's approval.

The sensitive, caring, and concerned teacher goes well beyond merely identifying what role a student is playing. Such a teacher seeks out the motivation behind the behavior. The teacher might check if the motivation is perhaps attention, power, revenge, achievement, affiliation, or a desire to be left alone. This is an especially difficult task for the teacher who must work with a class of twenty-five students, each of whom is unique.

With a class of twenty-five students, and depending on the course content and other aspects of the classroom situation, the teacher may enact any one or all of the following six roles observed by Ringwald et al. (1971):

1. **The Expert:** concerned primarily with the transmission of facts and information.
2. **The Formal Authority:** concerned with evaluation and control.
3. **The Socializing Agent:** concerned with serving as a gatekeeper for his or her own "inner circle" of colleagues.
4. **The Facilitator:** concerned with helping students achieve their goals.
5. **The Ego-Ideal:** concerned with serving as a model of competence, excitement, and energy.
6. **The Person:** concerned with communicating a variety of roles, not simply the role of teacher.

The effective teacher who is able to determine the motivation of students also must be able to determine the roles he or she is playing and the motivation

behind them. The most effective teacher is one who understands the consequences of a particular role and therefore uses it to obtain some known desired
result. The effective teacher is able to adapt to the variety of situations that will
emerge in working with groups of students.

STAGES OF GROUP DEVELOPMENT

The roles of group members should become clearer as the stages of group
development are examined. Perhaps the clearest delineation of group stage development in the classroom has been presented by Stanford and Roark (1974)
as represented in Table 6.1.

Stage 1 is characterized by questions about belonging. These questions determine a need for orientation in an environment that is trusting, open, friendly,
and nonaggressive. The teacher can provide descriptions of what the class will
be like, overviews of the textbooks that will be used, details about meeting
times, and other required information in written form so that students can refer
to it when necessary. It is good to play some form of get-acquainted game so
that students can interact with each other as well as get acquainted with the
teacher. Teachers can model during this process.

Stage 2 is characterized by the establishment of norms for interacting with
each other. Limits and rules are set during this stage and teachers expect students to test any limits established. This is perhaps the most critical stage for
the teacher because students will learn whether the teacher will actually enforce
certain classroom rules and regulations. The teacher needs to be accepting of
student ideas while recognizing the place of feelings in the process.

Stage 3 is probably best understood as the "get the teacher" stage where
students are likely to see everything done by the teacher as wrong. Students
may argue that the rules should be changed. Subgroups will be established in
the class and one subgroup is likely to come into conflict with another subgroup. The teacher must be extremely careful to note that this is a normal stage
of group development and be very careful in handling hostility or conflict. The
teacher can serve as facilitator of students' expression of feelings as well as
helping students resolve conflicts.

Stage 4 provides some relief to the tension in the previous stage as students begin to resolve some of their differences in constructive ways. If students believe they have been heard, they are more willing to listen to others.

TABLE 6.1
Stages of Group Development

	Interaction Pattern	Process and Focus	Communication
Stage 1: Beginning	Randomness or leader-centered pairing and subgrouping	Confusion, searching, protective and seeking allies	Guarded, constricted, topic- and situation-centered
Stage 2: Norm Development	Erratic, tentative, usually leader-centered or leader-directed	Testing limits, seeking answers, trial-balloons leadership	Security-oriented, situation-centered, little self-disclosure
Stage 3: Conflict	Erratic; centered on one person and/or pair, depending on issue; or random	Confrontive, hostile; anxious conflict	One-way distorted labeling; some self-disclosure, usually in anger or retaliation
Stage 4: Transition	Less erratic patterns develop; less centered on leader	Vacillate between task and group concerns; focus on new norms and on personal feelings	Self-disclosure and feedback more open; less labeling
Stage 5: Production	Based on task at hand; usually work-dictated	Cooperation, group leadership, group is a group; *we* identify	Open, within limits of disclosure feedback, and intimacy norms
Stage 6: Affection	Group-centered but moving to individual focus	I-Thou interaction often; intimacy norms changed to more intimacy	More self-disclosure and risk; positive feedback
Stage 7: Actualization	Pattern appropriate to task; usually group centered	Flexible; moves from task to person to group as appropriate	Open, constructive, based on *being* rather than on needs

Note. Table based on information in "Classroom Ecology" by R. Sommer, 1967, *Journal of Applied Behavioral Science, 3,* pp. 489–503. Copyright 1967 by the Journal of Applied Behavioral Science. Reprinted by permission.

This communication will foster a sense of group cohesion in which genuine communication can take place with appropriate feedback and self-disclosure apparent.

Stage 5 is a refinement and further development of the shared-trusting level of cohesion that developed in the previous stage. The teacher becomes a "consultant" to the class and a true feeling of unity exists. There is a concern for the feelings of all in the class and feelings of loyalty to one another are high. Considering all the factors that might have an impact on a given classroom, probably only a few will reach this stage. Those who do are likely to spend most of their time at this stage, once it is reached.

Stage 6 is characterized by close personal interactions, and these relationships are likely to be seen as the primary task for the class. Students become interested in doing more personal things with each other and in avoiding attention to external accomplishments. An outsider may view a class at Stage 6 as having too much fun.

Stage 7 is characterized by a variety of individual learning styles, each of which is encouraged and accepted. Such a class will be as open to conflict as to cooperation. Open disagreement is assumed to be a part of any decision making because all decisions will be arrived at by consensus.

Discussion of the stages of group development has to be understood in light of the reality that no group will progress through the stages as clearly as they have been presented. Group member roles, both task and individual, will have a bearing on how well a class will negotiate the stages. When difficulty arises, groups will likely revert to a previous stage where they are more comfortable. The role of the teacher is crucial to the positive transition from one stage to another. An awareness of stage development, combined with empathy, genuineness, caring, and knowledge, should make for a good teacher.

GROUP GAMES AND TRAPS

The effective teacher is capable of viewing groups of students as able to learn to think for themselves, to locate information, evaluate it, and put it into action. The effective teacher believes that each student has a contribution to make to the group and that the teacher has a contribution to make, too. This teacher believes that, given enough relevant information and time to think about it, a group can decide what is best for its members better than the teacher can decide individually. The teacher makes information available to the group and helps them seek additional sources of information. The teacher facilitates group decisions and helps students find ways of measuring their progress and success. The teacher helps each member find a way to participate and a place in the group so that each student feels like they belong.

Despite all attempts at fostering a positive environment in which learning can take place, some pitfalls exist and should be avoided if the teacher is to develop the most promising learning environment. Newman (1974) identified five games students play that lead to entrapment of the teacher:

1. The **Who did it first** game. This game serves the group's needs by allowing individuals to blame others for their actions. Students will respond that "someone else did it first" as a means of detracting attention from themselves. Sometimes a general scapegoat may become identified in a classroom. This person becomes victimized and blamed for starting any negative events. Teachers must be aware of the difficulty in determining origins of behavior in specific episodes. The first person should not be blamed any more than other participants.

2. The **Fairness** game. Any person who recalls childhood must remember using the statement "it isn't fair" in an attempt to get additional consideration from parents and teachers. This game derives from sibling rivalries and is most often put into play when one desires to avoid a task or merely to watch the teacher become agitated. Teachers must work to avoid singling out a particular student or group of students to get special favors. Students will use this game to attack the teacher and will also blame other students for having received some advantage. This is not to say that all students must be treated alike. The effective teacher recognizes that the students in his or her class have individual needs and that individuals with different needs are to be taught differently.

3. The **Do-gooder** game. This game frequently involves the teacher who has entered teaching with some missionary zeal to do good deeds. Frequently this type of teacher determines self-worth and teacher-worth by helping the unfortunate. Such a mission is likely to produce phoney responses to students because the teacher is unable to be genuine and honest in a provocative situation. The goal is to be empathic toward students rather than sympathetic toward them.

4. The **Willing-sucker** game. The teacher will discover that in every group at least one student is vulnerable and easily manipulated. Students often find power in manipulating another to satisfy their own needs, while maintaining for themselves shelter from consequences. The goal of the

teacher is to try to catch the manipulating student in the process of revealing the observed dynamics.

5. The **Dare** game. This game is similar to the "willing-sucker" game but the participant is not easily manipulated. In fact, the "dare" game involves the issuance of a challenge so great that failure to live up to it would cause one to seriously question one's place in the group. The person offering the dare convinces himself or herself that failure comes from willingness to participate, not from actually losing. Strategies similar to disarming the willing sucker are useful in disarming the challenger of the "dare" game.

Activities included in Pfeiffer and Jones (1973–81), A *Handbook of Structured Experiences for Human Relations Training, Volumes 1–7,* may be useful in combatting the games, in getting the group started, in helping the group resolve conflict, or in providing individual feedback to a member of the class. The advantage of this activity series is that activities from a minimal level of involvement to a very intense level of involvement are included. Various activities are appropriate for each stage through which a group may be progressing. The activities are fun and provide further helpful insight into dynamics of group process.

The question of efficiency of group function will emerge over and over. The teacher must remember that the classroom group situation will not work perfectly, because human beings are not perfect. Success can be measured only in terms of progress toward an ideal. Teachers also must remember that a single failure does not mean total failure. One is inclined to view immediate results and to ignore possibilities of long-term efforts.

PARENT-TEACHER CONFERENCES

Two forms of activities involve interactions between teachers and parents: parent-teacher conferences and parent-education groups. Both of these activities were introduced in Chapter 5. (Parent-education groups were discussed in detail under the heading "Parent Effectiveness Groups.") The material presented here on student groups will be applicable to any other group the teacher encounters. The dynamics involved in working with parent groups is essentially the same as with any other group.

Parent participation is a key element in the education of their children. Parents must be encouraged to take an active role. Such involvement necessitates frequent contact between the teacher and parents. Some general points that must be considered in regard to parent-teacher conferences are as follows:

1. Did the teacher do groundwork prior to the conference so that parents are aware of what will be discussed? Parents also need an opportunity to prepare themselves.
2. Was the teacher able to establish a pleasant environment, free from threat?
3. Were all parties allowed time to voice concerns? The conference should not be viewed as one-sided, where the teacher "tells" parents what to do.
4. Was follow-up clear so that progress can be monitored? Were responsibilities clearly defined?

Davis and Davis (1981) identified some additional critical questions that require answers before the parent-teacher conference begins:

What do I want from the conference?
What are my strengths and weaknesses in the problem area?
What are my attitudes toward the child? The parents?
What are my feelings about conducting the conference?
If conflicts arise, which of my defenses are likely to emerge?
Will other school personnel be involved in the conference?
Is the conference to be held in a place where interruptions or noise
    may be expected?
What messages will make up the body of the conference?
What possible solutions will be discussed?
How will the conference be summarized? (pp. 47–50)

Teachers must view parents as natural allies in the process of educating children. Too frequently, parents and teachers become adversaries. Too frequently, teachers see parents only as one of the types described by Ryan and Cooper (1984):

1. Mrs. Mysonthegenius, who expects her average child to be a genius
2. Mrs. Putdown, a former teacher who quickly points out what is wrong with teacher and class
3. Mrs. Latecomer, who has no support for teacher or child and complains when problems naturally arise
4. Mr. Heavyhands, who knows how to handle child and encourages teacher to use the same techniques
5. Mrs. Youthinkyou'vegotproblems, who attends school conference and focuses on her problems and not on the child

TABLE 6.2
Characteristics of Defensive and Supportive Communication Climates and Verbal Indicators

Communication Behaviors Leading to Defensiveness	Communication Behaviors Leading to Supportiveness
1. *Evaluation:* to pass judgment on another, to blame or praise based on one's values; to make moral assessments of another; to question standards, values, and motives of another. Use of words like "good," "bad," "right," "wrong."	1. *Description:* nonjudgmental; to ask questions that are perceived as genuine requests for information; to present feelings, perceptions, or processes that do not ask or imply that the receiver change behavior or attitude.
2. *Control:* to try to do something to another; to attempt to change an attitude or the behavior of another; to try to restrict another's field of activity, choices (implied in attempts to change another person is that he is now inadequate). Use of words like "should," "ought to," "need to."	2. *Problem Orientation:* the opposite of persuasion. To communicate a "desire to work together," to define a problem and seek a solution; to imply that you have no preconceived solution, attitude, or method to impose; to allow the other to set his own goals, make his own decisions, and evaluate his own progress or to share with you in doing so.
3. *Strategy:* to manipulate others; to use tricks to involve another.	3. *Spontaneity:* to be straightforward and honest, to be free from deception; to communicate that you have no hidden motives directed toward that person.
4. *Neutrality:* to express a lack of concern for the other person; to communicate a detached "other person as an object: attitude.	4. *Empathy:* to express respect for the worth of the listener, to identify with his problems, share his feelings, and accept his emotions at face value.
5. *Superiority:* to communicate the attitude that you are "better than the other" in position, power, wealth, intellectual ability, physical characteristics; to raise feelings of inadequacy in the other. Use of self-references and comparative terms.	5. *Equality:* to be willing to enter into participative interaction with mutual trust and respect; to attach little importance to differences in talent, ability, worth, appearance, status, and power. Use of plural pronouns, e.g., "we."
6. *Certainty:* to appear dogmatic; to seem to already know all the answers; needing to win an argument rather than solve a problem; seeing your own ideas as "truths" to be defended. Use of symbols like "obviously," "certainly."	6. *Provisionalism:* to be willing to reconsider your own behavior, attitudes, and ideas; to investigate issues rather than take sides. Use of tentative language, e.g., "it seems like," "as far as I know."

Note. Reprinted with the permission of Simon & Schuster, Inc. from the MacMillan College text *Developing Skills for Human Interaction* by L. R. Heun and R. E. Heun. Copyright © 1978 by Merrill, an imprint of MacMillan College Publishing Company, Inc.

6. Mrs. Specialhelp, whose child is doing well but who is sure that his/her child needs special attention, possibly tutoring, and uses guilt to force teacher to help (pp. 94–96)

Heun and Heun (1978) summarized Jack Gibbs' research on communication behaviors that lead to *defensiveness* or *supportiveness*. Knowledge of these behaviors seems quite appropriate for parent-teacher conferences, and they are applicable in other settings as well. The behaviors are described in Table 6.2.

The parent-teacher conference, when handled properly, should serve as an excellent public relations and educational tool. An understanding of the preparation needed prior to the conference, of parent types, of communication behaviors, and of the need to evaluate the conference should enable the teacher to use conferences to their maximum potential. The parent-teacher conference should be used for all students, not only for those experiencing difficulty. Their use should be seen as a normal part of the school routine.

Quite frequently, a teacher may be called to lead or interact with other groups in the community. The teacher should view these offers as opportunities to use the many skills developed in working with a class. Again, the teacher is reminded that the same dynamics observed in a classroom or with a group of parents will emerge in any other group. Teachers learn from interaction with others just as students do. The more interactions the teacher has, the more likely it will be that he or she will find personal rewards in places other than the classroom. Students also should be encouraged to participate in other groups, both in and out of school. After all, human society is based largely upon the capacity of individuals to respond to the needs of other human beings, often in the context of a group.

REFERENCES

Benne, K. D., & Scheats, P. (1948). Functional roles of group members. *Journal of Social Issues, 4,* 41–49.

Davis, D. H., & Davis, D. M. (1981). Managing parent-teacher conferences. *Today's Education, 70,* 46–50.

Hearn, G. (1957). Leadership and the spatial factor in small groups. *Journal of Abnormal and Social Psychology, 54,* 269–272.

Heun, L. R., & Heun, R. E. (1978). *Developing skills for human interaction.* Columbus, OH: Charles E. Merrill.

Newman, R. G. (1974). *Groups in school.* New York: Simon and Schuster.

Pfeiffer, J. W., & Jones, J. E. (1973–81). *A handbook of structured experiences for human relations training,* Volumes 1–7. La Jolla, CA: University Associates.

Ringwald, B. E., Mann, R. D., Rosenwein, R., & McKeachie, W. J. (1971). Conflict and style in the college classroom: An intimate study. *Psychology Today, 4,* 45–47, 76, 78–79.

Ryan, K., & Cooper, J. M. (1984). *Those who can, teach.* Boston: Houghton Mifflin.

Schmuck, R. A., & Schmuck, P. A. (1988). *Group processes in the classroom.* Dubuque, IA: Brown.

Shaw, M. E. (1981). *Group dynamics: The psychology of small group behavior.* New York: McGraw-Hill.

Sommer, R. (1967). Classroom ecology. *Journal of Applied Behavioral Science, 3,* 489–503.

Stanford, G., & Roark, A. E. (1974). *Human interaction in education.* Boston: Allyn and Bacon.

Chapter 7

WORKING
WITH SPECIAL GROUPS

The purpose of this chapter is to set forth some procedures for teaching special populations in schools. Teaching special groups is a complex process because it involves interaction of factors related to the child, the school, the home, the community, and the government. Education of special populations necessitates coordination of services from various school and community resources.

Two specific categories of students will be discussed. First, some strategies for teaching African American students will be presented, because racial differences between African American and white students are of particular interest and importance to schools. Furthermore, many, if not all, approaches useful in teaching African American students apply to other minority groups as well.

The second part of this chapter focuses on students who are classified as "exceptional." This group includes those students who are classified as learning disabled, emotionally handicapped, mentally handicapped, or gifted/talented. Many of these students are taught in self-contained classrooms. Others are assigned to regular classrooms (mainstreamed), necessitating special understanding and techniques for teaching.

TEACHING AFRICAN AMERICAN STUDENTS

Among the areas of concern in teaching is the issue of cross-racial interaction. Whether races have been isolated from each other or whether they have had intensive interactions, beliefs about persons of a different race are generalized to other persons of the same race. Rokeach (1968) found that contact between Blacks and whites produced persons who were less prejudiced than when no contact occurred. Because mere contact does not eliminate prejudice, it is necessary to provide some means by which individuals may openly discuss their racial feelings. Sensitivity programs of racial awareness seem to offer the greater facility in helping persons come to grips with their emotional feelings regarding racial issues. While such racial awareness programs are useful, they must be developed in conjunction with specific skills training if the greatest benefit is to be realized.

Beck (1973) summarized, in tabular form (Table 7.1), some work by Bertram Lee and Warren Schmidt on relations between Blacks and whites. These data are presented so that both whites and Blacks can become more aware of assumptions and behaviors that block authentic relations. Assumptions and behaviors that facilitate more authentic relations are also presented. The data suggests that meaningful knowledge about both self and members of the different race is necessary from a theoretical level as well as from a practical level.

Adding more to this understanding, Cheek (1976) identified ten characteristics of African American persons that have evolved over a long period of a djustment. African Americans may possess any one or more of these characteristics:

1. Bidialectalism, which means a knowledge of standard English as well as a familiarity with or emphasis upon African American language or nonstandard English.
2. Cultural paranoia, a general distrust of whites until proven otherwise.
3. A preoccupation with race and its importance.
4. A seething aggression and pent up anger and rage.
5. A lack of loyalty to white institutions or organizations.
6. Conflict over whether to talk "white or black."
7. An alertness to preferential treatment given to whites.
8. An ability to "fake it" with white people and not reveal self.
9. A sensitivity to nonverbal cues such as body posturing, manner of walk, use of eyes, sucking of teeth, and facial expressions.
10. A suspiciousness and unconvinced attitude concerning patriotism, authority, the value of law, and hard work. (pp. 38–39)

Note that these characteristics are learned and are likely to appear somewhat different among African Americans from different social classes or geographical locations. One caution is that these characteristics should not be

TABLE 7.1

Toward More Authentic Interpersonal Relations Between Blacks and Whites

	Assumptions Which BLOCK Authentic Relations	Assumptions Which FACILITATE Authentic Relations
Assumptions Whites Make	• Color is unimportant in interpersonal relations. • Blacks will always welcome and appreciate inclusion in white society. • Open recognition of color may embarrass Blacks. • Blacks are trying to use Whites. • Blacks can be stereotyped. • White society is superior to Black society. • "Liberal" Whites are free of racism. • All Blacks are alike in their attitudes and behavior. • Blacks are oversensitive. • Blacks must be controlled.	• People count as individuals. • Blacks are human—with individual feelings, aspirations, and attitudes. • Blacks have a heritage of which they are proud. • Interdependence is needed between Whites and Blacks. • Blacks are angry. • Whites cannot fully understand what it means to be Black. • Whiteness/Blackness is a real difference but not the basis on which to determine behavior. • Most Blacks can handle White's authentic behavior and feelings. • Blacks want a responsible society. • Blacks are capable of managerial maturity. • I may be part of the problem.
Assumptions Blacks Make	• All Whites are alike. • There are no "soul brothers" among Whites. • Honkies have all the power. • Whites are always trying to use Blacks. • Whites are united in their attitude toward Blacks. • All Whites are racists. • Whites are not really trying to understand the situation of the Blacks. • Whitey's got to deal on Black terms. • Silence is the sign of hostility. • Whites cannot and will not change except by force. • The only way to gain attention is through confrontation. • All Whites are deceptive. • All Whites will let you down in the "crunch."	• Openness is healthy. • Interdependence is needed between Blacks and Whites. • People count as individuals. • Negotiation and collaboration are possible strategies. • Whites are human beings and, whether they should or not, do have their own hang-ups. • Some Whites can help and "do their own thing." • Some Whites have "soul."

117

	Behaviors Which BLOCK Authentic Relations	Behaviors Which FACILITATE Authentic Relations
Behaviors of Whites	• Interruptions. • Condescending behavior. • Offering help where not needed or wanted. • Avoidance of contact (eye-to-eye and physical). • Verbal focus on Black behavior rather than White behavior. • Insisting on playing games according to White rules. • Showing annoyance at Black behavior which differs from their own. • Expressions of too easy acceptance and friendship. • Talking about, rather than to, Blacks who are present.	• Directness and openness in expressing feelings. • Assisting other White brothers to understand and confront feelings. • Supporting self-initiated moves of Black people. • Listening without interrupting. • Demonstration of interest in learning about Black perceptions, culture, etc. • Staying with and working through difficult confrontations. • Taking a risk (e.g., being first to confront the differences). • Assuming responsibility for examining own motives—and where they are.
Behaviors of Blacks	• Confrontation too early and too harshly. • Rejection of honest expressions of acceptance and friendship. • Pushing Whites into such a defensive posture that learning and re-examination is impossible. • Failure to keep a commitment and then offering no explanation. • "In-group" joking, laughing at Whites—in Black culture language. • Giving answers Blacks think Whites want to hear. • Using confrontation as the primary relationship style. • Isolationism.	• Showing interest in understanding White's point of view. • Acknowledging that there are some committed Whites. • Acting as if "we have some power"—and don't need to prove it. • Allowing Whites to experience unaware areas of racism. • Openness. • Expression of real feelings. • Dealing with Whites where they are. • Meeting Whites half-way. • Treating Whites on one-to-one basis. • Telling it like it is. • Realistic goal-sharing. • Showing pride in their heritage.

Note. From *The Counselor and Black/White Relations* (pp. 63–64) by J. D. Beck, 1973, Boston: Houghton Mifflin. Copyright 1973 by Houghton Mifflin. Reprinted by permission.

assumed to exist simply because a person is African American. Instead, they are presented to provide additional understanding of some of the possible difficulties in interracial interactions.

Love (1977) presented an extensive list of teacher behaviors that get in the way of good interracial interactions in desegregated schools. Her list was revised to develop positive behaviors that should facilitate the teaching of African American students.

1 Hold high expectations of African American students.
   a Encourage African American students to excel.
   b Provide individual attention for African American students having difficulty in reading or math.
2 Use appropriate instructional materials.
   a Use textbooks that include African American viewpoints.
   b Supplement textbooks with materials and activities that foster a multicultural viewpoint.
   c Use bulletin board displays that recognize African American issues, holidays, contributions, heroes, etc.
   d Use African American persons as resources in the instructional program.
   e Include instructional materials that help students explore myths and stereotypes of racism.
3 Make every effort to foster interpersonal relations between teachers and African American students.
   a Relate to African American students as individuals.
   b Hold high standards for African American students.
   c Respond positively toward African American students' hair styles, music,clothing, and so forth.
   d Interact with African American students in out-of-class activities.
4 Group African American students on the basis of ability.
   a Use a variety of sources of information to determine class placements.
   b Examine standardized tests for sources of bias against African American students.
   c Seat students alphabetically in class.
5 Use counseling approaches appropriate to needs of African American students.
   a Encourage African American students to move into nontraditional career paths.
   b Help African American students prepare to take standardized tests.
   c Encourage African American students to become peer helpers for other African American students.

6 Encourage institutional practices appropriate for African American students.
  a Encourage schoolwide acknowledgment of African American holidays.
  b Initiate/facilitate interest clubs and extracurricular activities specific to the interests of African American students, e.g., Bid-whiz Club, Swahili Club.
  c Work to secure participation of African American students in the total school program.
7 Be honest in interactions with students.
  a Be willing to discuss "touchy" issues (busing, segregated housing patterns).
  b Assist students in examining conflicting racial feelings and attitudes.
  c Be open to discussions of incidents with racial overtones in the classrooms.
  d Be open to discussions of relationships between African American and white students.
8 Administer discipline fairly.

THE SELF-FULFILLING PROPHECY

Generally, research on intergroup-interracial education supports the thesis that teachers have lower expectations of African American students than of white students. Teachers also tend to have lower expectations of students from lower socioeconomic levels than from higher socioeconomic levels. Expectations are the lowest for "disadvantaged" African American students. A study by Cooper, Baron, and Rowe (1975) showed that lower class African American students were expected to receive lower grades than lower class white students, and lower grades than other lower class students, regardless of race. Although the African American middle class student was expected to achieve success equal to the white middle class counterpart, if he or she failed, external forces such as luck and task difficulty were held responsible. If the white middle class student failed, it was because of internal factors such as ability and effort.

In a study by Harvey and Slatin (1975), using a sample drawn from schools serving lower and upper middle class neighborhoods in a city of 100,000, teachers expected white children to succeed more often than African American children, regardless of perceived socioeconomic background.

Long and Henderson (1974) found that southern teachers expected less from African American students who scored low on I.Q. tests than they expected of low-scoring whites, and they expected less of African American students who were talkative and participated in class activities than they expected of white children who were active.

Rosenthal and Jacobsen (1968) discussed how teachers in schools located in lower class neighborhoods did not set standards as high as those in middle class schools, nor were they as concerned with bringing their children up to grade level. In the same vein, Silberman (1970) visited schools in ghetto areas and was surprised by the modesty of the expectations of teachers, supervisors, principals, and superintendents for students in their care.

Thus, if a tendency exists for many teachers to have lowered expectations for African American "disadvantaged" students, the question is "Why"?

According to Silberman, many teachers of African American children apparently believe (even if they do not admit it in their minds) that their students are intellectually inferior. Even when this attitude is unconscious, the teacher cannot avoid communicating it to the children in one way or another. Generally, explanations seem to be based on either the belief in inherent racial inferiority (as interpreted from I.Q. tests) or the premise that the environmental conditions in which many "disadvantaged" African American children live depresses the ability of these children to learn.

The first assumption is based mainly on the misinterpretation and emphasis of I.Q. tests. Teachers apparently attribute at least a rough predictive validity to readiness test scores in spite of evidence that the reliability and validity of these tests are weak. These teachers see the child as a fixed entity determined by heredity; the determinant is these tests. For them, the I.Q. scores are a meaningful guide to a child's potential, and they accept that these scores will follow the children for the rest of their lives (Silberman, 1964). Generally, those who expect less of African American students because of the low I.Q. scores have neglected to understand the limitations of tests and that scores may not be a true measure of intellectual competence because they do not take into account the factors of motivation and possible cultural bias.

The other explanation of intellectual inferiority rests on the thesis that when poor children enter school they are intellectually deficient because of deprivations in their environment. In other words, the culturally deprived child is unable to learn in the standard educational environment because no stimulation for educational achievement has occurred previously. Instead of viewing students as having cognitive differences in specific areas, some educators have generalized the social deprivation theories to imply that the "different" student is intellectually deficient, for example, assuming that poor children use an "impoverished mode of speech" which in turn degrades their thought because they are intellectually deficient and cannot succeed in academic endeavors (Ginsburg, 1972). Baratz and Baratz (1971) concur that the social deprivationists assume a *lack* of stimulation in "disadvantaged" African American children rather than a *difference* in environmental stimulation.

According to Clark (1965) the problem with the "socially neglected," "school retarded," "culturally impoverished," "culturally deficient" students is that they have been assigned generally negative terms and descriptions which in turn lower teacher expectations. "These children do not learn because those who are charged with the responsibility of teaching them do not believe that they can learn, do not expect that they can learn, and do not act towards them in ways which help them to learn" (p. 131). Weatherly and Lipsky (1977) agreed that when teachers are frequently presented with negative data about students, they may "adapt a defensive strategy aimed at absolving themselves of responsibility for the child's learning" (p. 189).

Understanding the background of students seems almost a necessity in forming realistic expectations, but deprivation theories can pose problems. Expectations are often lowered by empathic understanding. According to Silberman (1964), some books and in-service workshops designed to sensitize teachers and administrators to the problems of the "disadvantaged" backfire. By learning that African American youngsters fail through no fault of their own, some teachers may learn to understand and empathize with failure and thereby to expect it.

Therefore the conclusion is that the main consequence of lower expectations is that these expectations become self-fulfilling prophecies. Once an educational system is organized where children are placed in tracks in separate classrooms or within a single classroom, or where certain judgments about their abilities determine what they are taught or not taught, the results tend to justify the assumptions. Clark (1965) stated it thusly:

> Children themselves are not followed by the various euphemisms educators use to disguise educational snobbery. From the earliest grades, a child knows when he has been assigned to a level that is considered less than adequate. . . Those children who are relegated to the inferior groups suffer a sense of self-doubt and deep feelings of inferiority which stamp their entire attitude toward school and the learning process. . . But it all adds up to the fact that they are not being taught, and not being taught, they fail. They have a sense of personal humiliation and unworthiness. They react negatively and hostilely and aggressively to the educational system. They hate teachers,

they hate schools, they hate anything that seems to impose upon them this denigration, because they are not being respected as human beings, because they are sacrificed in a machinery of efficiency and expendability, because their dignity and potential as human beings are being obscured and ignored in terms of educationally irrelevant factors—their manner, their speech, their dress, or their apparent disinterest. (p. 128)

Silberman (1964) reported that Leacock and her observers were struck by the liveliness and eager interest of "disadvantaged" students in lower grades, in contrast to the possibility and the apathy observed later. In schools they studied, children's interest and eagerness had disappeared by the fifth grade:

What teachers and administrators communicate to lower class students is not middle class values but middle class attitudes toward lower class people and their role in society. The school, she writes, conveys a middle class image of how working class children are and how they should be—an image which emphasizes obedience, respect and conscientiousness . . . rather than ability, responsibility and initiative and which expects unruliness with regard to behavior and apathy with regard to curriculum. By conveying this image to their students, teachers perpetuate the very behavior they decry. And the behavior in turn confirms the teacher's initial expectation, thereby perpetuating the reign of error for still another generation of students. (p. 91)

The classic study of self-fulfilling prophecies was conducted by Rosenthal and Jacobsen (1968) in the South San Francisco Unified School District, a low socioeconomic area. The researchers randomly selected a large group of sixth graders who had recently taken a fairly nonverbal I.Q. test—the Flanagan Test of General Ability. Teachers were led to believe that the test measured potentiality for intellectual blooming. Within each classroom in the school, 20% of the children were randomly designated as "bloomers," and teachers were told to watch these students closely because they were likely to show a large increase in their intellectual performance during the school year. Eight months later when the entire group of sixth graders was retested, it was found that those students who had been randomly labeled "very bright" demonstrated significantly greater improvement in reasoning and total I.Q. than did the "nonblooming" children. The difference between the "blooming" children and the control children was especially pronounced in the lower grades. Students designated as bloomers not only performed better than the control students, but they also were reported to be happier, better adjusted, and more curious. Furthermore, teachers expressed more liking for the bloomers than for the controls.

An observational study done by Rist (1971) centered around one class of ghetto children during kindergarten, first, and second grade. The kindergarten teacher, who was African American, placed children in reading groups that reflected the social class composition of the students. Permanent seating arrangements were made the eighth day of school based on such factors as behavior, verbalization, dress, mannerisms, and physical appearance. Within a few days, only certain children were called upon to lead the class in the pledge of allegiance, read the calendar, lead the class to the bathroom, and perform other duties. These children were seated at a table near the teacher. Children at the outer tables were given a "no response" from the teacher at a ratio of three to one, as opposed to the nearer tables. As the year wore on, numerous instances were observed of children at far tables calling one another "stupid," "dummy," or "dumb-dumb." General grouping continued in the first and second grades. The second grade pupils at the table near the teacher were called "tigers" and the other two groups were called "cardinals" and "clowns."

In discussing the observation, the researcher noted that no matter how well a child in the lower reading group might have read, that child was destined to remain in the same reading group. This is in a sense another manifestation of the "self-fulfilling prophecy." A slow learner had no option but to continue to be a slow learner, regardless of performance or potential. The kindergarten teacher's initial expectations two years earlier as to each child's ability resulted in placement in a reading group, whether high or low, from which there appeared to be no escape. Though the analysis focused on the early years of schooling for a single group of African American children attending a ghetto school, the researcher felt the implications were far-reaching for those situations in which children from different status backgrounds were within the same classroom. "When a teacher bases expectations of performance on the social status of the student and   assumes that the higher the social status, the higher the potential of the child, children of low social status suffer stigmatization outside their choice or will" (p. 107). This observation brought out the problem that lowered expectations sometimes involve prejudice of class as well as color. In some cases, African American teachers also are capable of making unrealistic expectations of their students. Pedersen, Faucher, and Eaton (1978) concluded that if children are lucky enough to have a first-grade teacher who has high expectations for their achievement, they will be likely to develop positive self-concepts and be more successful in school.

Finally, Rubovits and Maehr (1973) found that academically gifted African American children were subjected to greater criticism by white teachers than were gifted white students. "In this regard, the present study provided what appears to be a disturbing instance of white racism. African American students were given less attention, ignored more, praised less and criticized more" (p. 217). Findings were suggested that it is the gifted African American student who is given the least attention and praise, and the most criticism, even when comparing him or her to a *nongifted* white student. Interestingly results showed that highly dogmatic teachers were more inclined towards the prejudicial pattern than less dogmatic teachers.

We hasten to point out that in spite of the research previously cited, several studies have disputed the findings of the role of teacher expectancy in achievement. According to O'Connell, Dusek, and Wheeler (1974), simply telling teachers that a student performs well is not enough to alter the student's performance. Part of the problem is that children are also influenced by the expectations of parents, peers, and administrators, so it is difficult to isolate the factor of teacher expectation. Clairborn (1969) found that when teachers perceived pupils to be of high potential, some of them, but not all, altered their behavior.

Therefore, teachers need to develop realistic expectations for all students, especially those from groups that differ from the majority. In order that the expectations be realistic, teachers should understand the problems students may face because of their membership in a special group. If students are overwhelmed by unrealistic expectations, whether too high or too low, they may fail and eventually lose confidence in themselves and in the school.

LESSON PLANS TO DEVELOP SELF-ESTEEM AND DIMINISH PREJUDICE

The objective of this section is to present a series of lesson plans that have the primary objective of building a sense of importance and self-worth in each child and that have the underlying theme that *all* persons are important. The ultimate goal is to diminish racial feelings in students by allowing them to discover that persons of other races are worthwhile individuals, not *in spite* of their differences but *because* of them. This effort requires revealing the fallacies in old tales and stereotyped generalizations that have been handed down from generation to generation, and demands honest expression of feelings, open discussions, and reevaluations of some erroneous ideas.

Cook (1951) said, "Reeducation along intergroup lines, if it is to be effective, should be started at the time children enter school" (p. 44). He went on to state that, "under conditions of urban life, prejudices are learned at such early ages as to make the reeducation of children in human relations a prime need at the elementary school level" (p. 51).

With this in mind, we advocate that these lessons begin in kindergarten and extend through high school. The deliberate education of the child about himself or herself and others is one of the obligations of the educator. Such learning cannot be left to chance.

To effectively present these lesson plans, the teacher may require some special training. It is necessary to be sure of the concepts one wishes to develop and to feel positively about them. Attending a workshop on intergroup education or interracial communication would be helpful; but if one is not available, good reference materials can be found in most libraries.

Although a series of lesson plans have been developed specifically to begin to address the development of self-importance and attack prejudicial behavior, these same concepts can be addressed in all subject matter areas. The teacher must constantly seek ways to incorporate intergroup/interracial education in history, geography, literature, social studies, arts, crafts, music, and all other subjects. The history of mathematics provides a good example of cross-cultural development. Biology is a place for teaching about the facts of racial differentiation and the weaknesses of "race" as a scientific concept (Domnitz, 1965).

Besides the formal learning situations, many instances will occur in the classroom and on the playground that will provide good opportunities for strengthening and supplementing ideas and concepts of behavior the teacher wishes to develop and reinforce. If a person can learn to hate and distrust others, he or she can learn to like and trust others as well. Educators advocate that, as much as possible, intergroup education be infused into regular curricular offerings.

Intergroup education is as important as teaching reading, mathematics, or language arts. As a result of carefully selected materials and methods, individuals can and will be changed, in their attitudes and behaviors toward persons of other groups, and toward members of whatever group they themselves belong to. The change will result in more acceptance of persons who differ and more acceptance of one's own differences from others (Grambs, 1967).

In utilizing the lesson plans the teacher should realize that they are merely outlines and be flexible in making changes where necessary to extend or expand areas that need more study in his or her specific situation. Lessons presented on the following pages are designed for elementary school students, but activities may be altered to be more age or grade appropriate. Each lesson is designed for approximately 30 minutes of class time.

These lesson plans were developed around parts of the book *Liking Myself* (1977) by Pat Palmer. This hand-lettered and illustrated book, which includes information on feelings, self-concept, and assertiveness, is recommended for children ages five to nine.

Lesson 1—Like Ourselves

To help create a relaxed, less formal atmosphere, the teacher arranges the chairs so that all students feel a part of the group. If an area is available where the students can sit on the floor, it may be used.

Before the discussion begins, talk about some of the rules to follow so that everyone can hear what is being said and have a turn to talk. Point out how important it is to listen to what others in the class have to say.

Introduce the lesson by asking students if they know that it is acceptable to like yourself and be your own best friend. Get a discussion going by asking such questions as: What does this mean? Do you like yourself? Are you your own friend? Allow the children to express their opinions freely and avoid showing dissatisfaction with their answers. If anyone in the class makes fun of another's answer, use this opportunity to tell the students that we all have different feelings about things, and that is acceptable. Everyone should say exactly what they feel without the fear of being criticized.

The discussion may not last too long the first time but will get longer as the students become accustomed to expressing their ideas in an environment conducive to free expression of thoughts and feelings.

End the lesson by telling the class members that you want them to feel good about themselves because it is acceptable to like oneself: Enjoy being yourself right now. Clap your hands. Give yourself a hug. Smile at yourself. Now share your good feelings with others by smiling at your neighbor. Reach out and touch a friend. Feel good about yourselves, feel good about each other.

Have the students ask a parent, brother, sister, or friend to tell them what that person likes about them and bring the answers to class for the next lesson. Older students may be asked to write down the information.

Lesson 2—Like Others

Have the students make tags of brightly colored paper that say, "I like me." Pin them on the students and encourage them to wear the tags all day. This will help develop interest among the other classes and at home.

Have each child get a partner, sit facing each other, and take turns telling the other about some of the things he or she likes about self. What each child will point out can be very revealing. Comments made can help students see their fellow students in a different light. Have the class members change partners two or three times. Have as many African American/white pairs as possible, and encourage the children to try to find different things to say about themselves with each new partner.

After finishing this activity, ask the class members if anyone learned something about a partner that had not been known before. Allow students to share what they learned. Conclude the lesson with "I like myself. I like you. Let's give ourselves a pat on the back today."

If class pictures have been taken, use these to make a bulletin board, but if they are not available, ask the students to bring in a snapshot to use. If necessary, bring a camera and take your own pictures.

Arrange the pictures on a bulletin board with a characteristic describing the person. Every few days change the characteristic yourself or have students add different ones. Be sure at some point to include as a characteristic that a person is African American or white.

Lesson 3—At Times, I May Not Like Self

The first two lessons were about liking yourself and that it is acceptable to like yourself and to be your own friend. The idea to be developed in Lesson 3 is that possibly there will be times when a person might not like himself or herself. To feel this way sometimes is natural and acceptable. Explore why a person feels this way, what may cause these feelings, and what should be done about them.

Begin this discussion by asking each class member to think of a time when he or she did not like self. If you have a hard time getting ideas from the class, give an illustration of your own, such as when you had not performed well on a test. In fact, for the teacher to share personal feelings with the class during these discussions is a good idea. It is good for students to understand that the teacher has some of the same feelings as other individuals.

After getting some ideas from class members, try to get them to discover reasons behind their feelings of not liking themselves. What were the causes or circumstances that precipitated these feelings? Then ask the class what they did to get rid of them.

End the lesson on a positive note. Tell the students that these feelings of not liking oneself are acceptable, but of course, we want to like ourselves most of the time.

Lesson 4—Feeling and Feeling Talk

This lesson involves feelings and "feeling talk." Start this lesson by smiling at the class and asking them what you might be feeling. Yawn and rub your eyes, frown, or show amazement and ask students what your feelings might be. Get the students to name some different feelings. You might want to list them on the chalkboard. Ask if they have some feelings that they like and some that they dislike. Have them explain why.

The idea in this lesson is that you should listen to your feelings because they tell you when you need to take care of yourself. Sometimes feelings are hidden. Ask class members to describe a situation when they kept their feelings to themselves. Discuss how it felt to keep it inside instead of talking to someone about how they felt.

Is it all right to feel anger? Discuss this question, then tell the class that anger is an acceptable feeling. Ask them about other feelings and if they are acceptable. Leave them with the idea that feelings of anger and fear are acceptable.

Now that all feelings have been established as acceptable, the teacher needs to develop how one expresses these feelings without hurting or upsetting another person. Palmer (1977) suggested some good examples to follow, such as: I am angry. I am sad. I want to be left alone. I feel very upset right now.

It may take much discussion for students to recognize and understand that the secret to feeling talk is to start with "I" instead of "You." Say, "I am mad" instead of, "You make me mad."

Play the "I Think, I Feel, I Want Game" (Palmer, 1977, p. 35). Each child chooses a partner and they sit facing each other. They start each sentence with one of the three previous statements. To help the students get started, teachers may ask them to tell how they would feel if a great big bear wandered into the room. How would they feel if everyone was invited to a birthday party except them? How would they feel if an African American boy or girl asked them to a party? How would they feel if a white boy or girl invited them to a party? How would they feel if someone called them a derogatory name? How would they feel if someone used an undesirable racial designation in addressing them?

Children need to learn to express their feelings to others, and these activities with partners are a step in that direction. By learning to talk openly in the classroom with a partner, they may carry it over into other situations at school and at home.

Encourage the students to use feeling talk with their friends and family. The teacher should be aware of situations at school in which students can be reminded to express themselves with feeling talk.

Lesson 5—Think, Feel, Want

This lesson reinforces feeling talk by having the children play the "I Think, I Feel, I Want Game" but little differently than it was done in Lesson 4. Have different pairs of students volunteer to act out with words how they feel about certain situations. The teacher might want to use a situation that has occurred at school that needs some redirecting in the feeling talk used or the student's reaction to the situation.

If the teacher cannot develop original situations to use, he or she might refer to open-ended scripts that J. D. Grambs (1968) included in the appendix of *Intergroup Education.* In their book *Role Playing for Social Values,* Shaftel and Shaftel (1967) offered original and stimulating unfinished stories for classroom use.

Lesson 6—Like You for Various Reasons

Have the children make tags of paper containing the words "I like you." The idea on which to work in this lesson is that we like people for many different reasons, but we should not dislike a person just because of skin color.

Many different materials exist that a teacher may use to help children see African American persons in a more realistic light. The teacher may read a story about an African American family or show a film that depicts good interracial interactions. Regardless of the material used, the presentation of material should be followed by a good, open discussion so that students have an opportunity to express their ideas and feelings and the teacher can point out some fallacies in thinking. Time, often much time, is required for students to change their ways of thinking, and one such lesson probably will not be enough. At this point the teacher may need to present additional lessons using moral dilemmas (see example in Chapter 2).

Lesson 7—Different and Acceptable

The theme for this lesson is, "You can be different and still be acceptable." Have students think of at least one way they differ from the person sitting in front of or behind them. If any handicapped children are in the class or school, this lesson is good for exploring those differences and for helping students understand handicapping conditions.

Ask different pairs of children to volunteer to be in front of the class. Ask how they are different from each other. When a white and African American child are paired together, get the children to point out differences in hair texture. Have students explore differences in skin texture.

After pointing out some obvious physical differences, ask the class if they can identify other ways people are different. The teacher may have to give examples, such as one student is a good basketball player and another can draw well. Go into as much detail as needed and be open and honest in discussion of these differences. Do not avoid anything students bring up.

Write across the board "It's OK to be different." Ask students to look around them in school and at home to discover ways in which they are different from others and how others are different from them. While thinking of these differences, remember that we must learn to appreciate differences because "Different is OK."

Lesson 8—Differences Are Essential

Today make tags that contain the words "It's OK to be different." On a flannel board arrange three or four identical human figures. Start the discussion by asking the students to choose which one of the figures is "Mary." Of course, they cannot do this by looking at them because they are all the same. Ask students if there might be some way in which they could tell the females apart if they looked identical. They might suggest such things as the way they talked, acted, or walked. After getting answers to this question, go a step further and ask what would we do if everyone not only looked alike but acted alike and talked alike. Get the class members to see that this would make for a very boring world. Differences are important.

On the flannel board, arrange figures of peoples of different ages, race, size, and sex. After pointing out all the differences the class can identify, tell the students that not only are these people different, but these differences are important. Suggest ways they think they are important. Whatever their answers, probe as to why they feel this way.

This lesson can be concluded by stating that each one in the class is important just because they are themselves, and they don't need any other reasons. They are different from each other and these differences are important.

Lesson 9—I Am Important

The tags the children are to make and wear today contain the words "I am Important." Ask students what they have been thinking regarding being important. Have they had any new ideas and thoughts on being important? After this discussion, point out to the class that if they are important, then everyone else is important, too. Try to get students to tie in all the different ideas that have been themes of the last eight lessons—that we should like ourselves; that we should like others; that feelings are acceptable and it is important to use "feeling talk" to express ourselves; that differences are acceptable—in fact, they are necessary for a better, more interesting world; that we do not dislike a person because he or she is different; and that everyone is important.

Summary Regarding Lesson Plans

These lesson plans are only skeleton ideas. Each presents a slightly different idea or concept that the teacher might wish to expand.

The teacher may want to spend two, three, or more time periods on any one idea. Considerable time might be spent on African American/white relations as a final (tenth) lesson. With older children, the teacher should adjust the content to more age- or grade-level appropriate material.

These lesson plans could be used as a spring board, a stepping stone, a beginning for the development of the teacher's own ideas. Remember that the educational task is to recognize contemporary needs and to develop deliberate exercises for educating and reeducating students about the many groups that make up America, its history, and the world in which we live.

OTHER RACIAL-ETHNIC GROUPS

The same strategies, techniques, and personal belief system necessary for teaching African American students are useful in working with any other racial or ethnic group. No less sensitivity is needed in working with Chicanos, Latinos, American Indians, or Asian Americans than is needed for African Americans.

Teachers should seek to understand children's behavior in terms of all the forces that tend to have an impact on their behavior. The cultural background may provide some useful information in helping teachers to understand children from diverse backgrounds. Teachers are cautioned to remember that generalized cultural differences may serve to hamper educational advancement because, it appears, culturally different subgroups are alike in many ways. The "self-fulfilling prophecy" pattern should be avoided with all racially different groups. Washington and Lee (1981) summarized the challenge thusly:

School administrators, teachers, and counselors must share responsibility to develop innovative educational philosophies and methods that meet children's needs. In meeting the needs of [culturally different] children, school personnelmust challenge false assumptions about the cognitive skills and affective states of [culturally different] children. Secondly, school personnel must actively seek stronger relationships with . . . parents and community groups. Third, advocacy roles for [culturally different] children must become integral tasks of educators. This advocacy role should evolve from the institutions' recognition of cultural divergence. (p. 64)

EDUCATION OF EXCEPTIONAL CHILDREN

When the 94th Congress of the United States enacted a law in 1975 providing for the "education of all handicapped children," the status of public education began a rapid change. What has come to be referred to generally as P.L. 94-142 (the 142nd law passed by the 94th Congress) was designed to

assure that all handicapped children (between the ages of 3 and 21 inclusive) have available to them, . . . a free appropriate public education which emphasizes special education and related services designed to meet their unique needs, to assure that the rights of handicapped children and their parents or guardians are protected, to assist States and localities to provide for the education of all handicapped children, and to assess and assure the effectiveness of efforts to educate handicapped children. (Section 3 of the Act)

The law specifically defined some of the terms used in the act. The term "special education" means

specifically designed instruction, at no cost to parents or guardians, to meet the unique needs of a handicapped child, including classroom instruction, instruction in physical education, home instruction, and instruction in hospitals and institutions. (Section 4 (a) (16) of the Act)

The term "related services" was defined as including

transportation, and such developmental, corrective, other supportive services (including speech pathology, audiology, psychological services, physical and occupational therapy, recreation, medical and counseling services) as may be required to assist a handicapped child to benefit from special education, and includes the early identification and assessment of handicapping conditions in children. (Section 4 (a) (17) of the Act)

"Free appropriate public education" was defined in the law as

special education and related services which (A) have been provided at public expense, under public supervision and direction, without charge, (B) meet the standards of the State educational agency, (C) include and appropriate preschool, elementary, or secondary school education in the State involved, and (D) areprovided in conformity with the individualized education program required. (Section 3 (c) of the Act)

The required "individualized education program" means a

written statement for each handicapped child developed in any meeting by a representative of the local educational agency or an intermediate education unit who shall be qualified to provide, or supervise the provision of, specially designed instruction to meet the unique needs of handicapped children, the teacher, the parents or guardian of such child, and whenever appropriate, such child,which statement shall include (A) a state of the present levels of educational performance of such child (B) a statement of annual goals, including short term instructional objectives, (C) a statement of the specific educational services to be provided to such child, and the extent to which such child will be able to participate in regular educational programs, (D) the projected date for initiation and anticipated duration of such services and (E) appropriate objective criteria and evaluation procedures and schedules for determining, on at least an annual basis, whether instructional objectives are being achieved. (Section 4 (a) (19) of the Act)

Each state has the responsibility to develop eligibility criteria, assessment and screening procedures, and process procedures for developing the Individualized Education Program (IEP). To help understand these areas, we have chosen samples from some states to illustrate how the eligibility criteria (Table 7.2) are identified and how guidelines are developed for comprehensive screening and assessment (Table 7.3).

The tasks involved in the development of the IEP for each handicapped child are probably best understood if one follows through the steps involved. The IEP is to be completed by a team of persons. Team members usually are selected from among the following:

1. principal (or designee) as chairperson
2. teacher referring child
3. chairperson for special education (or designee)
4. teacher of exceptional children
5. psychologist
6. social worker
7. school counselor
8. speech, language, and hearing specialist
9. physician or school nurse
10. physical therapist
11. occupational therapist
12. physical education teacher
13. recreation specialist
14. referring agency personnel
15. parent(s)

The steps involved in the development of the IEP are described in the following eleven steps:

STEP 1 Identifying Information

Information including the child's name, birthdate, age at time of the IEP development, school, and class should be filled in wherever requested on the form.

If the child spends part of his or her time in one class (such as a learning center) and part of the time elsewhere (such as in a regular class), both locations should be noted.

STEP 2 Hours/Days Per Week in Mainstream

Note how much time the student will receive instruction in a regular classroom with nonhandicapped students. Also note hours and days per week in regular and/or adaptive physical education.

TABLE 7.2
Definitions of Children With Special Needs (Sample State)

The term "children with special needs" includes, without limitation, all children who, because of permanent or temporary mental, physical, or emotional handicaps, need special education, are unable to have all their educational needs met in a regular class without special education or related services, or are unable to be adequately educated in the public schools. It includes those who are academically gifted, autistic, behaviorally-emotionally handicapped, deaf-blind, hearing impaired, mentally handicapped, multi-handicapped, orthopedically impaired, other health impaired, pregnant, specific learning disabled, speech-language impaired, traumatic brain injured, and visually impaired. The terms used in this definition are defined as follows:

1 *Academically Gifted.* Those who demonstrate or have the potential to demonstrate outstanding intellectual aptitude and specific academic ability. In order to develop their abilities, these students may require differentiated educational services beyond those ordinarily provided by the regular school program.
2 *Autistic.* A severe and chronic developmental disorder that affects communication and behavior. The essential features include disturbances of
   a Developmental rates and/or sequences
   b Responses to sensory stimuli
   c Speech, language and cognitive capacities
   d Capacities to relate to people events and objects
   Associated features include stereotyped motor patterns and erratic expression of emotions.
3 *Behaviorally-Emotionally Handicapped.* Students who, after receiving specially de-signed educational support services and intervention strategies in the regular educational setting, still exhibit patterns of situationally inappropriate interpersonal or intrapersonal behavior of such frequency, duration, and intensity to disrupt the student's own learning process. Frequency, duration, and intensity are long-standing patterns of behavior that occur regularly and often enough to interfere consistently with the student's own learning process. A behavioral-emotional handicap is evidenced by one or more of the following characteristics that cannot be attributed primarily to physical, sensory, or intellectual deficits:
   a Inability to achieve adequate academic progress (not due to a learning disability)
   b Inability to maintain satisfactory interpersonal and/or intrapersonal relationships
   c Inappropriate or immature types of behavior or feelings under normal conditions
   d A general pervasive mood of unhappiness or depression
   e A tendency to develop physical symptoms, pains or fears associated with personal or school problems
   The term does not include the socially maladjusted student unless it is determined that he or she is also behaviorally-emotionally handicapped.
4 *Deaf-Blind.* Students have concomitant hearing and visual impairments, the combination of which causes such severe communication and other developmental and

TABLE 7.2 (*Continued*)
Definitions of Children With Special Needs (Sample State)

educational problems that they cannot be accommodated in special education programs solely for deaf or blind children.

5　*Hearing Impaired.* Those with hearing losses who are handicapping educationally and developmentally and who, with or without amplification, may require various instructional modifications and related services in order to make full use of their learning opportunities. This term includes all hearing losses ranging from mild to profound.

6　*Mentally Handicapped.* Refers to significantly subaverage general cognitive functioning and a reduced rate of learning. This condition exists concurrently with deficits in adaptive behavior, is manifested during the developmental period, and adversely affects the student's educational performance.

7　*Multihandicapped.* Students have a pervasive primary handicap that is cognitive and/or behavioral in combination with one or more other handicaps, the combination of which causes such developmental and educational problems that the children cannot be accommodated in special programs that primarily serve one area of handicapping condition.

8　*Orthopedically Impaired.* Students possess a severe orthopedic impairment that adversely affects their educational performance. The term includes impairments caused by congenital abnormalities and impairments from other causes.

9　*Other Health Impaired.* Students have chronic or acute health problems which cause limited strength, vitality, or alertness to such an extent that special educational services are necessary. The health problems may include heart conditions, chronic lung disease, tuberculosis, rheumatic fever, nephritis, asthma, sickle cell anemia, hemophilia, epilepsy, lead poisoning, leukemia, diabetes, genetic impairments, or some other illness which may cause a student to have limited strength, vitality, or alertness, adversely affecting educational performance or developmental progress.

10　*Pregnant Students.* Students who, because of their pregnancy, require special educational and/or related services other than that which can be provided through regular educational services.

11　*Specific Learning Disabled.* An inclusive term used to denote various processing disorders presumed to be intrinsic to an individual (e.g., acquisition, organization, retrieval, or expression of information; effective problem-solving behaviors). Those students who, after receiving instructional intervention in the regular education setting, have a substantial discrepancy between ability and achievement. The disability is manifested by substantial difficulties in the acquisition and use of skills in listening comprehension, oral expression, written expression, reading, and/or mathematics.

12　*Speech-Language Impaired.* A disorder in articulation, language, voice, and/or fluency which may range in severity from mild to severe; may be developmental or acquired; and pupils may demonstrate one or any combination of the four parameters listed above.

(*Continued on next page*)

TABLE 7.2 (*Continued*)
Definitions of Children With Special Needs (Sample State)

A communicative difference/dialect is a variation of a symbol system used by a group of individuals which reflects and is determined by shared regional, social, or cultural/ethnic factors and should not be considered a disorder of speech or language. The components of speech-language impairment include:

a Articulation. An abnormal, nondevelopmental production of phonemes (speech sounds). Types of misarticulations include omissions, substitutions, and distortions.

b Language. The impairment of comprehension and/or production of an oral communication system. The disorder may involve the form of language (phonologic, morphologic, and syntactic systems), the content of language (semantic system), the function of language (pragmatic system), and/or any combination of the above:

   (1) Form of language. Phonology is the sound system of a language and the linguistic rules that govern it. Morphology is the rule system that governs the structure of words and the elements of meaning used in their construc tion. Syntax is the linguistic rules governing the order and combination of words to form sentences, and the relationships among the elements within a sentence.

   (2) Content of language. Semantics refers to the content or meaning of words and utterances.

   (3) Function of language. Pragmatics refers to the social use of language and its appropriateness in a given situation.

c Voice. An abnormal production of pitch (e.g., range, inflection, appropriateness), intensity (loudness), resonation (e.g., excessive nasality), and quality (e.g., breathiness, hoarseness, and harshness)

d Fluency. A disruption in the normal, rhythmic flow of speech that interferes with communication. The disorder may include, but not be limited to, frequency of dysfluencies, duration of dysfluencies, struggle and avoidance characteristics, and types of dysfluencies (repetition—phrases, whole words, syllables, and phonemes; prolongations; and blocks)

13 *Visually Impaired*

a "Functionally blind" are those who have so little remaining vision that they must use Braille as their reading medium.

b "Partially seeing" are those who have a loss of vision but are able to use regular or large type as their reading medium. These will generally be children who have a visual acuity between 20/70 and 20/200 in the better eye after correction.

c "Legally blind" are those who have a visual acuity of 20/200 or less in the better eye after correction or a peripheral field so contracted that the widest diameter subtends an arc no greater than 20 degrees.

Note. From *Procedures Governing Programs and Services for Children With Special Needs* (pp. 1–5), 1991, Raleigh, NC: Department of Public Instruction (No copyright).

TABLE 7.3
Comprehensive Screening and Evaluation (Sample State)

Screening and evaluation are the responsibility of the school-based committee and professionals qualified to administer and determine the results of certain technical tests and procedures which are designed to screen or evaluate a pupil's strengths and weaknesses in specific areas of learning and/or behavior. Such professionals might be available within the city and the county school administrative units or from other appropriate agencies (e.g., mental health centers, public health departments, and developmental evaluation clinics):

1 **Parental Permission.** When initial screening and/or evaluation procedures require the administration of instruments, interviews, or other procedures used selectively with an individual child, (not given to everyone in the child's class, grade, or school), written parental permission must be obtained. The local education agency shall send a written prior notice to the parent(s) or guardian(s).

2 **Screening.** Screening should be done to determine if the child is eligible for further consideration for special education services. Appropriate screening may eliminate unnecessary referrals for psychologicals and other in-depth assessment. The child's existing school records, including work samples, shall be collected and analyzed. Other screening information could include physical health information, educational data, and informal social behavior data.

3 **Evaluations/Screenings.** The evaluations and screening of an exceptional child must be multi-factored and multi-disciplinary in order to provide a comprehensive view of the child from the perspective of the school, home, and community. In addition to ability and achievement data, information on physical condition, sociocultural background, and adaptive behavior in the home and school should be gathered and considered, and weight should be given to each.

4 **Parental Consent.** If the parent(s) or guardian(s) consents, the local educational agency shall provide or cause to be provided an appropriate evaluation. If the parent(s) or guardian(s) does not consent, the local educational agency may obtain a due process hearing on the failure of the parent to consent.

5 **Types of Evaluation/Screening.** Types of evaluations and screenings fordetermining eligibility for special educational services include, but are not limited to, the following areas:
   a Educational/developmental
   b Psychological
   c Adaptive behavior
   d Motor
   e Vision and hearing
   f Medical
   g Speech-language
   h Audiological
   i Otological
   j Opthalmological or optometric
   k Vocational

(Continued on next page)

TABLE 7.3 (*Continued*)
Comprehensive Screening and Evaluation (Sample State)

6 **Validated Instruments.** Tests and other evaluation materials must have been validated for the specific purpose for which they were used.

7 **Racially and Culturally Unbiased Evaluations.** All test and evaluation materials and procedures utilized for the purposes of evaluation and placement of children with special needs will be selected and administered so as not to be racially or culturally discriminatory. Such materials and procedures will be provided and administered in the child's native language or mode of communication, unless it clearly is not feasible to do so. No single procedure shall be the sole criterion for determining an appropriate educational program for a child. Test results should accurately reflect the child's aptitude, achievement level, or whatever other factor the test purports to measure, rather than reflecting the child's impaired sensory, manual, or speaking skills, except when such skills are the factors which the tests purport to measure.

Note. From *Procedures Governing Programs and Services for Children with Special Needs* (pp. 25–26), 1991, Raleigh, NC: Department of Public Instruction (No copyright).

STEP 3 Special Notations

In this area, the team should note any information that is relative to the child's well being and ability to profit from an educational program. This might include use of medication, significant allergic conditions, eating problems, particular fears, need for frequent rest periods, and so forth.

STEP 4 Student Profile
(Outlining Areas of Need or Concern)

The first task of the team in the planning function is to review the information gathered during the child evaluation process. This information should be viewed from the perspective of usefulness to the team as a basis for developing an IEP.

Using this information, the team should list the child's present level of performance in each learning area, including both strengths and weaknesses and areas possibly in need of intervention from support services. Areas to be considered as a minimum should include academic achievement, language development, psychomotor skills, social adaptation, self-help skills, pre-vocational and vocational skills, as well as any other relevant areas.

STEP 5 Prioritized Annual Goals
(Long Term—as Related to Present Level of Performance)

One of the first decisions the team has to make in developing and implementing the IEP is where to start. This process is called prioritizing, which means deciding which needs should be addressed first. The following is a list of critical areas to consider in making this important decision:

a. Priority parental concerns
b. Priority teacher concerns
c. Appropriate developmental sequences of tasks or behaviors that appear to be the most modifiable, as determined from baseline assessment data, including the child's strengths, weaknesses and learning style.

Goal statements will be used as a basis for specifying services that the child will receive. The number of goal statements needed is dependent upon the child's need and may range from one to several. Care should be taken not to have so many goals that accomplishment is impossible. In the case of a child with many needs, the team should concentrate initially on high priority goals, and later move to other areas.

STEP 6 Writing Short-term Instructional Goals

For each of the long-term goals outlined in Step 5, the team will develop several short-term objectives for the instructional program, that is, statements describing, in specific, objective and measurable terms, the intermediate steps which together will help the child accomplish the goal. Short term, in this case, refers to several periods of time within the long-term goal; the actual length of time chosen is up to the team. For example, team members may choose to set short-term objectives to correspond in time to each reporting period. Or they may choose to set weekly objectives or biannual objectives.

STEP 7 Services and Resources

Specific educational and/or support services and resources should be listed for each of the short-term instructional goals stated in the plan. These statements will be in general terms and will define the service areas in which implementation will occur, including, for instance, regular or special classroom instruction, transportation, social services, or therapy.

STEP 8 Persons(s) Responsible for Implementation

Within each service or goal area, the team should assign a specific person to be responsible for seeing that objectives in his or her service area are met. This person will in most cases be the implementer who will later develop the Individual Implementation Plan for that area.

STEP 9 Review Dates

According to P.L. 94-142 a review must be done at least on an annual basis.

STEP 10 Recommendations and Justification for Placement

The final task of the team in completing the IEP will be to decide upon a placement recommendation. This placement should reflect the program provided by the school system where the services are needed by the child, as already indicated on the form, where it will be delivered best. It also should reflect state criteria for eligibility and the capabilities of the school system. A short justification for the selection of a particular placement option should be written by the team.

STEP 11 Completion of Forms

Once the plan has been determined, all the information should be recorded on a form. Dates on which meetings were held should be noted and each person who participated should sign the form. Copies should be distributed to appropriate persons.

The knowledge about P.L. 94-142, eligibility criteria, screening procedures, and the steps involved in the development of the Individual Education Program is pertinent to all classroom teachers. The "least restrictive environment" clause [Section 612 (5) (B) of the Act] suggests that not all children will be educated in special classes. The clause does not mandate that all children be "mainstreamed" into regular classes; in fact, the term "mainstream" is not used anywhere in the legislation. Realistically, the regular classroom teacher will have responsibility for many children who, as a result of an IEP developed along the lines recommended previously, are defined as handicapped in P.L. 94-142. Teachers are reminded that government regulations involving the education of handicapped children change frequently. A careful review of regulations on a periodic basis should ensure that teachers are operating with the most recent information.

The most frequent structure the regular classroom teacher is likely to find is a "handicapped" child placed in the regular classroom where supportive help is provided by a resource teacher. This structure allows the resource teacher to intervene educationally with individuals who can remain in the regular classroom environment. The resource teacher suggests remedial strategies and procedures that the regular teacher incorporates in teaching the identified students. The resource teacher also can provide diagnostic or prescriptive information to the regular teacher. This demands that the regular teacher implement educational as well as remedial goals and objectives, with support and direction from the resource teacher. In this model, the resource teacher and the regular classroom teacher are jointly responsible for record keeping and general monitoring of the student's progress. This is true even where identified students receive direct instruction from the resource teacher within the classroom.

This model is designed only for children for whom the regular classroom, supplemented with resource support, is the "least restrictive educational environment." To ensure maximum benefits from such an arrangement, the regular classroom teacher should be given class size consideration when the classroom is assigned one or more handicapped students.

Once a handicapped student has been assigned to a regular classroom teacher, that teacher is responsible for implementing recommendations made in the IEP. The teacher should develop an Individual Implementation Plan which will include specific learning activities (methods, materials, and media) to monitor performance. These learning activities are best stated as behavioral objectives. McAshan (1970) and Kibler, Barker, and Miles (1974) stated that behavioral objectives must include four components:

1. **Who.** State the name of the child who is to perform the activity.
2. **Who will do what.** State the response expected from the child once he or she has learned the skill.
3. **Under what conditions.** Specify how much aid, what type of assistance, or the particular circumstances in which the child will perform the behavior.
4. **To what degree of success.** Specify how successfully the child must perform the task toreach the criterion established. There is a relationship between conditions and degree of success. If conditions are too difficult for the child, then a 90% or 100% level of performance cannot be expected.

Having to confront the requirements of P.L. 94-142 will likely prove stressful for the regular teacher. The challenges presented by the presence of a handicapped child in the regular classroom are likely to necessitate significant changes in the regular classroom environment. The following two examples demonstrate some of the concerns of teachers.

Case Illustration: Math Teacher

I am glad that I was invited to this meeting. I understand that the special education people are required to write an Individualized Education Plan on each special student to assure that each child is placed properly. That is exactly why I am here. I want to say, for the record, that Frank West is inappropriately placed in my math class.

When I spoke to Frank's special class teacher I made it clear that I was willing to experiment with Frank. I'd seen him around—a sort of surly, withdrawn kid—but he didn't look as retarded as the others in that class. His teacher said that Frank was ready to do more math work, and she told me that he could add, subtract, multiply, and divide and that he had a good understanding of multiple operations. Well, the kids in my class, which is business and shop math, can do about that much. Truly, some do much less, but I figured that Frank would fit right in.

Well, his teacher was right. Frank has all of the operations learned, but the kid can't reach much beyond a second grade level! What that means is he can't follow directions in his math book when I assign a page, and he can't read any of the word problems, banking directions, puzzles, or anything else. To top it all off, his penmanship is horrendous! He can barely do any cursive writing.

I sympathize with the special ed teacher's situation. The pendulum swings again and now we're turning handsprings trying to include the slower kids in the "mainstream." I think it's a fine idea for those who can do the work. But I have 18 other kids in Frank's math class and I can't spend all my time with him. He knows he's below average. Don't make it worse on Frank by keeping him in my room. Put him back where he belongs.

Case Illustration: Shop Teacher

I am the industrial arts teacher at Crescent Point High School. I've been here for 12 years and I teach basic manual training, metal and automotive shop. I have had Frank in my classes all three years.

Kids—they're all the same to me. Special ed kid, slow learner, tough guy, you name it. We set up the rules right away and none of them give me any major trouble or back talk.

Now, we all know that the kids who take the entire sequence of Industrial Arts courses are not your college bound, upper middle class kids. The kids I teach are the potential drop outs, blue collar and military material. I teach them to work quickly, efficiently, to get the job done on time and to obey orders—all the skills they'll need to hold down a job later.

West follows directions well enough but I always pair him with one of the better readers in the group. He can barely read, but he pays attention and get his jobs finished. I do some basic reading with the students who can't read. I go over new words that apply to each project and have the kids read, write, and spell each word before they begin a new project. West learns the words well enough, will get them on paper into sentences, if he feels like it, and remembers them pretty well. The boy can really do it if he tries.

But I can't hold up the whole class for the few who have special problems, and when West gets behind he's not the kind of kid you're dying to help. He gets mean. I caught him smoking in the auto body shop (the day he was trying to avoid a difficult assignment) and I explained that I'd have to turn him in. He cussed something fierce and slammed a hammer into a pile of metal scraps. When he's angry he mutters under his breath—he wouldn't dare talk to me that way aloud—and he is a very difficult kid to get along with.

I'm not suggesting that he be removed from shop. No, he needs the mechanical skills so he won't end up on welfare, leeching off the taxpayer's money. But there's a lot of water gone over the dam. He's not a kid with whom I particularly want to work, but he should graduate from high school. If he'd quit fooling around and change his attitude, he could make it.

Questions

The following questions are based on the two preceding cases:

1. What are your spontaneous responses to the concerns raised by the teachers?
2. In what ways do you agree with "regular" teachers in these situations? In what ways do you agree with efforts to "mainstream" the students involved?

3. Based on your responses to the two previous questions, what directions do you think the rest of the meetings will take?
4. What would you recommend for Frank West? Why?
5. Based on all available information, what outcomes do you foresee?

Suggestions for Teaching Handicapped Students

The regular classroom teacher can take steps to make the job of teaching handicapped students easier. These steps are as follows:

1. Seek training that is specifically concerned with teaching handicapped students.
2. Be aware of individual abilities of students and accept them as individuals who can and want to learn.
3. Reinforce positive self-concepts in handicapped children. Help "regular" students accept the handicapped and work toward meeting their needs.
4. Work closely with teachers of handicapped children, vocational education teachers, vocational rehabilitation counselors, school counselors, and other personnel to make sure that instruction is appropriate for the handicapped.
5. Refer special problems to special teachers when necessary but try to deal with minor problems on an individual basis in the classroom.
6. Work closely with the special teacher in grading the students on an individual basis rather than comparing them with "regular" students.
7. Adjust teaching techniques so that all students can succeed in learning.
8. Use a multi-media approach in teaching handicapped students. Employ a wide range of instructional methods in teaching.
9. Inform handicapped students that you expect them to learn, but be certain that your expectations of them are reasonable and realistic.
10. Demonstrate a genuine interest in all students, including the handicapped.
11. Become involved in joint planning efforts with other teachers who are serving the same students.
12. Learn about available community resources and how to use them to serve the handicapped.

TEACHING THE GIFTED OR TALENTED

We cannot discuss special populations in the schools without giving some attention to those students who are academically gifted or possess some exceptional talent. The school environment should be such that the maximum number of gifted or talented students will emerge. Such an environment should stimulate gifted or talented students to participate actively in a school, class, or small group to accomplish some undertaking or to engage in some creative endeavors.

The gifted or talented student, no less than the average child or the handicapped child, must have experiences through which he or she can discover potential and significant ways to use that potential. *Intelligence or talent has no functional importance until it is directed toward some significant purpose.* Equally important, the gifted or talented student must discover his or her limitations.

The academically gifted child frequently finds great satisfaction in reading. This ability may be useful in allowing the gifted student to tutor other students in the class. The gifted or talented student needs to participate in many varied activities in the school if their giftedness or talent is to be encouraged. The school has an obligation to provide for each student experiences that will further that student's power to create in fields where special aptitudes exist.

Sensitive teachers and counselors must work to maintain a proper balance between the intellectual and social interests and contributions of gifted or talented students. This balance is absolutely necessary if these youth are to gain and retain social leadership and social effectiveness.

REFERENCES

Baratz, S. S., & Baratz, J. C. (1971). Early childhood intervention. *Challenging the myths: The schools, the Blacks and the poor.* Cambridge, MA: Harvard Educational Review Reprint Series, Number 5, 111–132.

Beck, J. D. (1973). *The counselor and Black/white relations.* Boston: Houghton Mifflin.

Cheek, D. K. (1976). *Assertive Black...puzzled white.* San Luis Obispo, CA: Impact.

Clairborn, W. L. (1969). Expectancy effects in the classroom: A failure to replicate. *Journal of Educational Psychology, 60,* 377–383.

Clark, K. B. (1965). *Dark ghetto: Dilemmas of social power.* New York: Harper and Row.

Cook, L. A. (1951). *Intergroup relations in teacher education.* Washington, DC: American Council of Education.

Cooper, H. M., Baron, R. M., & Rowe, C. A. (1975). The importance of race and social class information in the formation of expectancies about academic performance. *Journal of Educational Psychology, 67,* 312–319.

Domnitz, M. (1965). *Educational techniques for combating prejudice and discrimination and for promoting better group understanding.* Hamburg, Germany: UNESCO Institute for Education.

Ginsburg, H. (1972). *The myth of the deprived child.* Englewood Cliffs, NJ: Prentice-Hall.

Grambs, J. D. (1968). *Intergroup education.* Englewood Cliffs, NJ: Prentice-Hall.

Harvey, D. G., & Slatin, G. T. (1975). The relationship between a child's SES and teacher expectations: A test of middle class bias hypothesis. *Social Forces, 54,* 140–159.

Kibler, R. J., Barker, L. L., & Miles, D. T. (1974). *Objectives for instruction and evaluation.* Boston: Allyn and Bacon.

Long, B., & Henderson, E. H. (1974). Certain determinants of academic expectancies among southern and nonsouthern teachers. *American Educational Research Journal, 11,* 137–147.

Love, B. J. (1977). Desegregation in your school: Behavior patterns that get in the way. *Phi Delta Kappan, 59,* 168–170.

Lovinger, S. L. (1979). *Learning disabilities and games.* Chicago: Nelson Hall.

McAshan, H. H. (1970). *Writing behavioral objectives: A new approach.* New York: Harper & Row.

O'Connell, E. J., Dusek, J. B., & Wheeler, R. J. (1974). A follow-up study of teacher expectancy efforts. *Journal of Educational Psychology, 66,* 325–328.

Palmer, P. (1977). *Liking myself.* San Luis Obispo, CA: Impact Publishers.

Pedersen, E., Faucher, T., & Eaton, W. (1978). A new perspective on the effects of first grade teachers on children's subsequent adult status. *Harvard Educational Review, 48*, 1–31.

Procedures Governing Programs and Services for Children With Special Needs (1991). Raleigh, NC: Department of Public Instruction.

Public Law 94–142, *Education for All Handicapped Children Act,* November 29, 1975.

Rist, R. (1971). Student social class and teacher expectations. *Challenging the myths: The schools, the Blacks and the poor.* Cambridge, MA: Harvard Educational Review Reprint Series, Number 5, 70–109.

Rokeach, M. (1968). *Beliefs, attitudes and values: A theory of organization and change.* San Francisco: Jossey-Bass.

Rosenthal, R, & Jacobsen, L. (1968). *Pygmalion in the class room: Teacher expectation and pupils' intellectual development.* New York: Holt, Rinehart & Winston.

Rubovits, P. C., & Maehr, M. L. (1973). Pygmalion Black and white. *Journal of Personality and Social Psychology, 25*, 210–218.

Rules governing programs and services for children with special needs. (1978). Raleigh, NC: Division for Exceptional Children, State Department of Public Instruction.

Shaftel, F., & Shaftel, G. (1967). *Role playing for social values: Decision making in the social studies.* Englewood Cliffs, NJ: Prentice-Hall.

Silberman, C. E. (1964). *Crisis in Black and white.* New York: Random House.

Silberman, C. E. (1970). *Crisis in the classroom: The remaking of American education.* New York: Random House.

Washington, V., & Lee, C. C. (1981). Teaching and counseling the Black child: A systemic analysis for the 1980's. *Journal of Nonwhite Concerns, 9*, 60–67.

Weatherly, R., & Lipsky, M. (1977). Street-level bureaucrats and institutional innovation: Implementing special education reform. *Harvard Educational Review, 47*, 171–197.

UNIT IV
ENCOUNTERING
PROBLEMS

Chapter 8

TEACHING STUDENTS WITH SPECIAL PROBLEMS

This chapter developed in response to the need for teachers to understand several specific problems likely to be confronted in the line of duty. The needs of all students must be recognized and met if students are to develop their fullest potential. For the most part, the teacher must recognize special problem areas and initially deal directly with the student and the problem area.

Some students who have problems may be identified easily. The delinquent student may be easily recognized, especially if the delinquent behavior occurs in the classroom. But for many other students in need of special help, the need is not so apparent. Some aspects of drug or alcohol abuse, for example, are not readily identified. Less obvious are frustrations with the loss of a parent through divorce or death, which often go unnoticed. A seriously withdrawn child may appear to be merely shy or quiet. All students experiencing one of these problems must be identified before they can be helped—whether that help is to be provided by the classroom teacher or by a person to whom the classroom teacher has made a referral.

This chapter discusses four of the special problem areas teachers are likely to face—drug and alcohol abuse, students from single-parent families, delinquent students, and death and dying.

DRUG AND ALCOHOL ABUSE

The percentage of high school students who use or have used alcohol has remained fairly stable over a six-year period, but the use of other drugs has dropped off, according to a nationwide survey of more than 16,000 students conducted by the University of Michigan Institute of Social Research.

The study, "Student Drug Use in America: 1975–1980," reported that 72% of the students were using alcohol in 1980, compared with 68% in 1975. A total of 9.1% of the 1980 class reported daily marijuana use, compared with 10.7% in 1978. Among the 1980 respondents, 65% reported having tried an illicit drug. For marijuana, alcohol, and cigarettes, most initial experiences took place before tenth grade (NIAAA Information and Feature Service, p. 1). Newcomb and Bentler (1989) reported that experimental use of tobacco products has the widest prevalence during preadolescence and 99% of seniors have had some experience with alcohol. The purpose in this section is not to review the causes of alcohol or drug abuse, or to provide in-depth information regarding types or classification of drugs. Rather, we approach the area of alcohol or drug abuse as an area in which teachers might do some teaching (drug education).

Drug education is a controversial topic in schools. Many educators argue that the less said about the subject the better. This group of educators argue that drug education programs educate toward use of drugs rather than away from use. Many drug education programs have involved inexperienced and unknowledgeable but well meaning teachers telling students a number of inaccurate or slanted facts about drug use. Researchers have found that students taught extensive factual information about drugs later used more drugs than students who were not taught facts (Larimer, Tucker, & Brown, 1970). These presentations were designed to convince students that drugs are bad.

Newcomb and Bentler (1989) concluded that factors associated with initial involvement with drugs include peer influences (modeling use, provision of substances, and encouraging use); social structural variables such as socioeconomic status (heavier use among devalued populations); family role and socialization variables (greater use in disturbed families, with adult drug-use models, and with lack of religious commitment); psychological variables, such as self-esteem (low self-esteem leading to greater drug use); behavioral variables, such as deviant behaviors or lack of law abidance; emotional variables, such as need for excitement; and psychopathological variables, such as stressful life events, depression, and anxiety (p. 245).

Students need to learn that drugs in themselves are neither good nor bad, but what people do with them does make them good or bad. Drug education programs should focus on the behavioral realities associated with drug use and not on the drugs themselves. Many a well-meaning teacher has spent too much time talking about slang terms used for drugs and not enough time with the part these drugs are playing in the lives of real people. Drug education programs must provide students with all the information and understanding they need to make realistic decisions about their involvement with drugs. Students will not make decisions on drug information alone. Students will take drug facts and incorporate these facts into their own value systems. Therefore we advocate that drug education programs be geared toward value orientation and decision making.

Not only do a variety of value orientations exist in our society, but these orientations also are different across generations. Youngsters are quick to point out laws that give immediate access to alcohol at 18 or 21 years of age. Young people also use the alcohol abuse statistics to point out inconsistencies regarding alcohol and marijuana use. These details should not become the major focus of drug education programs, although they are likely to when drug facts become the primary focus of programs.

According to Slimmon (1975) the goal of values education is to help students become aware of what they cherish and to refine their tendencies for action to the point where they become dependable references for responsible decision making. The advantage of using values education as a means of teaching about drugs is that it forces teachers and students to think about the process taking place in the classroom. In other words, the approach takes the information about drugs, much of it confused or incorrect, examines it, organizes it, and eventually makes some sense out of it. This process may involve correcting some of the ideas about drugs that students reveal. This becomes the appropriate time to teach drug "facts."

One study by Swanson (1974) assessed junior high school student evaluations of a drug education program taught by values-oriented and traditionally oriented teachers. The values-oriented teachers used values clarification activities and the traditionally oriented teachers used a lecture-discussion format. Students rated the values-oriented teachers as more informed, more relevant, and more sincere than the traditionally oriented teachers.

In a study designed to measure the effectiveness of a drug prevention education program in grades two through six, Kearney and Hines (1980) reported that children significantly increased their feelings of self-worth, their decision-making abilities, and their factual knowledge about drugs, and improved their attitudes toward use and misuse of drugs. Teachers in the experimental group used self-esteem experiences, values and decision-making activities, and drug information in their teaching. The success of this Appleton, Wisconsin project led it to be disseminated for replication nationwide via the National Diffusion Network.

We should hasten to add that values education or values clarification are not without their critics. Chng (1980) summarized four major criticisms of the approach. First, the contention is that values clarification focuses on the process of valuing and is free of moral communications. Chng argued that before one can discuss process, one must have relevant information. A second criticism centers around "ethical relativism," or the belief that all values are equally valid and morally defensible. Chng argued that much more is involved in the question of whether one should or should not use illicit drugs. Third, a criticism is leveled at the Coronado Program, which claimed to be value free, yet the program had as one objective the education of students against drug misuse. Finally, a criticism is leveled that suggests that youngsters have not developed a substantial value system and are likely to rely too heavily on peer pressure.

Brooks (1971) summarized the problems with many drug education programs and offered a suggestion for improving them. He said:

> Past experiences in the area of drug education have produced mostly negative results. The general kind of drug education that's been provided our schools and with which we've trained our teachers has been inclined to turn kids on to drugs instead of turn them off. So we're seeing the necessity of some radical changes in the field of teaching teachers to teach about drugs. (p. 127)

Two additional activities related to drug and alcohol abuse are presented to assist teachers in working with students. The first activity involves physical signs teachers might use to determine possible student involvement with drugs or alcohol. This list was provided by Moses and Burger (1975):

1. A sudden and continuing drop in school grades
2. Class cutting and truancy without apparent reason or shame
3. A marked mood change unrelated to normal adolescent behavior
4. Constant depression, extreme belligerence towards [teachers]
5. A change in friends to those his [or her] parents disapprove of
6. A sudden refusal to bring new friends home
7. A drifting away of older friends and neighbors. (p. 212)

The second activity is to compare characteristics of persons who use drugs to those who do not. In a study of suburban Westchester County, New York, Tec (1972) revealed the following:

1. The less satisfaction adolescents derive from various aspects of their high school status the more likely they are to use marijuana.
2. The greater the number of teachers with whom students are pleased, the

less likely they are to use marijuana with regularity, and the more likely they are to be totally disinterested in ever using it. Similarly, the greater the number of teachers that students feel are pleased with them, the less likely they are to be regular marijuana users, and the more likely they are to be total abstainers.

3. Students who aspire to become the "best" athletes constituted the lowest proportion of marijuana users.

4. Students who aspired to become professionals (doctors, scientists, lawyers, etc.) were less likely to use marijuana than those who had no plans at all. Students who aspired to become artists comprised the highest proportion of marijuana users. Students who aspired to be laborers or tradespeople were not as prone to use marijuana as most other groups.

So what should teachers do? All teachers, regardless of the discipline taught, should incorporate some drug education into the curriculum. The school counselor often can serve as a consultant in planning this instruction. Most school systems have materials that can be used in planning for such instruction. Teachers can develop a special unit that focuses on drug and alcohol, to be used during the school year. Teachers may begin to examine their own feelings and emotions as well as their roles and relationships with students. Teachers must view drug education as an ongoing process, to be used throughout the year. If the values clarification approach is used, it offers an opportunity for teachers to talk about drug problems without talking about drugs.

And what is a teacher to do when a student is suspected of using and/or abusing drugs and alcohol? First, the teacher reviews the communication techniques discussed in Chapter 4. These techniques should prove quite useful as the teacher attempts to establish a relationship with the student so as to help the student feel at liberty to discuss any problems. The goal of the teacher in these discussions should be to get the student to examine his or her value system, to sort out and analyze reasons for decisions, and eventually to come to grips with why they do the things they do. This should be done in a nonjudgmental atmosphere in which the student is able to examine the probable consequences of decisions made.

Second, when teachers feel they are not capable of handling a situation, it is appropriate to consult with other professionals or refer the student to the school counselor. Including others in the process of identification and counseling not only helps the student, but also helps the teacher learn new behaviors and methods for dealing with future problems.

The best way to deal with any problem is to prevent it from happening. The most effective manner for handling drug use among children and teenagers is to educate youngsters and prevent the use and abuse of drugs before they occur. Peer programs appear to have the strongest effect on several outcomes for the average teenager. The enhancement of social skills and assertiveness is predicted to reduce drug use or prevent the initiation of drug use for the typical teenager.

STUDENTS FROM SINGLE-PARENT FAMILIES

Perhaps the most traumatic event in a student's life is the loss of a parent. Children depend on their parents for love and security, and a bonding system develops early in life. When a parent leaves this relationship, the loss is often shattering. Frequently this loss occurs without the child having been prepared. The loss for younger children is hard to comprehend and makes little or no sense; often the loss causes disruption, agony, insecurity, guilt, isolation, and feelings of being different, all of which are an expected part of the emotional picture.

The divorce rate in the United States has doubled since 1965. Almost half of the nation's juvenile population has been touched by divorce; some nine million children now live in single-parent families. The "typical" American family no longer exists. In the United States, about 15% of all families at any given time are single-parent units. Seventy-five percent of all divorces occur in households with children less than 18 years old. In 1979, the estimate was that one out of six school children lived with only one parent (Hammond, 1979). By 1989, that estimate had risen to one out of three. Thirty percent of these children live in stepfamilies. The other 70% live with their mothers or fathers alone (Clarke-Stewart, 1989). McLanahan (1986) reported that divorce reduces the child's school achievement, chances of high school graduation, and completed years of schooling. There are substantial long-term effects on the child's later economic well-being from experiencing a divorce or separation.

As these statistics suggest, a growing number of children will come to school having experienced the loss of a parent from the home. Many of these children will adjust to the loss with relative ease. They will not require special attention from school officials. Others will require teachers and the school in general to alter typical methods for relating with students.

Teachers are often the last to know that a student's parents are divorcing. Some parents worry about prejudicing their child's teacher against the child by labeling them a "child of divorce." More likely is the failure of many parents to understand that a major crisis in the life of a child does appear to show repercussions in behavior and performance in school. Nor do parents seem to realize that in order to relate constructively to alarming changes in the child's behavior, the teacher needs to know about underlying problems.

Many teachers can be immediately sensitive to a child's distress and respond accordingly. Some teachers may expect children to separate their personal family difficulty from academic performance and continue to function academically as if nothing has happened. Some students will be able to do this sorting, but they are likely to be exceptions to typical behavior.

Kelly and Wallerstein (1976a, 1976b, 1977) have studied effects of parental divorce on children. They have not found defined stages of response. They have concluded that the effects are shared, age-related responses which are tied to the child's developmental stage, environment, and relationship to both parents. Among the responses that may be expected are guilt, denial, and fantasy to cope with the guilt; temper tantrums; restlessness; irritability; moodiness; a sense of vulnerability; and manipulative and exploitative tendencies. Clarke-Stewart (1989) reported that boys in families in which the parents subsequently divorced were more impulsive and aggressive than boys in nondivorcing families. They exhibited the following symptoms: headaches, fatigue, weight loss, depression, anxiety, and mood swings.

According to Kelly and Wallerstein (1977) some children appear to be helped through their crisis by a close relationship with and friendly reliance on a special teacher. Younger children may climb into the laps of teachers to receive nurturance and solace. Older youngsters sometimes stay close to teachers to receive assurance that they are doing their school work satisfactorily. Preadolescent and adolescent youngsters frequently seek to discuss their situation with someone outside the family. The teacher is frequently the person to whom these youngsters turn for an empathic ear.

Teachers need and want to know what can and cannot be done to help the student through this disrupting period. What the student seeks and needs more than anything else is closeness, love, and understanding. One thing the teacher can do is refer the child to the school counselor during periods of stress. In some instances, the school counselor will not be available to step in and offer comfort during the rough periods in the child's life. Therefore, the teacher may be expected to provide support to the child. Teachers can accept responsibility for developing some basic "counseling" skills that can assist in this process. Moreover, schools can increase the opportunities for teachers to learn such techniques through in-service workshops.

Four ways are suggested in which the classroom teacher can respond to these changes and help the student cope with the turmoil and emotional upheaval he or she is experiencing. The first step is teacher awareness. The classroom teacher who knows about and is sensitive to stress in children is a rich resource for children and their parents. It is important for a teacher who observes some sudden change in behavior or other symptoms suggestive of stress to discuss the observations with the child and/or parents before the child's learning is seriously compromised.

Second, teachers can become aware of and act on knowledge about the child's situation. The empathic teacher can recognize the child's distress and provide an environment that makes the most of the child's efforts to cope. The teacher's action may be to acknowledge the child's temporary difficulty in meeting classroom responsibilities; it may be to indicate support by saying something like, "I know this is a hard time for you."

Third, teachers can be resources in the development and incorporation of curriculum and attitudinal changes in the classroom. There may be no solace in numbers, but classroom teaching that acknowledges the many variations in family life can help children feel more secure within their own family structure, even if it appears different to them.

Fourth, teachers need to know their own personal feelings about divorce and children of divorce. Santrock and Tracy (1978) reported a study of teacher education students who viewed a film about a boy at home, at school, and on the playground. One group was told that the boy was from a single-parent home and the other group was told that the boy was from an intact (two-parent) home. The teacher education students were asked to rate the boy on 10 personality traits. Those who were told that the boy was from a single-parent home rated him significantly lower in happiness, ability to get along with others, emotional adjustment, and morality. They rated him significantly higher in introversion, anxiety, and deviance. There was no significant difference in the ratings the two groups gave on need for achievement, aggressiveness, and sex-role adjustment. Participants also were asked to predict the boy's school behavior. Those who were told he was from a single-parent home predicted (at a significant level) that he would have difficulty coping with stressful situations at school, and rated him lower in popularity with classmates, likelihood to assume a leadership position, and likelihood to work well unsupervised.

This study suggests the need for teachers to examine their personal attitudes in order to avoid the "self-fulfilling prophesy" that children of divorce are different from what they really are. Children will respond to the expectations of teachers, and teachers' expectations about children of divorce need to be objective and realistic.

Clay (1980) reported that teachers and schools need to become more accessible to both parents of the children of divorce. She reported that single parents are concerned because schools tend to relate to children as though they have two parents in the home. School activities are often held at inaccessible times for parents, and single parents are often unable to provide transportation so that their children can participate in extracurricular activities. Clay also reported that single parents often find that teachers blame all behavior problems on the home situation without exploring other causes.

Ricci (1979) found that cards for parents' addresses and phone numbers have space for only one address and phone number. Report cards and notices are often sent to only one parent. She reported that the 1974 Buckley amendment denies access to the school records to the parent without custody. Both divorced parents, however, can communicate to the school, in writing, that they both are interested in the child's welfare and progress.

Damon (1979) provided a list of ten tips for teachers in dealing with children who are in crisis situations because of the loss of a parent through divorce:

1. Know your own feelings about separation and divorce.
2. Be alert to personality and behavior changes.
3. Seek support and information from colleagues and parents. Establish a rapport with parents through conferences, class newsletters, notes home, positive comments to students, telephone conversations, etc.
4. Provide time to talk with students about separation and divorce.
5. Find out custody and visitation responsibilities and be prepared to accept some assignments that may be late because of a visitation arrangement that may have hindered the child from completing the assignment on time.
6. Be alert to whether the child is sleeping and eating properly.
7. Provide time for students to talk about their feelings and to describe what is happening when and if they want to, without the teacher commenting in a helpful, "teacherly," or judgmental manner. Being a listener who is trying to understand without doing more than that can be a tremendous support, provided it is done sincerely and as regularly as is realistic.
8. Provide students with many positive comments and opportunities to excel and be in charge.
9. Share aspects of your own life and family background.
10. Do not presume anything. In many instances a separation or divorce may improve the home life of the child. (p. 72)

Clarke-Stewart (1989) added to this list by suggesting that teachers should

1. Try to be well-informed about what to expect from children under these circumstances
2. Recognize that these children need support and sympathy, not judgmental evaluations and criticism
3. Give children whose parents have just split up a break for some period of adjustment and transition
4. Raise the consciousness of all students about what divorce means and what children whose parents are divorcing might be experiencing

As divorce statistics continue to rise and as more and more families become part of these statistics, the classroom teacher is faced with the problem of helping children from these families cope with the realities of their world. Teachers can expect some of these children to bring frustrations into the classroom that they cannot handle alone. The emotional response to the loss of a parent emerges in the classroom. *Teacher awareness and willingness to provide a supportive setting to these youngsters will make schools more responsive to changes caused by divorce.* By doing so, teachers and schools can continue to meet their responsibility of helping all children learn to the level of their potential.

DEATH AND DYING

Death and dying are subjects that are often evaded in our society. They are, however, as much a part of human growth and development as being born. It may seem strange to consider death as a part of the life cycle, but it is, because it brings partial closure to a life story.

Children cannot avoid the death experience. Most children lose a pet to death. Robinson (1978) reported that one in every 20 children will lose a parent during childhood. Hymovitz (1979) estimated that children will see 18,000 deaths on television by the time they are 14 years old. Many of these media deaths are presented in a distorted manner in which the "bad guy" gets killed. Children frequently see death in this sense as punishment.

Teachers need to examine their own attitudes toward death, understand the grief process, and learn some typical reactions of children to death. The interest in death and death education emerged as a major topic of discussion with the work of Elizabeth Kübler-Ross (1969). Many teachers may have developed reactions to death that will hinder their work with a child who has experienced the death of a loved one. Sylvia Plath (1972) described her experience of crying at her father's grave years after his death:

> I remembered that I had never cried for my father's death. My mother hadn't cried either. She had just smiled and said what a merciful thing it was for him that he had died, because if he had lived, he would have been crippled and an invalid for life, and he couldn't have stood that, he would rather have died than had that happen. (p. 137)

The gestaltists would call Sylvia Plath's experience one of unfinished business. Teachers should explore their own personal lives to determine if areas of unfinished business exist surrounding the area of death. It seems safe to say that a teacher who brings unfinished business to discussions about death will have difficulty relating to students on the subject. Teachers should seek in-service training, read books, and talk with other persons about the topic of death. Teachers can explore their own attitudes by anticipating reactions from students and imagining how they would handle them. Role playing these situations should prove to be quite useful in this exploratory process.

These personal attitudes are influenced by those of our society. What are the attitudes and factors that influence how we see death? First, many have tried to accept and transcend death through a religious belief in some form of after-death existence, which minimizes the importance of physical death. Secondly, many believe in a kind of social mortality, which is the belief that people live on through what they create—their work or their children. If these beliefs are held, they help us assuage the threat of death.

Another factor that has lead to the difficulty of dealing with death is urbanization. People living in cities are further removed from the experience of the cycle of life and death than are people who live in agrarian societies. We live and work in controlled environments which make us feel almost independent from natural forces. The accent in our urban societies is on fast-paced, efficient activity, and this is seen as vital to our survival. Many see death from a distance; thus, we have little experience death, which leads to difficulty in coping with it.

Advances in medical science are another factor that influences us. The use of antibiotics and vaccines, heart-lung machines, artificial kidneys, refined surgical procedures, respirators, and so forth to prolong life and delay extensive suffering and early death gives a presumed sense of mastery over death. The need for thoughts concerning the meaning of life and death therefore seem less important.

Secularization is another factor that leads to difficulty in dealing with death. A value system not based on religion or metaphysics experiences more difficulty because death becomes almost impossible to comprehend. The complete extinction of one's self with no redeeming features and no moral significance is an extremely frightening possibility.

In our society, these factors are primarily responsible for the general attitude our society has toward death: denial. Emphasis is placed on living, on being young, and on being vigorous.

Teachers' attitudes related to death can play an important role in the quality of instruction on the subject. These attitudes may have developed because of personal fears, lack of knowledge, or lack of experience. Before the teacher can face death education seriously, these attitudes must first be explored and, where appropriate, altered so that better teaching can take place.

Second, the teacher must obtain information and understanding of the grief process. Dying individuals, families of dying individuals, and families of the dead all go through similar stages in reaction to death. Kübler-Ross (1969) identified five stages in her book *On Death and Dying.* They can be summarized as follows:

Denial and Isolation. "No, not me." This is the typical reaction of the dying person or the person who faces the death of a loved one. It helps cushion the impact of awareness that death is inevitable.

Rage and Anger. "Why me?" There is resentment that others will remain healthy and alive. God is frequently the special target for this anger because he is regarded as imposing the death sentence arbitrarily. Kübler-Ross suggested to those who are shocked at this expression of anger that "God can take the anger."

Bargaining. "Yes, me, but just let me live until . . ." The fact of death is accepted but an offer is made to bargain for more time. Often this bargain is made with God, even though the person may not have been religious. The person may promise good behavior in exchange for another year of life.

Depression. "Yes, me." First the person is sorry for all the wrongful deeds committed. Later a state of grief is entered which is in preparation for death. The person may not want to see anyone and may be quite withdrawn. The message is that unfinished business is being finished and the person will be able to "let go peacefully." This stage is painful for mourners, but it is worse for the dying person who now realizes that everything will be lost.

Acceptance. "My time is very close now and it is all right." When the earlier stages have been satisfactorily expressed, the individual is accepting of death. This stage is neither happy nor unhappy. "It is devoid of feeling but it is not resignation, it is really victory."

Not all people experience these stages in sequence. Sometimes people move beyond and then regress to an earlier stage. The stages may serve as a framework for teachers to understand the grieving process.

A third area of concern of the classroom teacher should be to gain an understanding of the emotional responses of children to death. There appears to be a developmentally related understanding of death (see discussion of Piaget's stages in Chapter 2). Gordon and Klass (1979) have discussed the understanding level of children at various ages. Children from 3 to 5 years old appear to be ignorant of the meaning of the word "dead." They may be interested in the word although their concept is probably limited or erroneous. Children between the ages of 5 and 9 years begin to understand the meaning of the word "dead" and can associate the word with "the end." Younger children in this age group are often preoccupied with the coffin, the grave, and the service. By age 8, a questioning interest in what happens after death is developing. Children 9 to 10 years old appear ready for a full explanation of death. They understand the concept but define it in reference to biological events. From about 11 years on, children seem to respond to death much as adults do. In other words, they are more likely to experience the five stages of death referred to earlier. As they get older (upper teens), they are able to discuss death according to social value and meaning (war, abortion, murder, suicide).

While the topic of death may produce anxiety among school personnel, the topic of suicide may be an even greater one for educators to discuss. We believe that suicide should be discussed just as any other means of death. We would like to use this opportunity to provide readers with a list of signs that may be useful in determining when students are at risk of suicide. While no list will provide all warning signs, this list does offer useful indicators that should be used as a basis for class discussion, so students may become alert to these signs, as well as for discussions with students who exhibit these signs. These characteristics were developed from an adolescent suicide sample in Los Angeles County and were reported by Bensley and Bertsch (1987):

- In almost every instance, the adolescents had multiple, unexpected separations from their parents during the first three years of their lives.

- All felt that there was no real communication or there were no emotional ties in their families.
- Only 10% felt that they could talk to their parents when they were troubled.
- All thought about suicide, off and on, for the five years preceding their attempts.
- More than 60% had attempted previously.
- In 25% of the families involved, one of the parents had attempted suicide.
- A relative or a close friend of 45% of the suicidal young people had attempted suicide.
- In 88% of the families, one or both natural parents were absent (i.e., divorced, separated, or death).
- More than 75% of the parents had been married more than once.
- Many of the adolescents felt that they had to contend with an unwanted stepparent—a feeling that was often mutual.
- Nearly 65% of the youngsters were in families in which someone had suffered a serious illness, usually in the two-year period prior to the attempted suicide. That illness had put the teenager into somewhat of a maternal role.
- About 85% of the adolescents had physical complaints (e.g., headaches, stomach aches, and a general malaise) (p. 19).

In his book *Helping Children Cope with Grief,* Alan Wolfelt (1983) offered caregiver behaviors that are appropriate for teachers. He identified 13 dimensions "typical of what frequently is exhibited by children experiencing grief" (p. 13). The 13 dimensions are shock/denial/disbelief/numbness; lack of feelings; physiological changes; regression; "big man" or "big woman" syndrome; disorganization and panic; explosive emotions; acting out behavior; fear; guilt and self blame; relief; loss/emptiness/sadness; and reconciliation. For each dimension, Wolfelt discussed and illustrated what occurs with children who experience grief as a result of loss of a dear one. Wolfelt then provided caregiving behaviors that could be used by teachers. Two of the most fundamental behaviors are creating an atmosphere for children's questions and creating a caring relationship.

With this information the teacher may still have questions about how to proceed with death education. Keith and Ellis (1978) stated that teachers may encounter many of the same objections to death education as are raised against sex education. Hymovitz (1979) suggested that death education should be consistent with the age, maturity, readiness, and receptivity of learners. Freeman (1978) recommended that input be requested from parents, the principal, and the curriculum consultant before death education is begun. In fact, she stated that permission to participate is not a bad idea. She identified several questions the teacher must confront before attempting death education: Should death education be integrated into other studies? Will exercises be frightening to children? What are the religious and sociological implications of teaching about death?

What should be the goals of death education? Hymovitz (1979) identified the following:

1. To teach that death and dying are part of life and living.
2. To help students to manage realistically with the idea of their own death and the deaths of significant others.
3. To help implement necessary institutional and attitudinal changes through death education.
4. To appreciate the impact of death upon the human creative impulses in music, art, religion, literature, and philosophy.
5. To broaden the conceptualization and interpretation of the meaning of life's end in order to live more fully in the time given to us.
6. To understand our common destiny as part of the effort to cherish, to dignify, and to respect, individually and collectively, our precious and unique cultural, religious, historical, and artistic contributions. (p. 104)

Bensley and Bertsch (1987) suggested the following behaviors when a school experiences death among its students or staff:

1. Confirm the incident with immediate family, police, and/or hospital personnel.
2. Call a meeting of all faculty and staff to enable them to express their feelings and receive accurate information.
3. Call on resource personnel (natural helpers) and request that they help.
4. Set up a number of rooms in the building as "discussion" rooms. Make it clear that students may attend a discussion if they wish and can return again throughout the day.
5. If the administration decides not to continue a normal class schedule, provide options for those students who do not wish to be involved in the activities related to the incident (p. 18).

Just as taboos on many other topics of discussion are in the process of dissipation, so must the taboo of death education in the schools dissipate. The authors believe that teachers have a moral obligation to include death education in the curriculum. Teachers must relate to all responses of children, including their responses to death. *Teachers must help youngsters learn to deal comfortably and productively with death at the same level at which they relate to other areas of their lives.*

JUVENILE DELINQUENCY

It is estimated that the population of persons between the ages of 10 and 17 numbered 29.4 million in 1978. The number of delinquency cases that reached the courts in 1978 was 1.3 million (U.S. Bureau of the Census, 1980). In the latter 1970s and continuing into the 1980s, problems of the juvenile offender received considerable interest through prevention programs as well as through state legislation that attempted to reduce the numbers of juvenile offenders in the community. All resources in communities are being evaluated as means of helping reduce levels and rates of delinquent crimes. The school is being viewed as a primary resource in this effort.

Lewis, Battistich, and Schaps (1990) presented a four-part etiological model of adolescent problem behavior, intended as a framework for bringing research and theory in child development into the design and evaluation of prevention programs:

1. Poor socialization practices in the family lead to low attachment to parents, resistance to authority, and early behavioral and emotional problems (e.g., aggression, withdrawal, anxiety, depression), as well as developmental deficits (e.g., poor attention span, poor impulse control).
2. Problems resulting from poor socialization in the family lead to early emotional and conduct problems in school. These problems in social relationships tend to persist and to be aggravated by the responses of teachers and peers, leading to social isolation or rejection, anxiety, insecurity, and continued problems with authority.
3. By mid to late elementary school, persistent problems in social adaptation have led to decreased learning. Resulting academic problems lead to increased anxiety, insecurity, depression, and social isolation and rejection from more competent peers, and the beginning of alienation from school.
4. School problems lead to disillusionment with schooling, withdrawal of effort, and rebelliousness, which contribute to further academic failure. Lack of success at conventional pursuits leads to increased alienation from academically and socially competent peers and affiliation with similarly alienated peers. Associa-

tion with delinquents leads to increased delinquency, drug use, resistance to authority, alienation from conventional society, and rejection of social norms and values, as well as continuing academic problems and a high probability of early school exit. (pp. 38-40)

Dunham and Alpert (1987) reminded us that if a student is misbehaving in school, does not like school, has friends who are dropping out and getting into trouble, and has a marginal or weak relationship with his parents, there is a very high risk of dropping out. The greater the degree of any of these factors, the greater the degree of risk.

Using available data it is possible to conclude that an organized social environment may be a primary factor influencing both delinquent and law-abiding behavior, and that to reduce the delinquent behavior, the social environment needs to be altered. Further, it appears that school is the single most influential social environment with respect to delinquent behavior. This recognition leads to a needed change in the school environment to affect the curriculum. This change is aimed at providing more organized educational experiences designed to tackle the problem. It necessitates that the school work with other community agencies that also have interests in youth and the elimination of delinquency.

In recent years the juvenile justice system has received considerable attention as it suggested reforms and programs aimed at prevention. Attention has focused on the group of children often classified as "undisciplined." They are children who are truant from school, who have run away from home, or whose parents find them too difficult to manage. They have not yet committed an act for which, if they were an adult, they could be prosecuted. The estimate is that children in this category now occupy more than 40% of the caseload of juvenile courts. Several states (including New York and North Carolina) have enacted legislation designed to divert these "undisciplined" youth from the system designed for those who have committed a crime. Efforts are dependent upon the community to develop alternative programs for these children in community-based residential treatment facilities. The development of community-based facilities means that the public schools must provide programs for many students who would have previously been sent to "training schools."

Several attempts have been made in an effort to keep delinquent youth in school. According to Schaum (1978), an In-School Alternative Learning Program offers good possibilities. With the aid of school supervision and with a highly structured center designed to encourage discipline, learning, individual counseling, and group counseling techniques, the program shows promise for academic achievement for the delinquent. Four ingredients are necessary for success of this program:

1. The student must be confronted with a positive program of academic achievement.
2. Nothing less than complete adherence to the rules should be accepted.
3. The school psychologist or counselor must be involved because the student needs much help in order to reject irresponsible behavior patterns.
4. There must be an opportunity for the student to participate in group counseling with a variety of peer personalities under the guidance of a counselor, so that some reconstruction can begin. (p. 280)

This program takes place mainly in the classroom. The school counselor arranges the student's schedule so that the student has regular class assignments that are coordinated with work in the In-School Alternative Learning Center. During the course of the program, participating students were restricted in their interactions with other students and were monitored daily on their progress. The restrictions seemed to produce motivation to achieve and return to the regular school routine.

Toth (1979) described a Life Skills Course designed to facilitate the assimilation of youthful offenders in the regular schools. Students selected to participate in the program were on probation, had poor socialization skills, especially with authority figures, and were considered to be "high-risk" with regard to school drop-out and/or further involvement with the law. The course was designed for ninth graders and focused on communication, problem solving, values, law, preemployment training, sexuality, and drugs. Role playing situations based on the students own experiences served as the vehicle through which content was presented.

The program is expensive because one professional works with a small number of students. Yet the success of the program, where students have remained in school during their first year of high school, cannot be measured in monetary value.

These are but two of the many examples of programs designed to help delinquents remain in school. Because of such programs and the results obtained, the future may be much better for the young delinquent, and schools may have a major role in the change. These young people need assistance and guidance from teachers and counselors who are able to see their needs and help them learn to function in society.

The most ambitious efforts in the school cannot prevent delinquency. The school personnel must work cooperatively with other community agency personnel in developing programs for this segment of the school population. Pink (1984) provided some direction toward rethinking prevention strategies for controlling juvenile delinquency:

1. The schooling experience is the critical factor in the development of adolescent identity and careers.
2. Intervention in schools offers the best opportunity to develop effective prevention.
3. Recent research on school improvement and effectiveness suggests both content and process for such intervention.
4. Articulating the relationship between schooling and early occupational careers must be made more explicit.
5. The juvenile justice system must work in concert with school districts and other community service agencies to orchestrate change in school, social, and occupational arenas to maximize youths' successful experiences.

Lewis, Battistich, and Schaps (1990) presented a list of characteristics of an effective school-based program:

1. Programs should be clearly derived from theoretical models that recognize the multiple determinants of drug use, unprotected sexual activity, and related problems.
2. School-based prevention programs should be directed at influencing the general social milieu of the school.
3. Programs that promote positive influences on social development may be more effective than programs that attempt to counteract negative influences.
4. Prevention programs should be comprehensive and long-lasting.
5. School-based prevention programs should be integral to the school curriculum.
6. Prevention programs should begin prior to the emergence of problem behavior.
7. Prevention programs must carefully monitor the implementation process to ensure that the programs are delivered as intended. (pp. 41-43)

The teacher who works with a delinquent student should first recognize that this type of student is unique from those who are not potential delinquents. These youngsters often lack an adequate self-concept, have poor judgment, and cannot maintain an appropriate balance between their own needs and the needs of others. The teacher who seeks to help each student achieve and retain confidence and self-respect is setting a basic foundation necessary for preventing delinquency and for helping those who have already become a part of the delinquent subculture. It is a tremendous professional challenge.

To provide assistance in helping children and their parents gain a better self-concept, Frey and Carlock (1991) stressed that developing a healthy self-concept is a process and that the self-concept changes as one develops, interacts with the environment, and assimilates what one has learned and experienced. In their book *Enhancing Self Esteem,* they suggested activities that teachers could use. Building a positive rather than a negative self-concept requires time, interaction with people who care. Teachers can have a significant role in the process.

REFERENCES

Bensley, L. B., & Bertsch, D. P. (1987). Confronting grief. *The School Administrator, 44*, 17–19.

Brooks, H. B. (1971). Teaching teachers to teach about drugs. *NAASP Bulletin, 55,* 127–134.

Chng, C. L. (1980). A critique of values: Clarification in drug education. *Journal of Drug Education, 10,* 119–125.

Clay, P. (1980). The schools and single parents: Accessibility is the key. *NAASP Bulletin, 64*, 40–43.

Clarke-Stewart, K. A. (1989). Single-parent families: How bad for the children? *NEA Today, 7,* 60–64.

Damon, P. (1979). When the family comes apart: What schools can do. *National Elementary Principal, 59,* 56–75.

Dunham, R. G., & Alpert, G. P. (1987). Keeping juvenile delinquents in school: A predictive model. *Adolescence, 22,* 45–57.

Freeman, J. (1978). Death and dying in three days? *Phi Delta Kappan, 60,* 118.

Frey, D., & Carlock, C. J. (1991). *Enhancing self-esteem* (2nd. ed.). Muncie, IN: Accelerated Development.

Gordon, A. K., & Klass, D. (1979). *They need to know: How to teach children about death.* Englewood Cliffs, NJ: Prentice-Hall.

Hammond, J. M. (1979). A comparison of elementary children from divorced and intact families. *Phi Delta Kappan, 61,* 219.

Hymovitz, L. (1979). Death as a discipline: The ultimate curriculum. *NAASP Bulletin, 63,* 102–106.

Kearney, A. L., & Hines, M. H. (1980). Evaluation of the effectiveness of a drug prevention education program. *Journal of Drug Education, 10,* 127–134.

Keith, C. R., & Ellis, D. (1978) Reactions of pupils and teachers to death in the classroom. *The School Counselor, 25,* 228–234.

Kelly, J. B., & Wallerstein, J. S. (1977). Brief interventions with children in divorcing families. *American Journal of Orthopsychiatry, 47,* 23–29.

Kelly, J. B., & Wallerstein, J. S. (1976a). The effects of parental divorce: Experiences of the child in early latency. *American Journal of Orthopsychiatry, 46,* 20–23.

Kelly, J. B., & Wallerstein, J. S. (1976b). The effects of parental divorce: Experiences of the child in later latency. *American Journal of Orthopsychiatry, 46,* 256–269.

Kübler-Ross, E. (1969). *On death and dying.* New York: Macmillan.

Larimer, G. S., Tucker, A., & Brown, E. F. (1970). Drugs in use. *Pennsylvania Health, 31,* 2–11.

Lewis, C., Battistich, V., & Schaps, E. (1990). School-based primary prevention: What is an effective program? *New Directions for Child Development, 50,* 35–59.

McLanahan, S. (1986). Family structure and the reproduction of poverty. *American Journal of Sociology, 90,* 873–901.

Moses, D. A., & Burger, R. E. (1975). *Are you driving your children to drink? Coping with teenage alcohol and drug abuse.* New York: Van Nostrand Reinhold. *NIAAA Information and Feature Service,* No. 84, June 1, 1981, p. 1.

Newcomb, M. D., & Bentler, P. M. (1989). Substance Use and abuse among children and teenagers. *American Psychologist, 44,* 242–248.

Pink, W. T. (1984). Schools, youth, and justice. *Crime and Delinquency, 30,* 439–461.

Plath, S. (1972). *The bell jar.* New York: Bantam Books.

Ricci, L. (1979). Divorce, remarriage and the schools. *Phi Delta Kappan, 60,* 509–511.

Robinson, C. M. (1978). Developmental counseling approach to death and dying education. *Elementary School Guidance and Counseling, 12,* 178–187.

Santrock, J. W., & Tracy, R. L. (1978). Effects of children's family structure status on the development of stereotypes by teachers. *Journal of Educational Psychology, 25,* 276–281.

Schaum, M. (1978). Delinquent behavior comes from delinquent minds. *The School Counselor, 25,* 276–281.

Slimmon, L. (1975). Affective education as both a prevention and a treatment modality. In E. Senay, V. Short, & H. Alksne (Eds.), *Developments in the Field of Drug Abuse* (pp. 710–717). Cambridge, MA: Schenkman.

Swanson, J. C. (1974). Junior high student evaluations of drug education by values and traditional oriented teachers. *Journal of Drug Education, 4,* 43–50.

Tec, N. (1972). Some aspects of high school status and differential involvement with marijuana: A study of suburban teenagers. *Adolescence, 7,* 1–28.

Toth, V. A. (1979). Assimilating offenders in schools. *School Guidance Worker, 4,* 48–50.

U.S. Bureau of the Census. (1980). *Statistical Abstract of the United States: 1980.* Washington, DC.

Wolfelt, A. (1983). *Helping children cope with grief.* Muncie, IN: Accelerated Development.

Chapter 9

SPECIAL PROBLEMS
OF TEACHERS

Without question, teachers must be prepared for the many challenges that will confront them in their career. With all the demands made on teachers for the physical, intellectual, social, and moral development of students assigned to them, no wonder stress-related problems and eventual burn-out develop for many of them. This chapter was developed to forewarn teachers about the special problems they can expect to encounter in their chosen career and to provide them with some practical suggestions for dealing effectively with those problems.

Teachers must reconcile the discrepancies among their expectations for themselves, the system's expectations of them, and the reality of the classroom situation itself. Teachers must be willing to operate from a position of trial and error, without fear of making mistakes. They also must realize that the path to success in teaching is different for each teacher. The entire contents of this book are designed to make smooth the transition from pre-service education to actual teaching, and to provide some basis for in-service learning for those already active in the teaching profession.

PROBLEMS AND DIFFICULTIES
OF BEGINNING TEACHERS

Charters (1970) reported that 79.2% of males and 65.5% of females survived longer than the first year of teaching. Mark and Anderson (1978) found that 81% of males and 82.1% of females survived the first year of teaching. The latter data suggested that the percent surviving was better than the preceding data indicated, but there is still a steep decreasing survival slope over time. In an NEA nationwide opinion poll conducted by McGuire (1979), one-third of the respondents said they would not choose teaching again if they could go back to college and start over, and 40% said they did not plan to remain in teaching until retirement.

Despite the importance of the first year of teaching, it is a relatively new area for research. In order to evaluate and revise present teacher/counselor preparation programs, objective information about relevant attitudes, problems, and concerns faced by beginning teachers or counselors is needed. Housten and Felder (1982) characterized the first experiences of new teachers as more a test of survival than a time of personal growth and development.

Collea (1972) considered the intentions, self-perceptions, and role perceptions of first-year teachers, as a means of assessing their verbal behavior patterns. Data suggested that the various intentions of first-year science teachers were in conflict. While beginning science teachers' desire to motivate students increased, their desire for student participation in classroom activities decreased. Moreover, Collea found that these teachers experienced a conflict in role perception; they felt that their principals wanted them to encourage and praise their students more but, at the same time, to exercise their authority in the classroom. The first-year science teachers found at the end of the year that they were not only more direct in their classroom behavior but they were also motivating students less and having less student participation. Finally, data have suggested that role perceptions of beginning science teachers moved away from their principals' perceptions of the teachers' verbal behavior in the classroom.

The results of Collea's 1972 study are consistent with those of Moskowitz and Hayman (1974). They studied the teaching behavior of "best," typical, and first-year teachers in three urban junior high schools. Of primary interest in this investigation was the behavior of new teachers, the way they changed over time, and how their behavior compared with the behaviors of best and typical experienced teachers. Moskowitz and Hayman suggested that beginning teachers are unprepared to deal with the difficulties they face, and that pre-service preparation of teachers might be appropriate for helping teachers in this situation. This idea, however, is devoid of hard research evidence.

At the start of the school year, Moskowitz and Hayman employed the Flint Interaction Analysis System to collect observational data in the classrooms of the three groups of teachers. Anecdotal records also were kept. Results indicated a number of significant differences in teaching behavior between the "best," typical, and beginning teachers during the first contact with classes. Like Collea (1972), Moskowitz and Hayman found beginning teachers to be very direct with students. This behavior increased with time. And yet, their classroom situations rapidly deteriorated. Best teachers, however, used more indirect behaviors and joked more. The beginning teachers criticized student behavior more and more frequently at each successive observational period, indicating that beginning teachers were increasingly having control problems and that students were out of order.

One implication of the Moskowitz and Hayman investigation is that beginning teachers need specific training in how to establish an appropriate relationship with students from the beginning of their teaching assignment.

Nickel, Traugh, and Tilford (1976) studied concerns and problems of first-year junior high school teachers. To identify these problems and concerns, a workshop involving 25 first-year junior high teachers from a medium-sized urban school district was held. The rationale for this method was to allow for interaction among teachers and between teachers and administration. A modified version of the confrontation meeting model designed by Richard Beckhard was utilized. Concerns and recommendations were organized into the categories of student behavior, teaching methodology, school environment, and community-school relations, and were presented to the Deputy Superintendent.

Nickel, Traugh, and Tilford suggested that first-year junior high school teachers perceived themselves as being inundated by problems with which they felt ill-prepared to cope. They concluded that the problems and concerns brought up by the 25 teachers who participated in the workshop highlight several points that are important both to school districts and to teacher education programs. The concerns ranged over many issues affecting public education, for instance, racial integration, individualized instruction, and discipline. Discipline was the chief concern of 10 of the 25 participants. The researchers stressed that school districts need to encourage communication between teachers and administrators.

Fuller and Brown (1975) found that the concerns of teachers could be divided into three groups, with each group being representative of a particular level of teacher experience. The three groups are:

1. Survival concerns: These are concerns about one's adequacy and survival as a teacher, about class control, about being liked by pupils, about supervisors' opinions, about being observed, evaluated, praised, and failed. These are concerns about feel-

ings, and seem to be evoked by one's status as a student. Pre-service teachers have more concerns of this type than in-service teachers.

2. Teaching-situation concerns: These are concerns about having to work with too many students or having too many noninstructional duties, about time pressures, about inflexible situations, lack of instructional materials, and so on. These frustrations seem to be evoked by the teaching situation. In-service teachers have more concerns of this type than pre-service teachers.

3. Pupil concerns: These are concerns about recognizing the social and emotional needs of pupils, about the inappropriateness of some curriculum material for certain students, about being fair to pupils, about tailoring content to individual students, and so on. Although such concerns cluster together, they are expressed by both pre-service and in-service teachers. This may be because such concerns are associated with characteristics which cut across experience or because in-service teachers feel such concerns more while pre-service teachers express more concern about everything than do in-service teachers. (pp. 37-38)

Veenman (1984) found the prominent problems of beginning teachers centered around classroom discipline, control, and management; motivation of students; individual differences of students as a result of mixed-ability grouping; identification of appropriate instructional levels; self-evaluation of one's teaching; assessment of student progress; relations with school administrators and colleagues; and relations with parents. While these problems were fairly universal, they did vary by educational system, type of school, subject taught, age of students, or the school's policy on grouping of students.

The first-year teacher should not be expected to know everything experienced teachers know. The pre-service experience, including student teaching, cannot possibly alert the prospective teacher to everything that needs to be known. Experienced teachers can do much to help beginning teachers adjust to the many realities they face. In-service experiences should provide beginning teachers with the opportunity to have their many concerns addressed.

In an attempt to promote the transition from teacher education to professional practice, several states have initiated competency programs for beginning teachers. Georgia, South Carolina, Florida, and North Carolina are among the states with such programs. The program in North Carolina, named the Quality Assurance Program, is designed to couple observations of teachers with traditional paper-and-pencil tests, as well as to evaluate teacher training institutions in the state.

Ward (1981) reported requirements used in several states for certification of teachers. First, students planning to major in education must pass a basic skills test in reading, writing, and mathematics before entering teacher preparation programs. Second, students must complete a full semester of student teaching that includes a performance evaluation. Third, students must pass a written test in the subject matter areas for which certification is desired. Teacher training institutions use data from this measure to evaluate their programs. Finally, the program includes in-the-classroom observations by three persons: the school principal, the peer teacher, and a person from a regional assessment center. The observation is geared to provide the beginning teacher with helpful information about their strong and weak points. South Carolina reported that 60% of beginning teachers had mastered all competencies during the first year of the program and that 85% of the teachers reported the evaluation to be a good experience.

Thies-Sprinthall and Gerler (1990) reported on a teacher induction program that provides beginning teachers with peer support in counselor-led support groups. They concluded that this special version of small-group counseling "in an atmosphere free of evaluation can add to the effectiveness of mentoring and clinical supervision. New teachers can face themselves under such conditions and refocus their own concerns from self to the teaching process, and then to their students" (p. 22).

The beginning teacher is likely to face numerous unanticipated challenges in the first several years of teaching. No beginning teacher can afford to ignore these special challenges. Not every beginning teacher can be an expert instructor, but no one preparing to teach should lose sight of the fact that skillful teaching is the distinguishing mark that all teachers should strive to attain.

STRESS AND ANXIETY IN TEACHING

We currently live in an age of stress. The teaching profession is not exempt from encroachments that serve to make teaching itself a source of anxiety. Once viewed as a stable profession, education is crumbling under pressure to make it responsible to all persons served and to make it solve general societal problems.

Selye (1978) has defined stress as the "body's nonspecific response to any demand [physical, social or psychological] placed on it, whether that demand is pleasant or not" (p. 60). He described unpleasant or negative stress as "distress" and coined a new term, "eustress," to describe pleasant or positive stress. The goal then, according to Selye, is to cultivate positive attitudes toward distress, thereby turning it into eustress. The way in which this intention is accomplished is by quickly forgetting the negative incidents and avoiding carrying grudges. One should seek, instead, one's own level of stress, choose one's own goals, and finally, look out for self by being necessary to others and thereby earning their goodwill. One is thus enabled to define a given situation or event as either distress or eustress, defeating or motivating.

Stress can have either short-term or long-term effects on the body. Short-term stress can be positive and helpful. It may serve as the motivator to complete a task or to improve performance in a given area. Long-term stress is a negative experience which frequently manifests itself in increased body movements, insomnia, and irritability. It causes discomfort and a desire to leave the uncomfortable situation.

Alley (1980) identified four sources of stress. Such categorization of stress is necessary so that one may develop strategies for reducing the negative impact of stress. Alley's four sources are as follows:

Personal. This area includes inner fears, inner drives, ambition, compulsiveness, energy, and the need to feel needed and successful.

Interpersonal. Family relations, illnesses of children, interactions with students in classes, and conflicts with colleagues, are examples of interpersonal stressors.

Institutional. This category includes school policies, governmental regulations, and public pressures which are a source of stress.

Societal. Here the stressors are inflation, traffic, taxes, and smog. They relate to teaching only indirectly but are primary in their bearing on the lives of teachers. (pp. 7-8)

Perhaps the best known measure of stress is the Social Readjustment Rating Scale (Table 13.1) developed by Holmes and Rahe (1967). They assigned values to significant life-change units, emphasizing that both positive and negative changes increase the amount of stress in one's life.

One who wishes to complete this rating scale should identify the stresses that have occurred in his or her life over the last 12 months. Total the number of points for each item identified. If that total number of points exceeds 300 there is an 80% chance of illness in the near future; 150–299 points suggests a 50% chance of illness; and less than 150 points offers a 30% chance of illness. One should be cautious about absolute interpretations, because not all persons who go through these stressful events will become ill at the rates suggested.

TABLE 9.1
Social Readjustment Rating Scale

Rank	Life Event	Mean Value
1	Death of spouse	100
2	Divorce	73
3	Marital separation	65
4	Jail term	63
S	Death of close family member	63
6	Personal injury or illness	53
7	Marriage	50
8	Fired at work	47
9	Marital reconciliation	45
10	Retirement	45
11	Change in health of family member	44
12	Pregnancy	40
13	Sex difficulties	39
14	Gain of new family member	39
15	Business readjustment	39
16	Change in financial state	38
17	Death of close friend	37
18	Change to different line of work	36
19	Change in number of arguments with spouse	35
20	Mortgage over $10,000	31
21	Foreclosure of mortgage or loan	30
22	Change in responsibilities at work	29
23	Son or daughter leaving home	29
24	Trouble with in-laws	29
25	Outstanding personal achievement	28
26	Wife begin or stop work	26
27	Begin or end school	26
28	Change in living conditions	25
29	Revision of personal habits	24
30	Trouble with boss	23
31	Change in work hours or conditions	20
32	Change in residence	20
33	Change in schools	20
34	Change in recreation	19
35	Change in church activities	19
36	Change in social activities	18
37	Mortgage or loan less than $10,000	17
38	Change in sleeping habits	16
39	Change in number of family get-togethers	15
40	Change in eating habits	15
41	Vacation	13
42	Christmas	12
43	Minor violations of the law	11

Note. From "The Social Readjustment Rating Scale" by T. H. Holmes and R. H. Rahe, 1967, *Journal of Psychosomatic Research, 11,* p. 216. Copyright 1967 by Journal of Psychosomatic Research. Reprinted by permission.

Obviously some people handle these events in a manner that reduces negative effects. Individual differences cannot be ignored in gauging the physical and emotional reactions to a given event. Nevertheless, the conclusion does seem fairly clear: the more stress there is in one's life, the more likely one is to become a candidate for a stress-related illness.

What are the stress-related events associated with teaching? Cichon and Koff (1980) replicated the procedure employed by Holmes and Rahe and developed an inventory of the types of stress-related events typically encountered by teachers. The Teaching Events Stress Inventory (TESI) was compared by 5,000 teachers employed by the Chicago Board of Education (see Table 9.2).

The TESI is a rank-order indicator of the relative degree of stress produced by certain events involved in teaching. These 36 events are ranked from the most stressful to the least stressful. Correlation patterns suggested that the relative degree of stress assigned to an event was stable across the sample. That is to say that regardless of age, race, sex, marital status, type of school, school size, or previous physical or mental illness, teachers shared common perceptions about stress associated with the profession. Also, all events on the inventory are stress producing. When individual differences are taken into account, events in the least stressful area may be as significant to a teacher as a "more stressful" event may be to another teacher. This is so because teachers must deal not only with occupational stress (events from the TESI) but also with general life stresses (events from the Social Readjustment Rating Scale). Research does not offer insights into which set of events may be more stress producing. Regardless of the cause or nature of stress, teacher stress and anxiety will have a negative effect on students because the attention of the teacher under stress will focus on the stress, which will take precedence over direct teaching activities.

Evidence seems to indicate that the use of the term "burn-out" came into the professional literature when Freudenberger (1975) described feelings of many of his volunteers in free clinics. He recognized that the burn-out phenomenon is not unique to self-help groups but occurs among all workers regardless of the setting. He went on to say that burn-out operates differently in terms of degree from person to person. Maslach (1976) described persons who experience the most negative effects of on-the-job stress as psychologically "burned out" by the experience. Edelwich and Brodsky (1980) suggested a working definition of burn-out as

> a progressive loss of idealism, energy, and purpose experienced by
> people in the helping professions as a result of the conditions of

TABLE 9.2
The Teaching Events Stress Inventory (TESI)

Rank	Event
1	Involuntarily transferred
2	Managing "disruptive" children
3	Notification of unsatisfactory performance
4	Threatened with personal injury
5	Overcrowded classroom
6	Lack of availability of books and supplies
7	Colleague assaulted in school
8	Reorganization of classes or program
9	Implementing board of education curriculum goals
10	Denial of promotion or advancement
11	Target of verbal abuse by student
12	Disagreement with supervisor
13	The first week of the school year
14	Maintaining self-control when angry
15	Teaching students who are "below average" in achievement level
16	Maintaining student personnel and achievement records
17	Preparing for a strike
18	Supervising student behavior outside the classroom
19	Change in duties/work responsibilities
20	Dealing with community racial issues
21	Seeking principal's intervention in a discipline matter
22	Disagreement with another teacher
23	Dealing with staff racial issues
24	Teaching physically or mentally handicapped children
25	Dealing with student racial issues
26	Lavatory facilities for teachers are not clean or comfortable
27	Developing and completing daily lesson plans
28	Conference with principal/supervisor
29	Evaluating student performance or giving grades
30	Having a research or training program from "outside" in the school
31	Attendance at in-service meetings
32	Taking additional course work for promotion
33	Talking to parents about their child's problems
34	Dealing with students whose primary language is not English
35	Teacher-parent conferences
36	Voluntarily transferred

Note. From "Stress and Teaching" by D. J. Cichon and R. H. Koff, 1980, *NASSP Bulletin, 64,* pp. 96–97. Copyright 1980 by National Association of Secondary School Principals. Reprinted by permission.

their work. These conditions range from insufficient training to [student] overload; from too many hours to too little pay; from inadequate funding to ungrateful [students], from bureaucratic or political constraints to the inherent gap between aspiration and accomplishment. (p. 14)

Kossack and Woods (1980) have designed a *Teacher Burn-Out Checklist* (Table 9.3) to assess the degree to which teachers are experiencing the phenomenon. Not only does the checklist provide some indication of the relative degree of burn-out, but it should also serve as a general measure of how well a teacher is coping with the expectations of the profession.

The teaching profession is likely to experience burn-out more than other professional groups because the expectation that education should be a "cure-all" for the ills of society places an unusual burden on teachers. Recent legislation provides additional bureaucratic burdens with no increased incentives. Teachers enter the profession because they like children and because they want to help children prepare for adult roles and responsibilities. When some teachers realize that their efforts are not meeting with success, they are likely to feel burned out.

In an attempt to prevent some of the stress associated with beginning teaching, Purkerson (1980) suggested the following list to strengthen the survival skills of beginning teachers:

1. Make beginning teachers aware of non-teaching assignments before they show up for their first day of work.
2. Make sure that beginning teachers understand the legal requirements for in-service.
3. Go over the teaching contract.
4. Explain salary and benefits.
5. Help them wade through the maze of how data processing is done in school.
6. Review the hierarchical structure of local and state teaching organizations and educational systems.
7. Invite them to join professional organizations.
8. Orient them to the Code of Ethics.
9. Help them decipher the growing list of acronyms. (pp. 47-50)

Teachers have found a number of strategies useful for coping with the stress associated with their jobs. Wyly and Frusher (1990) reported that teachers tend to use self-directed, active strategies aimed at getting away from the classroom. Table 9.4 reports the results of their investigation of teacher coping strategies.

TABLE 9.3
Teacher Burn-out Checklist

DIRECTIONS: Circle YES for those symptoms of burn-out which apply to your situation; circle NO for those symptoms which do not relate.

YES   NO   1. *FEELING IRREPLACEABLE.* Do you have feelings that you are indispensable? Do you haul yourself to school despite illness? Do you accept additional duties out of obligation or   because you secretly believe no one else can do quite as good a job?

YES   NO   2. *PROFESSIONAL MARTYR.* Do you take work home only to find that you do not complete it? Do you find, though you do not do it, that the work dominates your environment, provoking guilt feelings?

YES   NO   3. *PRESSURE.* Have you overextended yourself at work/home? Do you feel persistent pressure—too much to do and too little time?

YES   NO   4. *PERSONAL HABITS.* Have you experienced relatively unusual changes in your personal habits lately? Do you have insomnia, colds, headaches, rashes lately? Do you find that you are taking more aspirin, sleeping pills, tranquilizers than you were a year ago? Are you drinking or smoking or eating more than a year ago?

YES   NO   5. *TROUBLE WITH RELATIONSHIPS.* Are you impatient, irritable lately? Are discipline problems more noticeable? Are you having more arguments with spouse/friends/strangers lately?

YES   NO   6. *LOW SELF-CONCEPT.* Do you find yourself with thoughts of self-blame, guilt, self-recrimination, anxiety? Do you feel powerless to make a difference with your students? Do you lack a feeling of success/challenge? Are you thinking, "Why am I bothering to do this?"

YES   NO   7. *DISSATISFACTION.* Do you feel as if nothing is going well? Do you find yourself talking about work most of the time, and are your conversations tending to be negative?

YES   NO   8. *EVASION.* Do you use more ditto/board/workbook activities, audiovisual materials, support personnel to remove you from direct contact with students lately? Have you taken a larger number of sick days of late?

YES   NO   9. *BOREDOM.* Do you "turn yourself off" as you enter the school? Do you feel as if you are operating as a robot, that you do not care enough to care? Have you lost your joy, enthusiasm?

(Continued on next page)

TABLE 9.3 (*Continued*)
Teacher Burn-out Checklist

YES   NO   10. *ANGER.* The anxiety felt by teachers often stems from the lack of something concrete to fight. This anxiety leads to frustration, pessimism, and then to anger. Do you feel like fighting?

YES   NO   11. *ESCAPE.* Do you hate coming to work? Do you get a knot in your stomach when you realize that the next day is a workday? Have you been tempted to drive on past the school, to move, to change jobs?

YES   NO   12. *BREAKDOWN.* Have you had severe physical or mental illness of late? Have you had ulcers, high blood pressure, hypertension, colitis, nervous disorders?

INTERPRETATION

Educators who answered YES to:	Are:
One to three questions	Coping well with teaching frustrations
Four to six questions	Slipping into warning stages; take preventative action
Seven to nine questions	Sliding into alarming burn-out reactions; take immediate action
Ten to twelve questions	Burned out; take remedial action

Note. From "Teacher Burn-out: Diagnosis, Prevention, Remediation" by S. W. Kossack and S. L. Woods, 1980, *Action in Teacher Education, 2,* pp. 29–30. Copyright 1980 by Action in Teacher Education. Reprinted by permission.

In terms of coping with job-related stress, a four-pronged attack to the problem is recommended. The first step is to recognize signs of stress. Signs may be physiological (increased heart rate, increased muscle tension, increased perspiration, decreased digestion), behavioral (difficulty in interpersonal relations, poor work performance or productivity, increases in amount of alcohol consumed, cigarettes smoked, or medications taken), or cognitive (negative self-statements, difficulty concentrating). The second step involves analyzing or determining the source(s) of stress. This can be accomplished by completing both the Social Readjustment Rating Scale and the Teaching Events Stress Inventory. Data from these two instruments should be useful in step three, the development of a stress management plan. A specific plan is to be developed which relates to the events found to be sources of stress. The following are general recommendations for coping with stress which are useful for all teachers regardless of the specific nature of their stressors:

1. Seek professional experiences beyond the classroom, such as workshops, and professional meetings.
2. Keep alert to changing methods and philosophies. Try different teaching approaches.
3. Subscribe to professional magazines.
4. Use few rather than many rules in the classroom. Set realistic, flexible goals.
5. Try to complete school work at school even if it means staying late.
6. Change teaching assignment, grade level, or school.

TABLE 9.4
Teacher Coping Strategies

Coping Strategies	Coping Strategies in Rank Order (%)
Exercise	54.6
Talk to a friend	46.1
Take action	44.8
Get away from it all	43.7
Engage in a hobby	42.7
Attend professional conferences (within past 2 years)	32.5
Use a support system	28.2
Visitation to other classrooms (within past 3 years)	20.2
Blow off steam	16.1
Exchange teaching (within past 3 years)	13.3
Job rotation (within past 3 years)	12.9
Change your view of the situation so it doesn't bother you	11.6
Apologize even though you were right	11.4
Take sabbatical (within past 3 years)	11.1
Keep it to yourself	10.3
Drink more coffee or soda or eat more	5.7
Smoke cigarettes	3.4
Drink alcohol	2.3
Take drugs or medicine	1.1
Act as though nothing much happened	1.1

Note. From "Stressors and Coping Strategies of Teachers" by Jeanine Wyly and Susan Frusher, 1990, *Rural Education,* 11, pp. 29–31. Copyright 1990 by Rural Education. Reprinted by permission.

7. Get plenty of sleep, maintain proper diet, relax, and exercise regularly.
8. Get involved in a hobby.
9. Maintain friendships with non-teachers.
10. Maintain a good sense of humor.
11. Don't be afraid to make mistakes.

The program of stress reduction should be implemented and evaluated. So many efforts have failed because teachers did not implement a plan, continue it for some reasonable length of time, and evaluate its effectiveness. The effectiveness of a stress management plan can best be measured by noting changes in those signs that were identified with stress.

Teachers must continue to explore new avenues that lead to stress reduction. Because it is virtually impossible to provide a workable plan for all stresses or stressors, we have included an annotated bibliography of 25 sources which should prove useful.

ANNOTATED BIBLIOGRAPHY ON STRESS MANAGEMENT

Archer, Jr., J. A. (1982). *Managing anxiety and stress.* Muncie, IN: Accelerated Development.

This book has a holistic approach to anxiety management and encourages you to examine your anxiety process from many different angles. Contains simplified techniques and emphasizes application with steps for practice and self-assessment discussion questions.

Benson, H. (1975). *The relaxation response.* New York: William Morrow.

Offers techniques for dealing with stress and anxiety in normal life. Presentation includes theory, medical information, and clear instructions.

Collins, G. (1977). *Relax and live longer.* Santa Ana, CA: Vision House.

Describes the causes of tension and the reasons people do not relax, and offers specific techniques that foster relaxation.

Cooper, G. L., & Payne, R. (1978). *Stress at work.* New York: John Wiley and Sons.

Focuses on research, prevention, and treatment of stress in various occupational categories. Attention is also given to the relationship between occupational environment and family life.

Culligan, M. (1980). *How to avoid stress before it kills you.* New York: Gramercy.

Focuses attention on normal stress and how to avoid distress or prolonged tension. Useful techniques are presented.

Forbes, R. (1979). *Life stress.* New York: Doubleday.

This book deals with stress in the home, stress involved in sexual relationships, stress caused by the redefinition of the role of women, and "stress seekers." Stress reduction "lists" are offered to change behaviors.

Frankl, V. (1971). *Man's search for meaning.* New York: Simon and Schuster.

The author describes personal experiences in a concentration camp and how he was able to develop meaning in his life. Useful for seeing how an extremely stressful situation contains potential for growth.

Freese, A. (1976). *Understanding stress.* New York: Public Affairs Pamphlets.

Presents causes of stress and the relationship between stress and illness. Offers a variety of stress reduction techniques.

Gawain, S. (1978). *Creative visualization.* Berkeley, CA: Whatever Publishing.

This book deals with relaxation techniques and creative ways to overcome negative concepts about life. Recommends fantasy as a useful technique.

Giammatteo, M. C., & Giammatteo, D. M. (1980). *Executive well-being: Stress and administrators.* Reston, VA: National Association of Secondary School Principals.

Designed for school administrators but useful for teachers as well. Contains numerous self-administered instructions to assess levels of stress. Emphasizes practical strategies for stress reduction.

Glasser, W. (1981). *Stations of the mind.* New York: Harper and Row.

Glasser suggested that stress results from outdated means of looking at situations. He offers techniques for changing behaviors by changing perceptions of events and experiences.

Gunderson, E. K., & Rahe, R. H. (Eds.). (1974). *Life stress and illnesses.* Springfield, IL: Thomas.

A collection of research reports on the relationship of stress to illness. Contains contributions from medical researchers from around the world.

Kinser, N S. (1979). *Stress and the American woman.* New York: Ballantine Books.

Discusses stressful situations unique to women from the perspective of women. Presents coping strategies. Extensive bibliography.

Koestenbaum, P. (1974). *Managing anxiety.* Englewood Cliffs, NJ: Prentice-Hall.

Contains an authenticity profile which the reader may complete as a measure of consciousness. Recommends the use of an E-I-F(emotional-intellectual-fantasy) Journal as a means of learning to like and appreciate self. The Pain Test is a self-administered instrument designed to measure how much negativity you experience in your life.

Litvak, S. (1979). *Unstress yourself.* Phoenix, AZ: Mainstream Publishers.

This work presents various levels of stress reducers from instant relief to long-range strategies. The author finds little use for definitions of stress and descriptions of stressful situations but instead recommends changes in lifestyles.

May, R. (1977). *The meaning of anxiety.* New York: Ronald Press.

Summarizes cultural, biological, philosophical, and psychological theories that seek to explain anxiety. Case studies are used to illustrate theories. Three self-administered checklists are offered to help reader explore anxiety.

Miller, W. C. (1979). *Dealing with stress: A challenge for educators.* Bloomington, IN: Phi Delta Kappa.

Presents major causes of stress, results of stress, and strategies for preventing stress. Written for school administrators but useful for teachers.

Mitchell, L. (1979). *Simple relaxation: The physiological method for easing tension.* New York: Atheneum.

Offers simple, practical methods of relieving bodily tensions and stress. Particularly useful for those who find it difficult to relax.

Phillips, B. (1978). *School stress and anxiety.* New York: Human Sciences Press.

Focuses on student stress and how to eliminate anxiety associated with academic achievement. Suggests activities for youth to learn to manage stress.

Powell, J. (1976). *Fully human, fully alive.* Niles, IL: Argus Communications.

Offers a five-step approach to becoming more fully functioning: accepting oneself; being oneself; forgetting oneself in loving; believing; and belonging.

Samuels, M., & Bennett, H. (1974). *Be well.* New York: Random House.

Presents a guide to rest, relaxation, and restoration. Attention is given to health and ease as opposed to stress and disease.

Schuller, R. H. (1978). *Turning your stress into strength.* Irvine, CA: Harvest House.

Offers an approach to eliminating stress based on a religious point of view. Shows how stressful situations can be turned into positive perspective.

Selye, H. (1974). *Stress without distress.* New York: Lippincott.

Summarizes much of the research on stress. Theoretical and philosophical presentation of medical phenomena in lay terminology.

Sharpe, R., & Lewis, D. (1977). *Thrive on stress.* New York: Warner Communications.

Self-directed guide to reducing stress based on programmed behavior. Discusses how stress can be turned into positive experience for the individual.

Unger, L. (1976). *Walking: The perfect exercise.* San Luis Obispo, CA: Impact Publishers.

Presents a step-by-step approach to relief of stress through walking.

REFERENCES

Alley, R. (1980). Stress and the professional educator. *Action in Teacher Education, 2,* 1–8.

Charters, W. W. (1970). Some factors affecting teacher survival in school districts. *American Educational Research Journal, 7,* 1–27.

Cichon, D. J., & Koff, R. H. (1980). Stress and teaching. *NASSP Bulletin, 64,* 91–104.

Collea, F. P. (1972). First year science teacher: A study of his intentions, perceptions, and verbal behaviors. *School Science and Mathematics, 72,* 159–164.

Edelwich, J., & Brodsky, A. (1980). *Burn-out.* New York: Human Sciences.

Freudenberger, H. J. (1975). The staff burn-out syndrome in alternative institutions. *Psychotherapy: Theory, Research and Practice, 12,* 73–82.

Fuller, F. F., & Brown, O. H. (1975). Becoming a teacher. In K. Ryan, *Teacher Education* (pp. 25–52). Chicago: University of Chicago.

Holmes, T. H., & Rahe, R. H. (1967). The social readjustment rating scale. *Journal of Psychosomatic Research, 11,* 213–218.

Houston, W. B., & Felder, B. D. (1982). Breaking horses, not teachers. *Phi Delta Kappan, 63,* 457–460.

Kossack, S. W., & Woods, S. L. (1980). Teacher burn-out: Diagnosis, prevention, remediation. *Action in Teacher Education, 2,* 29–35.

Mark, J. H., & Anderson, B. D. (1978). Teacher survival rates: A current look. *American Educational Research Journal, 15,* 379–383.

Maslach, C. (1976). Burned-out. *Human Behavior, 6,* 16–22.

McGuire, W. H. (1979). Teacher burn-out. *Today's Education, 68,* 5.

Moskowitz, G., & Hayman, J. L. (1974). Interaction patterns of first-year, typical and "best" teachers in inner-city schools. *The Journal of Educational Research, 67,* 224–230.

Nickel, J., Traugh, C., & Tilford, M. (1976). Confrontation meeting: Identifying first year junior high school teachers' problems. *The Clearing House, 49,* 358–360.

Purkerson, R. A. (1980). Stress and the beginning teacher: And the walls came tumbling down. *Action in Teacher Education, 2,* 47–50.

Selye, H. (1978). Eustress. *Psychology Today, 11,* 60–70.

Thies-Sprinthall, L. M., & Gerler, E. R. (1990). Support groups for novice teachers. *Journal of Staff Development, 11,* 18–22.

Veenman, S. (1984). Perceived problems of beginning teachers. *Review of Educational Research, 54,* 143–178.

Ward, B. J. Summer (1981). Beginning teachers must make the grade. *National Assessment of Educational Progress Newsletter, 14,* 3.

Wyly, J., & Frusher, S. (1990). Stressors and coping strategies of teachers. *Rural Education, 11,* 29–31.

UNIT V
GATHERING CAREER
AND EDUCATIONAL
INFORMATION

Chapter 10

CAREER DEVELOPMENT

This chapter is organized into three sections. Section one describes the major changes or crises that may contribute to the high unemployment rate among teenagers, minorities, and women. In the second section, four career developmental theories are examined. These theories are included as a guide to helping students select careers. The goal of section three is to assist teachers who need to develop a career education program that may be incorporated into the curriculum.

Since the early 1900's, counseling has had a strong association with career development and has been an integral part of education. A primary objective of current school counseling programs is to provide students with the means of making the transition from school to work an easy one. Career preparation must be a main thrust of every school curriculum. However, the barriers that may prevent students from making career choices and decisions must be understood by teachers.

FACTORS THAT CONTRIBUTE TO MAJOR CHANGES IN INDIVIDUAL CAREER DEVELOPMENT

Drop-Outs

A considerable number of students drop out of school when they reach the legal age (16 years old in most states). Many of these students claim, as their major reason for leaving, that "school is a waste of time because it doesn't prepare me for a job." They also report that the classes they are required to take are not relevant, not interesting, or boring. In addition, some students come from homes that are experiencing financial difficulties. One or both parents may be unemployed and the family is finding that they are unable to pay bills. This condition may force students to leave school and seek full-time employment. However, after dropping out, students often find it difficult to secure worthwhile employment because of their lack of education. Some of them eventually return to school in the evenings and obtain a high school diploma.

Pregnancy

A teenager who becomes pregnant often leaves school to give birth. After the birth, her problems may continue. For example, many of today's pregnant teenagers are unmarried and will have no one to care for the child. Some of them return home and their parents help rear the child. While some of these teenagers may return to school, some never do. Their career goals may be postponed for many years.

Drug and Alcohol Abuse

Drug and alcohol abuse by students is widespread. Teachers may find that, regardless of grade level, students are smoking marijuana and drinking alcoholic beverages regularly. These students may even come to class under the influence of drugs and alcohol. Because of a decreased level of awareness, these students often fall asleep in class and fail to do their school work. In addition, continued use of drugs and alcohol may cause them to be absent from school, to drop-out, and/or to encounter serious health problems.

Teenage Delinquency

Some teenagers find themselves in trouble with the police and may have a record before completing their teen years. Sometimes students find a need to steal and break the law in other ways to support a drug and alcohol habit. Some of these teenagers may spend time in detention homes or jail. Students who are doing time may experience difficulty in preparing for a career. When these teenagers are released, they often find it difficult to obtain employment.

Minorities and Women

While membership in either of these groups does not suggest characteristics similar to those of the other groups in this section, minorities and women both have unique career needs. Some writers have gone so far as to suggest that existing career development theories do not address the unique needs of minorities and women. Nevertheless, large numbers of minority persons are unemployed, many because they were drop-outs or push-outs, became pregnant, were delinquent, or became involved in drugs or alcohol. Others have suffered simply because of their membership in a minority group.

Many of the factors mentioned above may contribute to unemployment or underemployment of minorities and women. In addition, to compound their problems, these students graduate from high school only to find that they do not have the skills necessary to enter the world of work. The goal of every school should be to prepare all students to become fully employable when they graduate.

Teachers must educate their students not only in subject matter areas but also about career opportunities. Most teachers have some knowledge about opportunities available to students in the community. Using community resources, knowledge of career theories, and specific information about students, teachers can incorporate career information in the curriculum.

Activities

1. *Interview an administrator or a school board member. What career programs, if any, have been developed to help the potential drop-out?*
2. *Are there any agencies in your community that help the pregnant teenager? If so, how does the agency help?*
3. *Where can a teenager with a drug- or alcohol-related problem go for help in your community? How do those agencies work with the schools?*
4. *Visit a detention home in your community. What provisions does it have, if any, for the career training or education of the teenager?*
5. *Visit your local state employment service. What types of jobs are being filled by minorities and/or by women? Describe any special programs available to members of either group.*

CAREER DEVELOPMENT THEORIES

This section was designed to introduce the teacher to four career development theories. The first theory, the trait and factor approach, was selected because of its historical significance. The second, Anne Roe's theory, was selected because it assumes that a child's home environment influences career decisions. John Holland's theory was selected because of its wide use in interest inventories. It is based on the premise that people seek work environments that are congruent with their personality types. Finally, Donald Super'stheory was selected because it views career development as a life-long process. Teachers desiring more detailed explanations of these career theories or others are referred to the list of references provided at the end of this chapter.

Trait and Factor Theory

In the early 1900s, Frank Parsons (1909) became interested in finding work for Boston's unemployed. Although Parsons is considered to be the "father of guidance," he was an engineer and lawyer. His trait-and-factor approach to finding jobs for people was rather mechanical and straightforward. The procedure, which he called "true reasoning," consisted of three steps:

1. A clear understanding of yourself, your aptitudes, abilities, interests, ambitions, resources, limitations, and their causes.
2. A knowledge of the requirements and condition of success, advantages and disadvantages, compensation, opportunities, and prospects in different lines of work.
3. True reasoning on the relations of these two groups of factors. (p. 5)

The trait and factor approach used the interview to determine the client's aptitudes, interests, and abilities. During Parsons' time, no aptitude, interest, or ability tests were available. His approach assumed that the counselor or helper knew something about the world of work. Finally, the counselor attempted to match the client with a job.

Two limitations of the trait and factor approach must be noted. First, it assumes that an individual is best suited for only one job. Second, it is based on the belief that an individual must make a choice at a given time. Nevertheless, the trait and factor approach did find jobs for people who otherwise would have continued to be unemployed.

The trait and factor approach is considered to have major shortcomings in comparison to newer theories that stress the importance of one's self-concept and the life-long process of career development. However, Parkinson, Bradley, and Lawson (1979) compared the three steps of Parsons' theory to recent theories and concluded that:

Step 1 sounds much like sell-concept theory today.
Step 2 sounds like information seeking based on socioeconomic reality.

Step 3 sounds like the beginning of a decision-making model.
(p. 127)

Despite the limitations of the trait and factor approach, some counselors still use a similar three-step method in counseling clients about careers.

Anne Roe's Theory

Anne Roe's (1956) theory of career development began with a study of the personalities of famous scientists. She concluded that the different personality types of these scientists were related, in part, to their early childhood experiences, needs, and genetic factors, and, therefore, that these influences contribute to the selection of a career. In addition, her theory combined the ideas of Garner Murphy and Abraham Maslow. Roe's theory is presented in Figure 10.1 (Roe & Seigelman, 1964).

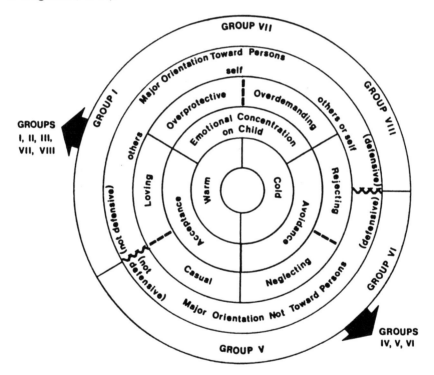

Figure 10.1. Ann Roe's Theory of Career Development. *Note.* From *The Origin of Interest. The APGA Inquiry Series*, No. 1 (p. 6) by A. Roe and M. Seigelman, 1964, Washington, DC: APGA. Copyright 1964 by APGA Press. Reprinted by permission. No further reproduction authorized without written permission of the American Counseling Association.

Groups I, II, III, VII, and VIII represent service, business, business organization, general cultural, and arts and entertainment occupations respectively. Groups IV, V, and VI include technological, outdoor, and science occupations.

To read the schematic presented in the figure, begin by examining the innermost circle. This circle contains the words "cold" and "warm." These refer to the type of environment in which children are reared.

Children reared in a "cold" environment may have had parents who avoided them or placed a great deal of emotional attention on them. For example, in an avoidance environment, parents may either neglect or reject their children. In an overly emotional environment, parents may either overprotect or place too many demands on their children.

The child reared in a "warm" emotional environment may have been reared by parents who were accepting. An accepting environment provides children with a loving or casual climate.

Depending on the type of environment in which children are reared, they may eventually choose an occupation whose major orientation is toward or not toward persons. Occupations that are oriented primarily toward persons may include service, general cultural, and arts and entertainment groups. Occupations not oriented toward persons may include outdoors and science groups.

Let us examine a particular occupation, that of the pharmacist (Group VI), using Roe's theory. According to Roe's theory, the pharmacist had early home relationships that were cold, with parents who avoided the child. These early home relationships resulted in their becoming non-person-oriented. Although pharmacists may enjoy working with people, the majority of their work involves working with things.

Roe's theory has two major limitations. First, many factors influence the home environment of children. Second, parent behaviors in child-rearing practices may not be consistent.

Activities

Teachers may easily utilize the following exercise in helping students consider occupations. This exercise incorporates the concepts of Roe's theory, strengths of family heritage, and Ginzberg, Ginzberg, Axelrad, and Herma's (1951) fantasy and tentative stages.

Dickenson and Parmerlee (1980) used an Occupational Family Tree as a career counseling technique. Students were asked during the fantasy to select an occupation and tentative stages based on the occupation of the family member to whom they felt the closest and with whom they identified. The authors suggested using the following questions:

> *How do you feel about the occupations of your relatives (proud, embarrassed, and so forth)?*
>
> *On what basis do you feel they want you to select the specific occupation (statements, hints, threats, and so forth)?*
>
> *Do your present occupational interests fit both your abilities and the need for such workers (aptitudes, job trends, and so forth)?*
>
> *List several low status (e.g., low pay or low prestige) jobs/careers that have some positive stereotypes (bus driver, hospital aid, and so forth).*
>
> *List several high status (e.g., high pay or high prestige) jobs/careers that have some negative stereotypes (car dealer, attorney, and so forth).*
>
> *What are the satisfactions from occupations your family has enjoyed most (leisure time, travel, living conditions, and so forth)?*
>
> *Which family member are you most like (characteristics, interests, abilities, and so forth)?*
>
> *What personal work habits or characteristics have made your family successful/satisfied and unsuccessful/dissatisfied on the job? (pp. 102–103)*

This activity should be completed by the reader. What have you learned about the relationship between your home environment and your occupation?

Holland's Theory

John Holland's (1973) theory of career development is based on the interaction between a person's personality type and work environment. He believed that people can be characterized according to six personality and environmental types. These types are realistic, investigative, artistic, social, enterprising, and conventional. A description of each type is follows.

Realistic (R). The realistic individual may be described as conforming, practical, and thrifty. These individuals enjoy working with things. Some realistic occupations include skilled tradesman, mechanic, machine operator, and grinder.

Investigative (I). The investigative individual may be described as analytical, intellectual, and precise. These individuals enjoy working with ideas. Some investigative occupations include physician, natural scientist, engineer, and engineering technician.

Artistic (A). The artistic individual may be described as imaginative, orig-inal, and idealistic. These individuals enjoy working in the arts. Some artistic occupations include artist, musician, and actor.

Social (S). The social individual may be described as friendly, kind, and understanding. These individuals enjoy working with and being with people. Some social occupations include teacher, counselor, and social scientist.

Enterprising (E). The enterprising individual may be described as ener-getic, self-confident, and talkative. These individuals enjoy working in sales. Some enterprising occupations include administrator, manager, and sales person.

Conventional (C). The conventional individual may be described as con-forming, efficient, and practical. These individuals like structure. Some conventional occupations include office worker, secretary, and clerk.

According to Holland (1973) the pairing of persons and environments leads to outcomes that include vocational choice, vocational stability, achievement, educational choice, personal competence, social behavior, and susceptibility to influence.

Holland also believed that interest inventories were really personality tests. He developed the Vocational Preference Inventory and the Self-Directed Search. These instruments are easy to administer and score. The six personality and environmental types are used in scoring and interpreting the instruments.

In addition to the above instruments, the Strong Interest Inventory (SII) also uses Holland's six personality and environmental types in its interpretation. The Strong contains 325 items divided into seven parts: occupations, school subjects, activities, amusements, types of people, preference between two activ-ities, and characteristics. Responses are recorded on a computer-scorable answer sheet.

To understand the results of either inventory, one must understand the rela-tionship among the six personality and environmental types, usually represented using a hexagon (see Figure 10.2).

The personality and environmental types that are adjacent to one another on the hexagon are more compatible than those that are diagonal to one another. For example, Investigative and Artistic types are more compatible than Investigative and Enterprising types.

Results of the Vocational Preference Inventory, Self-Directed Search, or Strong are returned to the individual. Together with the school counselor, the

Realistic   **Investigative**

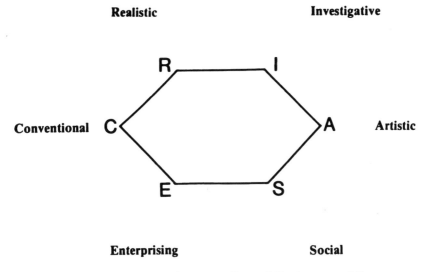

Conventional   **Artistic**

Enterprising   **Social**

Figure 10.2.   Holland's Six Personality and Environmental Stages.

individual determines his or her three-letter code. Examples of three letter codes are IAS, SAE, and IRE.

Using Holland's (1990) *Occupations Finder* and the three letter code, an individual will find useful occupational information. The *Occupations Finder* lists 1,346 occupations arranged according to the six types—Realistic, Investigative, Artistic, Social, Enterprising, and Conventional—which are divided into the three-letter codes. For each three letter code, a list of occupations, the nine digit number from the *Dictionary of Occupational Titles*, and the general education level are provided. For example, the three letter code "IAS" corresponds with the following occupations: economist, mathematician, and statistician.

Teachers desiring more information on John Holland's theory will find his *Making Vocational Choices: A Theory of Careers* an excellent resource.

Activity

Complete one of the following interest inventories: Vocational Preference Inventory, the Self-Directed Search, or the Strong Interest Inventory.

1. *What is your three-letter code?*
2. *Based on your three-letter code and a copy of the* Occupations Finder, *what occupations may be appropriate for you?*

3. *How do you feel about these occupations?*
4. *What have you learned about yourself that you did not know before?*
5. *Where may you find additional information about these occupations?*

Super's Theory

Donald Super (1957) formulated a theory that views career development as a continuous process covering the life span of individuals. His theory may be divided into four parts: self-concept, life stages, vocational maturity, and career patterns. These factors are indicated in the following twelve propositions offered by Super and Bachrach (1957):

1. Vocational development is an ongoing, continuous, generally irreversible process.
2. Vocational development is an orderly, patterned and predictable process.
3. Vocational development is a dynamic process.
4. Self-concepts begin to form prior to adolescence, become clear in adolescence, and are translated into occupational terms in adolescence.
5. Reality factors (the reality of personal characteristics and the reality of society) play an increasingly important part in occupational choice with increasing age, from early adolescence to adulthood.
6. Identification with a parent or parent substitute is related to the development of adequate roles, their consistent and harmonious interrelationship, and their interpretation in terms of vocational plans and eventualities.
7. The direction and rate of the vertical movement of an individual from one occupational level to another are related to his/her intelligence, parental socioeconomic level, status needs, values, interests, skill in interpersonal relationships, and the supply and demand conditions in the economy.
8. The occupational field the individual enters is related to his/her interests, values, and needs, the identifications he/she makes with parental or substitute role models, the community resources he/she uses, the level and quality of his/her educational background, and the occupational structure, trends, and attitudes of his/her community.
9. Although each occupation requires a characteristic of abilities, interests, and personality traits, the tolerances are wide enough to allow both some variety of individuals in each occupation and some diversity of occupations for each individual.

10. Work satisfactions depend upon the extent to which the individual can find adequate outlets in his job for his/her abilities, interests, values, and personality traits.
11. The degree of satisfaction the individual attains from his/her work is related to the degree to which he/she has been able to implement his/her self-control in his/her work.
12. Work and occupation provide a focus for personality organization for most men and many women, although for some persons this focus is peripheral, incidental or even nonexistent, and other foci such as social activities and the home are central." (pp. 118–120)

As the above propositions indicate, Super's approach to career development is comprehensive. He postulates that career development is a continuous process from birth to retirement. Many factors are involved in making adequate career choices. These factors include an individual's interests, abilities, and needs, and how these factors are influenced through parent identification, community makeup, and educational level. In addition, Super addresses the need for personal satisfaction which an individual can attain from an occupation. We will examine the elements of his theory.

Self-Concept. An individual's self-concept begins to form prior to adolescence with the identification of job models. A child's parents, teachers, and other significant adults play an important role in formulating a career choice. For example, a child may indicate a desire to become a lawyer just like his or her father or mother. As the child grows, he or she becomes aware of his or her interests, abilities, and needs. For example, a student who doesn't like math may decide against a career in engineering. A student will often select an occupation that is congruent with his or her self-concept. In addition, the amount of satisfaction one attains on the job is related to the self-concept. Super (1957) stated this succinctly: "The choice of an occupation is one of the points in life at which a young person is called upon to state rather explicitly the concept of himself, to say definitely 'I am this or that kind of person'" (p. 191).

Life-Stages. Super was influenced by Charlotte Buehler (1933) in formulating life stages of career development. Buehler believed that life was composed of separate stages: growth, exploration, establishment, maintenance, and decline.

Using the Life Stage concept of Super's theory of career development, an example will be presented to illustrate how someone may decide to become a teacher. A brief description of each of the five stages is presented in Table 10.1.

TABLE 10.1
Super's Conception of Life Stages and Development Tasks

Growth	Exploration
Birth	*14 years*
Self-concept develops through identification with key figures in family, and school needs and fantasy are dominant early in this stage; interest and capacity become more important with increasing social participation and reality testing; learns behaviors associated with self-help, social interaction, self-direction, industrialness, goal setting, persistence.	Self-examination, role try-outs, and occupational exploration take place in school, leisure activities, and part-time work.
	Substages
Substages	*Tentative* (15–17) Needs, interests, capacities, values, and opportunities are all considered; tentative choices are made and tried out in fantasy, discussion, courses, work, etc. Possible appropriate fields and levels of work are identified.
Fantasy (4–10 years) Needs are dominant; role-playing in fantasy is important.	
Interest (11–12 years) Likes are the major determinant of aspirations and activities.	*Task* Crystallizing a vocational preference.
Capacity (13–14 years) Abilities are given more weight, and job requirements (including training) are considered.	*Transition* (18–21) Reality considerations are given more weight as the person enters the labor market or professional training and attempts to implement a self-concept. Generalized choice is converted to specific choice.
Tasks Developing a picture of the kind of person one is.	*Task* Specifying a vocational preference.
Developing an orientation to the world of work and an understanding of the meaning of work.	*Trial—Little Commitment* (22–24) A seemingly appropriate occupation having been found, a first job is located and is tried out as a potential life work. Commitment is still provisional and if the job is not appropriate, the person may reinstitute the process of crystallizing, specifying, and implementing a preference.
	Task Implementing a vocational preference.

Note. From *Career Guidance through the Life Span* (p. 95) by E. L. Herr & S. H. Cramer, 1979, Boston, Harper Collins Publishers, Inc.

Establishment	Maintenance
24 years	*44 years*
Having found an appropriate field, an effort is made to establish a permanent place in it. Thereafter, changes which occur are changes of position, job, or employer, not of occupation.	Having made a place in the world of work, the concern is how to hold on to it. Little new ground is broken, continuation of established pattern. Concerned about maintaining present status while being forced by competition from younger workers in the advancement stage.

Substages

Trial—Commitment and Stabilization (25–30) Settling down. Securing a permanent place in the chosen occupation. May prove unsatisfactory, resulting in one or two changes before the life work is found or before it becomes clear that the life work will be a succession of unrelated jobs.

Tasks Preservation of achieved status and gains.

Decline

64 years

As physical and mental powers decline, work activity changes and in due course ceases. New roles must be developed: first, selective participant, and then, observer. Individual must find other sources of satisfaction to replace those lost through retirement.

Advancement (31–44) Effort is put forth to stabilize, to make a secure place in the world of work. For most persons these are the creative years. Seniority is acquired; clientele are developed; superior performance is demonstrated; qualifications are improved.

Tasks Consolidation and advancement

Substages

Deceleration (65–70) The pace of work slackens, duties are shifted, or the nature of work is changed to suit declining capacities. Many find part-time jobs to replace their full-time occupations.

Retirement (71 on) Variation on complete cessation of work or shift to part-time, volunteer, or leisure activities.

Tasks Deceleration, disengagement, retirement.

MA: Little, Brown, & Company. Copyright 1979 by Little, Brown, & Company. Reprinted by permission of

During the growth and exploration stages, an individual's self-concept is developing. It is during this period that an individual explores who he or she is and what he or she is capable of becoming. An individual learns much about self at home, at school, and at play. An individual also learns that he or she has certain needs, likes, and abilities. In addition, an individual discovers, through various activities, that certain things are easier to do than others.

In school, an individual may identify with his science teacher. This person may find that the work of the science teacher interesting and enjoyable. The individual's science teacher may have recognized this student's interest and taken a special interest in him or her. The science teacher is serving as the individual's role model.

At home, the student may role play a science teacher. He or she may use brothers, sisters, or peers to play the part of the students. In addition, the individual's parents may be very supportive of his or her desire to become a science teacher. They may purchase a science lab for their son or daughter to use at home to perform science experiments.

During his or her high school and college years, the individual will take courses that will enable him or her to reach the goal. It is during this time that the individual confirms whether he or she has the ability and interest to succeed. While completing an internship (practice teaching), the individual needs to determine whether he or she enjoys working with different kinds of students and whether the work provides satisfaction. At this time he or she is trying on the role to see if it is really a good fit.

After the training is completed, the individual enters the teaching profession. During the establishment stage, the person may decide that he or she would like to become a school principal. He or she becomes a principal after spending several years as an assistant principal. Most of the maintenance stage is spent as principal at three different schools. After thirty years of service to the school system, he or she is ready to retire. After retirement, the individual may choose to work as a teacher volunteer.

Vocational Maturity.   As a person passes through the life stages, each stage corresponds to some aspect in the development of the self-concept. For example, according to the information in Table 10.1, during the ages of 18–21 an individual begins to crystalize a vocational preference. More weight is given to reality considerations as one enters an occupation and attempts to implement a self-concept. The extent to which an individual satisfies this task during the life stage determines whether he or she is vocationally mature. A vocationally mature individual is ready to make a specific occupational choice.

Career Patterns.　A career pattern includes the number of occupations held by an individual from the first job to retirement, and the number of years each occupation was held. According to Osipow (1983), career patterns are the result of psychological, physical, situational, and societal factors. Therefore, needs, abilities, interests, values, family, and significant others all play a part in the career pattern of an individual. Each individual may have a unique career pattern. These factors were considered in Super's twelve propositions and are included in Table 10.1.

Career patterns may be stable, conventional, unstable, or multiple trial. These patterns take into account the occupational level attained by the individual, together with the sequence, frequency, and duration of employment in various occupations.

An example of a stable career pattern is the individual who enters an occupation after graduation and remains in the career until retirement. Physicians, lawyers, dentists, and chemists usually have stable career patterns. In the conventional pattern, a number of occupations are tried which ultimately lead to a stable occupation. For example, an individual may work as a lab assistant for a few years, return to school and become a medical technologist, and eventually become a medical technology teacher. This individual remains in the last occupation until retirement.

The unstable career pattern may occur among individuals who work for brief periods of time in various occupations. For example, a woman may work as a waitress, secretary, bookkeeper, salesperson, and factory employee. There is no clear pattern, only temporary employment in various occupations. An example of the multiple-trial pattern is the machinist who works in a factory. The machinist may move on to various factories but still work as a machinist until retirement. This person remains in the same occupation but performs the job at a number of different locations.

Activity

The following activity is designed to take the reader on a fantasy trip using Super's theory. You may wish to refer to Table 10.1 while completing the activity.

Think back in time when you were in the growth and exploration stages of life. Then answer each question as if you were in the growth stage and then the exploration stage.

1. *How do you feel about yourself during each of the two stages?*
2. *What factors (family background, economic, sociological, psychological, etc.) influenced you to become what you are today?*
3. *With whom, if anyone, did you identify? Why?*
4. *What occupation(s) did you try before entering or considering your present goal or occupation?*

Practical Applications of the Theories

The theories were included to help teachers guide their students in making career decisions. Six factors that must be considered include:

1. All individuals are unique and different. They have different abilities, needs, values, and interests. These factors may contribute to the occupations and life tasks that an individual chooses to pursue.
2. Individuals are influenced by their home, school, and community. They may play an important part in the career choices of students.
3. Teachers need to understand that career development is a continuous and life-long process. Career decisions are made when individuals are ready (vocationally mature) to make them.
4. All theories have limitations, but may be used as a guide to enhance the development or awareness of the world of work.
5. Teachers must be able to coordinate classroom learning with the world of work. They may incorporate a career program within their curriculum.
6. Students must be the ones to make the final choice about selecting an occupation. Students should not be forced to make any career decision before they are ready. There is no fixed time at which individuals must decide on a particular occupation.

If additional information about these or other career development theories is desired, the reader is directed to the bibliography and list of references located at the end of the chapter.

DEVELOPING A CAREER EDUCATION PROGRAM

Teachers must create an environment that is nonthreatening, nonjudgmental, and open to all ideas concerning careers. In addition, teachers may decide to incorporate some of the career developmental concepts into the curriculum. A career education program does not have to be a separate unit, but may combine career concepts with the subjects already taught in the school.

School subjects may easily be used as the foundation for teaching about careers. For example, mathematics teachers may explain how engineers, architects, and cashiers utilize mathematical concepts. Science teachers may illustrate how chemists, physicians, and waste water treatment operators use scientific concepts in helping people. English and social studies teachers may incorporate any of the occupations in teaching their subjects. For example, a research paper may be assigned in which students can explore their career aspirations, interests, abilities, and feelings of self, and indicate how these concepts might influence their occupational choice.

In developing a career education program, teachers need to consider the following: (1) writing objectives, (2) selecting appropriate activities, and (3) evaluating the program.

Writing Objectives

Because teachers have received training in their methods courses on writing objectives, this section will focus specifically on writing career objectives. Tennyson et al. (1980) suggested that teachers interested in incorporating career objectives into their curriculum should consider the following three points:

1. To provide experiences which will enable students to gain a fuller awareness growing out of the particular subject and how the subject-matter is used by workers in different occupations.
2. To contribute to the student's testing of reality by showing the relationship between requirements of these occupations and education or training needed to meet them.
3. To develop attitudes of respect for an appreciation of social usefulness of all types of work to which the subject may lead. (p. 11)

An example of a career objective for each grade level follows:

Elementary School Level. Students will be able to list occupations that are important to the operation of their school. For each occupation, students will be able to describe the training (i.e., subjects) that are needed to enter an occupation.

Middle School Level. Students will be able to list at least five occupations that are important to the community. For each occupation, students will be able to describe the training required to enter the occupation.

High School Level. Students will select an occupation that is of particular interest to them. For each occupation selected, students will research training required to enter the job. Students will pair off and role-play an interview for the selected occupation.

Before proceeding to the section on selecting activities, teachers should note that they may obtain useful information on developing a career education program from their State Occupational Information Coordinating Committee (SOICC). This agency publishes resource guides that contain teaching objectives, activities, and evaluation instruments on careers. In addition, SOICCs may conduct career workshops for your school district.

Once objectives have been written, teachers must select activities that may be used to satisfy the objectives.

Selecting Activities

Before selecting career activities, teachers need to be aware of the developmental stages of their students. It is important that the activities be informative as well as interesting. This section will describe some activities that have proven successful.

Elementary school students may become aware of a variety of occupations by having speakers come to class. For example, teachers may invite school employees to class to describe the training needed to do their job. The school principal, custodian, cafeteria worker, and counselor are usually willing to help. In addition, teachers may invite people from the community to visit the school and describe their occupations. For example, a teacher may invite a policeman, a fireman, a telephone worker, a utility employee, or a waitress to the class.

An interesting career guidance activity used with sixth-grade students was described by Splete (1981). In this activity, a teacher contacted the manager of a shopping mall and obtained permission to visit a store for two and a half hours. To guide the students' observation, the teacher prepared a questionnaire. Students learned how to figure sales tax and change, how to price items, and how to take inventory, and they learned about salesmanship and public relations. The activity permitted students to utilize mathematical concepts learned in school.

In another activity, Otto and Sharpe (1979) used seventh-grade students to examine the effects of a career exploration program on self–esteem, achievement motivation, and occupational knowledge. The students in the experimental group were given hands-on work experiences and group guidance activities supplemented by role-playing in the classroom. Three instruments were used: Self–Esteem Inventory, Programs of Educational and Career Exploration Knowledge Test, and a test of achievement motivation devised by Otto and Sharpe. Based on the results, the experimental group was significantly different from the control group, suggesting that, given an outstanding teacher and a well-designed, well-executed career exploration program, dramatic gains can be made in both the cognitive and affective domains.

In addition to activities involving resource people, discussions, field trips, and role-play, teachers may contact their SOICC agency, teacher centers, counselor, or school library to obtain career guides, games, films, and filmstrips on careers. Teachers also may wish to construct bulletin boards, develop a hobby center, and read stories about careers to their students.

Chapter 11 includes additional resources on career information that may be helpful to teachers interested in developing career activities.

Evaluating Career Education Programs

Once a career education program is developed and tested on a student population, it must be evaluated. Evaluation is used to determine whether the goals and objectives of the program were achieved.

In evaluating career education programs or objectives, tests are not necessary. Teachers may develop surveys, questionnaires, or rating scales. Evaluations do not have to be formal instruments. For example, teachers may ask students to tell them what they liked or learned from the activity. Regardless of the form used, teachers must use evaluations.

Activity

For your particular grade level, group, or subject, develop a career education program using the concepts developed in this section. For each objective, describe the activities and explain how you will evaluate the program.

BIBLIOGRAPHY

Brown, D., & Brooks, L. (1991). *Career counseling techniques.* Needham Heights, MA: Allyn & Bacon.

Crites, J. O. (1981). *Career counseling: Models, methods and materials.* New York: McGraw-Hill.

Ginzberg, E. (1972). Toward a theory of occupational choice: A restatement. *Vocational Guidance Quarterly, 20,* 169–176.

Herr, E. L., & Cramer, S. H. (1979). *Career guidance and counseling through the life span: A systematic approach..* Boston: Little, Brown.

Hoppock, R. F. (1976). *Occupational information* (4th ed.). New York: McGraw-Hill.

Isaacson, L. E. (1986). *Career information in counseling and teaching* (4th ed.). Needham Heights, MA: Allyn & Bacon.

Krumboltz, J. D. (1975). A social learning theory of career decision making. In Mitchell, A. M., Jones, G. B., & Krumboltz, J. D. (eds.), *A social learning theory of career decision making.* Palo Alto, CA: American Institute for Research.

McDaniels, C., & Gysbers, N. C. (1992). *Counseling for career development: Theories, resources, and practices.* San Francisco,   CA: Jossey–Bass.

Osipow, S. H. (1983). *Theories of career development* (3rd ed.). Englewood Cliffs, NJ: Prentice-Hall.

Roe, A. (1956). *The psychology of occupations.* New York: Wiley.

REFERENCES

Buehler, C. (1933). *The human life course as a psychological subject.* Leipzig: Hirzel.

Dickenson, G. L., & Parmerlee, J. R. (1980). The occupational family tree: A career counseling technique. *The School Counselor, 28*(2), 99–104.

Herr, E. L., & Cramer, S. H. (1979). *Career guidance through the life span: A systematic approach.* Boston: Little, Brown.

Ginzberg, E., Ginzberg, S. W., Axelrad, S., & Herma, J. L. (1951). *Occupation-

al choice: An approach to a general theory. New York: Columbia University Press.

Holland, J. L. (1973). *Making vocational choices: A theory of careers*. Englewood Cliffs, NJ: Prentice-Hall.

Holland, J. L. (1990). *The occupations finder*. Odessa, FL: Psychological Assessment Resources.

Osipow, S. H. (1983). *Theories of career development* (3rd ed.). Englewood Cliffs, NJ: Prentice-Hall.

Otto, F. L., & Sharpe, D. L. (1979). The effects of career exploration on self-esteem, achievement motivation, and occupational knowledge. *The Vocational Guidance Quarterly, 28*(1), 63-70.

Parkinson, T., Bradley, R., & Lawson, G. (1979). Career counseling revisited. *The Vocational Guidance Quarterly, 28*(2), 121–128.

Parsons, F. (1909). *Choosing a vocation*. Boston: Houghton Mifflin.

Roe, A. (1956). *The psychology of occupations*. New York: Wiley.

Roe, A., & Seigelman, M. (1964). *The origin of interests*. The APGA Inquiry series, No. 1. Washington, DC: American Personnel and Guidance Association.

Splete, H. H. (1981). Career guidance in the elementary school. *Elementary School Guidance and Counseling, 16*(1), 47–50.

Super, D. E. (1957). *The psychology of careers*. New York: Harper & Brothers.

Super, D. E., & Bachrach, P. B. (1957). *Scientific careers and vocational development theory*. New York: Teacher College Press.

Tennyson, W. W., Hansen, L. S., Klaurens, M. K., & Antholtz, M. B. (1980). *Career development education: A program approach for teachers and counselors*. A Minnesota Department of Education Publication and reprinted by the NVGA.

Chapter **11**

OCCUPATIONAL, CAREER, AND EDUCATIONAL INFORMATION

This chapter was written to enable teachers to find answers to occupational, career, and education questions students may ask. It introduces resources that may be used to obtain occupational, career, and educational information. Using these resources, teachers will be able to answer questions such as: "What training is required to become an electrician?" "Which colleges in the south have reputable biochemistry programs?" or "Where can I find information about becoming a lawyer?"

Section one describes the *Dictionary of Occupational Titles* (DOT), the *Occupational Outlook Handbook* (OOH), the *Encyclopedia of Careers and Vocational Guidance,* the *Guide for Occupational Exploration* (GOE), and the *Improved Career Decision Making in a Changing World.* Section two contains a description of preparation and training opportunities available to students in the school and community, and discusses on-the-job opportunities such as distributive education, cooperative training, and work experience. This section also includes information that teachers may use to help their students seek employment. In addition, teachers are provided with suggestions for assisting their students in preparing for the world of work.

Many students who graduate from high school attend educational institutions to prepare for the world of work. Students may need information on community colleges, two- and four-year colleges, and vocational and trade schools. It is important that teachers have some familiarity with the sources of such information. Examples of publications that contain information on colleges, universities, and trade schools are therefore described in the third section. Section four contains information on using the computer to obtain career information. Several computer programs dealing with careers are currently available. An example of a career system is described.

At the conclusion of each section, a number of activities are provided. The purpose of these activities is to give teachers and students interested in careers information an opportunity to gain experience in the use of the resources described.

CAREER INFORMATION RESOURCES

Dictionary of Occupational Titles (DOT)

The DOT may be purchased from the Superintendent of Documents, U.S. Government Printing Office, Washington, DC 20402. It was prepared by the U.S. Department of Labor's Employment and Training Administration. The DOT contains over 20,000 occupational definitions divided into seven parts: (1) Occupational Code Number; (2) Occupational Title; (3) Industry Designation; (4) Alternate Titles (if any); (5) Body of the Definition with lead statement, task element statement, and "may" items; (6) Undefined Related Titles (if any); and (7) Definition Trailer.

The occupational code is a nine-digit number, for example, 020.067-014 (mathematician). Each set of three digits has a specific purpose or meaning. The first set of digits identifies an occupational group. The first digit identifies the primary group. The nine primary groups are as follows:

0/1 Professional/Technical, and Managerial Occupations
2   Clerical and Sales Occupations
3   Service Occupations
4   Agricultural, Fishery, Forestry, and Related Occupations
5   Processing Occupations
6   Machine Trades Occupations
7   Bench Work Occupations
8   Structural Work Occupations
9   Miscellaneous Occupations

The second digit in the first set refers to a division within the group. The divisions within the 0/1 (Professional, Technical, and Managerial) group are:

00/01 Architecture, Engineering, and Surveying
02   Mathematics and Physical Sciences
03   Computer Related
04   Life Sciences
05   Social Sciences
07   Medicine and Health
09   Education
10   Museum, Library, and Archival Science
11   Law and Jurisprudence
12   Religion and Theology
13   Writing
14   Art
15   Entertainment and Recreation
16   Administrative Specializations
18   Managers and Officials
19   Miscellaneous Professional, Technical, and Managerial

The third digit defines the occupational group within the division. The occupational groups within the mathematics and physical sciences group are as follows:

020 Mathematics
021 Astronomy
022 Chemistry
023 Physics
024 Geology
025 Meteorology
029 Miscellaneous within this group

The middle three digits (digits four, five, and six) describe the worker functions performed in a given occupation. They refer to the degree to which the job relates to data, people, and things. The worker function codes are as follows:

Data (4th digit)	*People (5th digit)*	*Things (6th digit)*
0 Synthesizing	0 Mentoring	0 Setting up
1 Coordinating	1 Negotiating	1 Precision Working
2 Analyzing	2 Instructing	2 Operating-Controlling
3 Compiling	3 Supervising	3 Driving-Operating

Data (4th digit)	People (5th digit)	Things (6th digit)
4 Computing	4 Diverting	4 Manipulating
5 Copying	5 Persuading	5 Tending
6 Comparing	6 Speaking-Signaling	6 Feeding
	7 Serving	
	8 Taking Instruction	
	Helping	

The smaller the number in the middle three digits, the more complicated the tasks. Higher numbers represent tasks that are easier to perform.

The last three digits of the nine-digit code are used to differentiate a particular occupation from all others. If the first six digits of the code for a particular occupation are applicable only to that occupation, the final three digits are 010. If, however, there are three other occupations, for example, with the same first six digits, the last three digits for these occupations would be 014, 018, and 022, and so on, adding 4 to each successive occupation.

Let us analyze the nine digit DOT code for mathematician: 020.067-014.

First, find the first digit of the DOT code. The first digit, 0, denotes professional, technical, and managerial occupations. Next, examine the two-digit occupational division. In our example, this number is 02 and refers to occupations in mathematics and the physical sciences. Next, consider the occupational group, 020. This three-digit code refers to occupations in mathematics and includes occupations dealing with the development of methodology in mathematics, statistics, and so on.

The middle three digits of the code for mathematician are 067, corresponding to data, people, and things. The 0 in the data section refers to synthesizing data; the 6 in the people section refers to speaking-signaling; and the 7 in the things section refers to handling. Therefore, in this example, 067 means that an individual working in this occupation would be required to synthesize data, a highly complex task; speak with people; and handle things.

Finally, the last three digits in the example, 014, mean that there are more two occupations with the 020.067 code.

The DOT is a valuable resource for teachers seeking career information for their students. Teachers will find the DOT to be a handy reference and an excellent starting point for obtaining standardized occupational information.

Occupational Outlook Handbook (OOH)

A copy of the OOH may be purchased from the Superintendent of Documents, U.S. Government Printing Office, Washington, DC 20402. Like the DOT, the OOH was prepared by the U.S. Department of Labor and the Bureau of Labor Statistics. New editions of the OOH are published every two years. Sections on "How to Get the Most from the Handbook," "Where to Go for More Information," and "Tomorrow's Jobs" contain valuable information for those interested in exploring career options. In addition, all occupations described in the OOH are grouped into clusters. The clusters include industrial production, office, service, education, sales, construction, transportation, scientific and technical, mechanics and repairers, health, social science, and performing arts, design, and communication.

The *Occupational Outlook Handbook* may be used in conjunction with the *Dictionary of Occupational Titles*. For example, individuals may cross-reference DOT codes to the OOH. The OOH provides information on the projected growth of occupations. Information concerning the nature of the work, working conditions, training requirements, earnings, advancement opportunities, and sources of additional information are also included.

The OOH is easy to use. For example, suppose an individual is interested in finding information about being a pharmacist. An individual may locate pharmacist in the Alphabetical Index to Occupations and Industries or refer to the comprehensive section on occupations. The individual will find the following: the DOT number; a description of the nature of the work and working conditions; potential places of employment; training, advancement, and other qualifications; employment outlook; earnings and related occupations; and additional sources of information.

Occupational Outlook Quarterly (OOQ)

This book is published by the Superintendent of Documents, U.S. Government Printing Office, Washington, DC 20402. Like the OOH, the OOQ was prepared by the U.S. Department of Labor and Statistics. This quarterly updates occupational information contained in the previous edition of the OOH. It also reviews new career techniques and aids.

Encyclopedia of Careers and Vocational Guidance

The eighth edition is the most recent of this set of books published by J. G. Ferguson Publishing Company, Chicago, IL 60601 (W. E. Hopke, Editor-in-

Chief). It is a source of information that has proven valuable to those who need to assist individuals in choosing careers. The encyclopedia contains three volumes.

Volume I, *Reviewing Career Fields,* includes articles on timely career topics, such as "How to Understand Yourself—How to Discover and Evaluate Your Interests, Aptitudes, and Abilities"; "How to Use the Results of Guidance and Personality Tests"; "Where to Go for Information about Schools, Financial Assistance"; "How to Find a Job"; and "Changes in the World of Work". Also included in volume I are articles dealing with opportunities in major areas of work.

Volume II, *Selecting a Career,* contains articles on specific careers. The articles are divided among the following areas: professional, administrative, managerial, and technical occupations; clerical occupations; sales occupations; service occupations, agricultural, forestry, and conservation occupations; processing occupations; machine trade occupations; bench work occupations; structural work occupations; and miscellaneous occupations.

Volume III, *Selecting a Technician's Career,* contains information on technical fields. The occupations are grouped according to the major fields in which technicians work, for example, engineering, science, agriculture, conservation, broadcasting, medical, health, and so on.

For each occupation described in the *Encyclopedia of Careers and Vocational Guidance,* the following information is provided: definition, including the DOT code; brief history of the occupation; nature of the work; requirements needed to perform the occupation; methods of entering the occupation; advancement opportunities; employment outlook; earnings and conditions of the work; social and psychological factors; and sources of additional information. In addition, for most of the occupations covered, a cross-reference of additional articles related to the occupations is provided.

Guide for Occupational Exploration (GOE)

The GOE is issued by the Superintendent of Documents, U.S. Government Printing Office, Washington, DC 20402. It was prepared by the Employment and Training Administration of the Department of Labor and Statistics. It is designed to assist individuals looking for work that is congruent with their interests, skills, values, and abilities.

The GOE is organized into 12 interest areas, 66 work groups, and 348 subgroups. Each work group is described by providing answers to the following questions: "What kind of work would you do?"; "What skills and abilities do you need for this kind of work?"; "How do you know if you would like or could learn to do this kind of work?"; "How can you prepare for and enter this kind of work?"; and "What else should you consider about these jobs?" A list of DOT codes is provided for occupations classified under each of the work groups. Suggestions for using the GOE are included in the preface.

Military Career Guide

The *Military Career Guide* is available from the U.S. Military Entrance Processing Command, Chicago, IL. The guide was prepared by the Department of Defense. It contains descriptions of military occupations. Individuals who have taken the Armed Services Vocational Aptitude Battery (ASVAB) may, with the assistance of the school counselor or military representative, determine the military occupations for which they qualify. In addition, the *Military Career Guide* is cross-referenced to the DOT. Using the DOT, individuals may find related civilian occupations.

The *Military Career Guide* contains the following information: a description of each occupation, its physical demands, helpful attributes, its work environment, training provided, civilian counterparts, and opportunities.

Improved Career Decision Making in a Changing World (ICDM)

This volume, edited by Judith M. Ettinger, is available from Garrett Park Press, Garrett Park, Maryland. The ICDM is designed to help individuals use labor market information in locating career opportunities.

The book is divided into ten modules. Examples of some modules include "Theories of Career Development," "Developing An Awareness of Multicultural Issues," and "Specific Needs of Children At-Risk." Thirty-five activities are included. In addition, 16 appendixes are included which contain information on career software review guidelines, SOICC offices, NOICC staff, and sources of state and local job outlooks.

In addition to the resources just described for exploring career opportunities, teachers may wish to examine career systems such as *Career Job: A Career Exploration Program*, published by Social Studies School Service; *Occupational Library,* published by Chronicle Guidance Publications; or the *Career Information Kit,* published by Science Research Associates.

Activities

1   *Using the Dictionary of Occupational Titles*
    a   *Find the nine-digit occupational code for plumber, teacher, roller skater, and fire warden.*
    b   *For each occupation in (a), what are the alternate titles (if any)?*
    c   *For each occupation in (a), summarize the occupational definition.*
    d   *Find the occupations for the following nine-digit codes: 869.684 026, 074.381-010, 131.087.018, 629.381-014, and 549.132-034.*

2   *Using the Occupational Outlook Handbook, answer the following:*
    a   *What does a biomedical engineer do?*
    b   *Describe the working conditions of painters and paperhangers.*
    c   *What is the employment outlook for mechanical engineers?*
    d   *Where do geophysicists work?*
    e   *What is the training for a watch repairer?*
    f   *What are the average hourly earnings of a geographer?*
    g   *List three related occupations for landscape architect.*

3   *Using the Encyclopedia of Careers and Vocational Guidance, answer the following:*
    a   *What are three machine trades occupations?*
    b   *What is the possibility of employment in the medical and health services profession?*
    c   *If I am interested in the health services profession, where can I apply for financial assistance?*
    d   *What special requirements are needed to become a beauty operator?*
    e   *What does a political scientist do?*
    f   *What is the employment outlook for shipping and receiving clerks?*
    h   *What social and psychological characteristics must bellhops possess?*

4   *Using the Guide for Occupational Exploration (GOE), answer the following:*
    a   *What is the five-step process for using the GOE?*
    b   *Under what interest area would you find teacher?*
    c   *What kind of work would you do as a teacher?*
    d   *What skills and abilities do you need for this kind of work?*
    e   *What else should you consider about careers in teaching?*

5   *Using the Military Career Guide, select a military occupation that may interest you. For the occupation selected, respond to the following:*
    a   *What are the physical demands of the occupation?*
    b   *Describe the work environment.*
    c   *What training is provided?*
    d   *What are some related civilian occupations for your selected military occupation?*

VOCATIONAL TRAINING
AND EMPLOYMENT OPPORTUNITIES

Vocational Courses and Programs

Middle, junior high, and senior high schools may offer vocational courses. In addition, community colleges may have vocational and cooperative education programs. A description of some of these programs follow.

Agricultural Education.   Students interested in entering agricultural occupations such as horticulture, food processing, livestock; and feed, seed, and fertilizer sales may enroll in agriculture-related courses. High school students enrolled in agricultural courses may obtain practical experience through outside employment. These students usually take their classes in the morning and work in the job setting during the afternoon.

Business Education.   In middle and junior high schools, students may take courses in typing and office skills. While in high school, some students may elect to take additional courses in typing, business mathematics, shorthand, accounting, and data processing to help them prepare for careers in business. Some community college students may wish to develop these skills further by majoring in business. Students majoring in business or enrolled in business courses may obtain employment experience through the cooperative efforts of the school or college and employers.

Home Economics.   In some middle and junior high schools, students may be required to take home economics courses such as sewing and cooking. High school and college students interested in furthering their skills may take classes in food and nutrition, family life, clothing, and textiles.

Industrial Arts.   Industrial arts classes may help students in middle, junior high, and senior high schools discover and explore career opportunities in industry, and to determine whether they have the interests and abilities needed to succeed in this area. Some industrial arts classes are metal working, wood working, electricity, electronics, and graphic arts. These courses are usually open to all interested students in middle, junior high, and senior high schools.

Trade and Industrial Education.   Like industrial arts, the major purpose of trade and industrial education is to develop the skills needed and to prepare students for employment. Some of the classes offered in trade and industrial education include auto mechanics, carpentry, drafting, graphics, and welding.

Distributive Education.   The distributive education program is designed for high school students interested in entering the buying and selling occupations. Distributive education students may enroll in advertising, merchandising, marketing, and salesmanship courses while taking basic courses in mathematics and English. Typically, students enrolled in distributive education spend the morning in the classroom and the afternoon on the job. One may find distributive education students working in department stores, hotels, restaurants, and service stations. When distributive education students graduate from high school, they may enter the job market or continue in a distributive education program while in college.

Cooperative Education.   Cooperative education programs are available to middle school, junior and senior high, and college students enrolled in most of the programs discussed previously. The purpose of cooperative education programs is to enable students to learn skills necessary to succeed in business and industry. Cooperative education programs are carefully planned and coordinated by the school and the cooperating business or industry.

Depending on the school and the cooperative business or industry, students enrolled in cooperative education programs may select one of two alternatives. The first alternative may require students to work full-time for a specific period (six months)and attend school full-time for an equal amount of time. A second alternative may require students to work part-time while attending school on either a full-time or part-time basis. The students in the second plan usually work during nonschool hours.

Cooperative training programs benefit both students and employers. Because the students are trained by the company, employers may hire these students upon graduation. This practice aids the business or industry by reducing the training time needed to enter the occupation. In addition, it saves the company money. Students also benefit because they are able to earn money while in school and secure immediate employment upon receiving their diplomas.

Locating Employment for Students

This section provides suggestions for teachers interested in helping students find employment. The key to this effort is, "Know your community." Teachers need to become familiar with the businesses and industries in their community that employ the majority of the community's people. One resource is the yellow pages of the telephone book, which teachers may use to locate the names, addresses, and telephone numbers of the leading businesses and industries. Teachers may contact employers and invite them to speak to students about seeking employment with their company. In addition, teachers may wish to arrange tours of the business or industry.

Another source of employment information is the local state employment service, which may be found in the telephone book. It is a no-fee agency whose major purpose is to find jobs for people.

Teachers may invite employment interviewers or counselors to school to have them describe the many services offered by employment agencies. Students interested in receiving more help may schedule appointments with the representative for further employment assistance. At the agency, employment interviewers will help individuals determine the type of position sought. Employment interviewers may refer individuals to employment counselors who may administer the General Aptitude Test Battery (GATB).

To determine whether a specific occupation is available, employment interviewers check the job bank, which contains a number of positions currently open, usually printed on microfiche. The employment interviewer checks the various positions available to determine if any match the interests and abilities of the client. If a position is found, the employment interviewer contacts the employer and arranges an interview for the client.

Another method that teachers may use is to check the classified ads found in local newspapers. Classified ads are usually arranged according to major categories such as professional, sales, clerical, trades, and miscellaneous. Teachers may bring classified ads to class to assist students who are seeking employment.

Teachers may contact city, county, state, and federal personnel offices to obtain information about job vacancies. The local Chamber of Commerce also may provide teachers with information about occupational opportunities available in the community.

Activities

1. *Visit a high school and prepare a report about the vocational programs offered.*
2. *Visit a local State Employment Service and ask the employment counselor or interviewer to show you the job bank. What kinds of positions are available? What other services do they provide?*
3. *Arrange a field trip to a business or industry. What career opportunities are available?*

4. *Interview an individual in an occupation of interest to you. What are the requirements to enter the occupation? What are some advantages and disadvantages of the occupation?*

5. *Arrange to take a vocational aptitude and/or interest inventory. What do your results mean to you?*

COLLEGE AND UNIVERSITY INFORMATION

Students often have questions concerning program offerings at community colleges, colleges and universities, or vocational trade schools. For example, questions like "Does the University of Florida have a work-study program?" "Is there a college that offers courses in the circus?" or "Does the University of North Carolina have a School of Optometry?" are not uncommon.

Although no one would expect teachers to know the answers to all of the above questions, teachers should know where they might find the answers. The purpose of this section is to describe some of the resources that may be used to locate information on two-year colleges, four-year colleges and universities, and vocational and trade schools.

Primary Sources of Information

One of the best sources of information about the various schools are the schools themselves. High school counselors may have copies of current bulletins and catalogs of the colleges and vocational schools most frequently requested by their students. In addition, representatives from colleges, universities, and vocational trade schools may be invited to speak to students interested in attending their schools. For out-of-state schools, teachers may need to provide students with the school's address so they can send for information.

Schools may wish to purchase a commercially prepared college catalogue service. One such service is the *National College Catalog Service* (NCCS), Time Share Corporation, Box 974, Hanover, NH 03755. This service consists of college catalogs on microfiche. A school may purchase either a complete plan, which contains four- and two-year colleges; a plan with all four-year colleges and universities; or a plan with all two-year colleges. For each plan, a subscription service is available which will keep the plan current by providing microfiche of new catalogs every three months.

Schools may also order four-year and two-year college and university catalogs by state. A subscription service also is available for this plan.

Secondary Sources of Information

Many secondary sources of information on two-year colleges, four-year colleges and universities, and vocational and trade schools are available. Descriptions of some of these follow.

Barron's Guide to the Two-Year Colleges, Vol. I., Barron's Educational Series, Inc., 250 Wireless Blvd., Hauppauge, NY 11788. Volume I of Barron's Guide to the Two-Year Colleges is organized into three major sections. Section one lists and describes the two-year commuter colleges alphabetically by state. Sections two and three describe two-year residential colleges and four-year colleges that have two-year programs.

Each section includes the address and telephone number of the college with information about size, accreditation, type of admission, tuition and fees, degrees and programs offered, student-faculty ratio, and whether the school is on the quarter or semester system.

Volume II will be described in the section on trade and technical schools.

Lovejoy's College Guide, Clarence E. Lovejoy, Simon and Schuster, 1230 Avenue of the America's, New York, NY 10020. This book is divided into three major sections. Section one contains information about expenses, financial aid, grants, and admissions. Also included in this section are procedures for finding a college that is suitable to individual needs.

Section two contains an alphabetical index of professional and special programs. For example, students interested in majoring in music or art will find the information in this section helpful. Information concerning the accreditation status of the college or university is also included.

Section three contains an alphabetical school listing that includes a brief description of each school, its tuition and fees, and degrees offered.

Peterson's Annual Guide to Undergraduate Study, Joan Hunter, Editor, P.O. Box 2123, Princeton, NJ 08540. This book is divided into three major sections followed by two indexes. Section one contains a directory of basic college data with test score ranges. A directory of majors, college profiles, and how to apply for admission is also included. An in-depth description of the colleges and universities with programs offered is included in section two. Section three contains information about any specialized programs available (i.e., ROTC). Of the indexes, one is used for locating majors, and the other for locating information about a specific college or university.

The College Handbook, Maureen Matheson, Editor, The College Board, 888 Seventh Avenue, New York, NY 10019. *The College Handbook* is published every two years. It provides information about the number of undergraduates at each school, whether the school is on the semester or quarter system, admission requirements, tuition and financial aid, and where to write for additional information.

Barron's Profiles of American Colleges, Barron's Educational Series, Inc., 250 Wireless Blvd., Hauppauge, NY 11788. This two-volume work is similar in organization to *Barron's Guide to the Two-Year Colleges.* A major feature of this book is that, in addition to the regular colleges, it includes specialized colleges, including professional schools of art, music, theater arts, circus, etc. Admission to these schools is based on talent and special interest. Also included are colleges with religious affiliation, colleges offering ROTC, and external degree programs.

Colleges are listed under one of the following categories: most competitive, least competitive, and noncompetitive. The book also describes student life, sports, programs of study, admissions policies, and facilities available for the handicapped.

College Admissions Data Service, Orchard House, Inc., Balls Hill Road, Concord, MA 01742. The *College Admissions Data Service* is a two-volume work. Volume I contains information about colleges in the Northeast, the mid-Atlantic states, and the South. The mid-western and western colleges are contained in Volume II.

For each school listed, the following information is provided: (1) admissions requirements—the number of academic units needed, whether or not special admissions test scores (SAT or ACT) are required, application fee, and whether advanced placement scores will be accepted; (2) financial information—whether aid, loans, and employment are available; (3) faculty information—faculty-student ratio and the number of faculty holding bachelor's, master's, and doctor's degree; (4) other information—a description of extra-curricular activities, any special regulations, and whether the school is on the semester or quarter system.

The College Blue Book, Macmillan Information, A Division of Simon & Schuster, 866 Third Avenue, New York, NY 10022. *The College Blue Book* is a five-volume resource containing information about more than 3,000 colleges and universities in the United States and Canada.

Volume I. Narrative Descriptions. Volume I contains information about procedures for filing admission applications, description of the campus, entrance requirements, tuition and fees, and a description of the school's environment.

Volume II. Tabular Data. In Volume II, colleges are listed alphabetically by state or province. Also included is information about tuition, enrollment, faculty, accreditation, and the name of the registrar.

Volume III. Degrees Offered by College and Subject. Volume III is divided into two major parts. Part I includes a list of subject areas for which degrees are offered. Part II provides a listing of specific subject areas offered and degrees granted by one or more institutions of higher education.

Volume IV. Scholarships, Fellowships, Grants, and Loans. Volume IV includes information on the sources and availability of financial assistance and loans. For each loan, information about the amount of the loan, loan requirements, methods of distribution, deadlines, and application procedures are included. Volume IV also includes the names and addresses of sponsoring organizations; the academic level of the awards (colleges, prep and graduate schools); and a subject area index.

Volume V. Occupational Education. Volume V will be described under trade and technical schools.

VOCATIONAL AND TECHNICAL TRADE SCHOOLS INFORMATION

American Trade Schools Directory, Croner Publications Inc., 211-03 Jamaica Avenue, Queens Village, NY 11423. This directory contains approximately 9,000 public and private trade, industrial, and vocational schools throughout the United States and is revised annually. It is a loose-leaf book divided into two major parts. Part I lists the various subject areas in alphabetical order. Each subject area is listed by state and cross-referenced to Part II. Part II lists the trade schools alphabetically by state and town.

The *American Trade Schools Directory* is very easy to use. For example, suppose a student is moving to Wichita, Kansas, and wants to become a bartender. Is there a bartender school in Wichita? Using the directory, you look up bartender school find one listed under Kansas with a number, 55. Next, using Part II, you look up Kansas and 55. You find the following listing:

Kansas School of Bartending
2138 North Market Street
Wichita, Kansas 76214

This directory also includes code letters located next to the school's number. These codes indicate whether the school is public or private, its accreditation, and whether the school is for men or women or both.

Barron's Guide to the Two-Year Colleges, Vol. II, Barron's Educational Series, Inc., 250 Wireless Blvd., Hauppauge, NY 11788. Volume II contains an occupational program selector, which lists over 1500 vocational and technical programs at two-year colleges. Descriptions are provided of programs in the following areas: agricultural and environmental management, business and commerce, media and communications, health and public services, and engineering technology.

The College Blue Book Vol. V, Occupational Education, Macmillan Information, A Division of Simon & Schuster, 866 Third Avenue, New York, NY 10022. *The College Blue Book* includes over 8,000 business, trade, and technical schools. These schools are listed in alphabetical order and classified as allied medical, art, barber, business, correspondence, cosmetology, flight and ground, nursing, trade and technical, or two-year college. In addition, information about enrollment, tuition, contact persons, entrance requirements, description of the programs, and financial aid is included.

Activities

Using the references described in this section, answer the following questions. Be sure to include the title of the reference and page number where you found the answer.

1. *Does the University of Hawaii offer a master's degree in electrical engineering?*
2. *Does Lehigh University have a work-study program?*
3. *Find at least three two-year commuter colleges in New York City.*
4. *What is rolling admissions? Find at least one college in South Carolina that has rolling admissions.*
5. *Which university in Florida offers courses in the circus?*
6. *Does the university of Colorado have a philosophy department?*
7. *Are there any specialized accredited colleges in Missouri?*
8. *Is there a Baptist College in North Carolina that offers a major in history?*

9. *Is there a two-year college for women in Texas?*
10. *Is there a College of Optometry in Pennsylvania?*
11. *Is there a secretarial school in Omaha, Nebraska?*
12. *Can one obtain a master's degree in civil engineering at Rutgers University?*
13. *Is there an accredited barber college in Salt Lake City, Utah?*
14. *Name at least one art school in Georgia.*
15. *Where can one study cosmetology in Des Moines, Iowa?*

COMPUTER INFORMATION SYSTEMS

We are living in the computer age. Many elementary, middle, junior high, and senior high schools have purchased computers for teachers and students. Many occupational, career, and education software programs are available from commercial publishers. One does not need to be a computer expert to use these programs. Students may learn subjects and obtain college and career information using computer programs. Three examples of career and college software programs are the *Career Scan IV, College Scan IV,* and *SIGI Plus.*

The *Career Scan IV* and *College Scan IV* are published by the National Educational Software Services, Vernon, Wisconsin. Searches in both programs may take about 15 minutes. *Career Scan IV* includes over 700 occupations and contains nine question categories with 42 variables. The questions and variables cover lifestyles, abilities, school subjects, training or education required, interests, values, and job characteristics. In addition, each occupation is cross-referenced to the *Dictionary of Occupational Titles.*

The *College Scan IV* includes approximately 1200 colleges and universities and can search on more than 450 variables. The variables are arranged by topic and include programs of study; size, cost, location, and control; academic, environment; characteristics of the student body; institutional regulations; and athletic programs.

SIGI Plus, Educational Testing Service, Princeton, NJ 08541. *SIGI Plus* assists those seeking an occupation or career. It assesses values, interests, and skills. Once preferences are entered, *SIGI Plus* searches its library and locates careers that match the preferences. In addition, it covers major aspects of career decision making and planning using nine separate but interrelated sections. The sections include: (1) Introduction—What is SIGI Plus? (2) Self-Assessment—What do I want? and What am I good at? (3) Search—What occupations might

I like? (4) Information—What occupations might I like? (5) Skills—Can I do what's required? (6) Preparing—Can I do what's required?" (7) Coping—Can I do what's required? (8) Deciding—What's right for me? and (9) Next Steps— How do I put my plan into action?

All of the systems described above also provide the user with print-outs of the information collected. An advantage of having a computer system is that the student can use it independently. Students usually find the programs and systems easy to use. Most students enjoy interacting with the computer. The only limitation to using computer programs in school is the number of computers and programs available.

Teachers should obtain copies of the resources presented in this chapter and use them. They should also make use of the activities included at the end of each section to practice finding occupational, vocational, and educational information.

Many other excellent occupational, vocational, and educational publications are available, but due to space limitations, only a selected sample of informational resources could be included in this chapter. Some resources may or may not be suitable for your students. Likewise, it was not possible to describe all of the software programs. New software programs are constantly being written. Teachers should review the various resources and software before using them with students or purchasing them.

REFERENCES

American trade school directory. Queens Village, NY: Croner Publications.

Barron's guide to the two-year colleges (2 vols.). Woodbury, NY: Barron's Educational Series.

Barron's profiles of American colleges. Woodbury, NY: Barron's Educational Series.

Career information kit. Chicago, IL: Science Research Associates.

Career lab: A career exploration program. Culver City, CA: Social Studies School Service.

Career Scan IV. Verona, WI: National Educational Software Services.

College admissions data service. Concord, MA: Orchard House.

College blue book. (5 vols.). Riverside, NJ: MacMillan Professional Library and Services.

College Scan IV. Verona, WI: National Educational Software Services.

Dictionary of occupational titles (4th ed., 2 Vols). (1991). Washington, DC: U.S. Government Printing Office.

Ettinger, J. M. (Ed.). (1991). *Improved career decision making in a changing world.* Garrett Park, MD: Garrett Park Press.

Guide for occupational exploration. Washington, DC: U.S. Government Printing Office.

Hopke, W. E. (Ed.). (1990). *Encyclopedia of careers and vocational guidance* (8th ed.). Chicago, IL: J. G. Ferguson.

Hunter, J. (Ed.). *Peterson's annual guide to undergraduate study.* Princeton, NJ.

Lovejoy, C. E. *Lovejoy's college guide.* New York: Simon and Schuster.

Matheson, M. (Ed.). *The college handbook.* New York: The College Board.

Military career guide. Chicago, IL: U.S. Military Entrance Processing Command.

National college catalogue service. Hanover, NH: Time Share Corporation.

Occupational library. Moravia, NY: Chronicle Guidance Publications.

Occupational outlook handbook. Washington, DC: U.S. Government Printing Office.

Occupational outlook quarterly. Washington, DC: U.S. Government Printing Office.

SIGI Plus. Princeton, NJ: Educational Testing Service.

UNIT VI
OBTAINING AND USING
TEST AND NON-TEST DATA

Chapter 12

APPLYING STATISTICAL
CONCEPTS TO TEST DATA

Most teachers administer standardized tests; however, some have difficulty in interpreting the results. Although school counselors are responsible for the interpretation of standardized tests, teachers can learn to understand test interpretation as well. The foundation to interpretation of test results is understanding some basic statistical concepts. This chapter presents statistical concepts that teachers may use to describe and interpret test results.

ORGANIZING DATA

Ranking, frequency, and class intervals are three statistical concepts that may be used by teachers to organize data. The results of a science test administered to seventh grade students will be used to illustrate these concepts.

Ranking

One method for organizing test data is to rank order the data from high to low. To rank the science test results, list the scores from highest to lowest and assign the rank of 1 to the highest score, 2 to the next lower and so on until you have ranked all of the scores in the *distribution,* the arrangement of scores from high to low. For practice, use Data Set 1 to rank the scores on the science test for the seventh grade class:

Data Set 1

Student	Results	Student	Results	Student	Results
A	78	L	72	W	77
B	62	M	91	X	66
C	82	N	96	Y	60
D	84	O	83	Z	84
E	94	P	79	AA	73
F	86	Q	66	BB	84
G	84	R	65	CC	68
H	78	S	99		
I	97	T	71		
J	84	U	64		
K	66	V	98		

To rank the scores in Data Set 1, arrange the scores from the highest to the lowest. Assign the rank of 1 to the highest score, 2 to the next higher score, and so one until you have assigned the rank of 29 to the lowest rank. Table 12.1 illustrates the results of this ranking. If each student received a different score,

TABLE 12.1
Ranking of the Results from a Science Test
Administered to Seventh Grade Students
(Tied scores have not been adjusted.)

Rank	Student	Score	Rank	Student	Score
1	S	99	16	A	78
2	V	98	17	H	78
3	I	97	18	W	77
4	N	96	19	AA	73
5	E	94	20	L	72
6	M	91	21	T	71
7	F	86	22	CC	68
8	D	84	23	K	66
9	G	84	24	Q	66
10	J	84	25	X	66
11	Z	84	26	R	65
12	BB	84	27	U	64
13	O	83	28	B	62
14	C	82	29	Y	60
15	P	79			

TABLE 12.2
Assigned Ranks to Reflect Different and Same Scores

Rank	Student	Score	Rank	Student	Score
1	S	99	15	P	79
2	V	98	16.5	A	78
3	I	97	16.5	H	78
4	N	96	18	W	77
5	E	94	19	AA	73
6	M	91	20	L	72
7	F	86	21	T	71
10	D	84	22	CC	68
10	G	84	24	K	66
10	J	84	24	Q	66
10	Z	84	24	X	66
10	BB	84	26	R	65
13	O	83	27	U	64
14	C	82	28	B	62

the task would be complete. However, Table 12.1 indicates that identical scores were obtained for ranks 8 through 12, 16 and 17, and 23 through 25. Therefore, additional steps are necessary.

For example, an average rank must be assigned to each identical score.

For Ranks 8 to 12:

$$(8 + 9 + 10 + 11 + 12) = 50/5 = 10$$

For Ranks 16 and 17:

$$(16 + 17) = 33/2 = 16.5$$

For Ranks 23 to 25:

$$(23 + 14 + 15) = 72/3 = 24$$

Assign the rank of 10 to the ranks of 8, 9, 10, 11, and 12; the rank of 16.5 to the ranks of 16 and 17; and the rank of 24 to the ranks of 23, 24, and 25. These results are illustrated in Table 12.2.

Frequency

A frequency (f) is the number of times a given score occurs in a distribution. The frequency distribution for Data Set 1 is illustrated in Table 12.3.

The first step is to list the test scores from highest to lowest. List each score only once. Next, refer to Data Set 1 and determine the frequency by counting the number of times that a given score occurs. Place the total number of times the given score occurs under the heading of Frequency (f).

Although the scores are now somewhat organized, the array of numbers is still rather long and cumbersome. Another method of condensing the numbers—class intervals—is described in the following section.

TABLE 12.3
Frequency Table

Test Score (X)	Count	Frequency (f)
99	I	1
98	I	1
97	I	1
96	I	1
94	I	1
91	I	1
86	I	1
84	IIIII	5
83	I	1
82	I	1
79	I	1
78	II	2
77	I	1
73	I	1
72	I	1
71	I	1
68	I	1
66	III	3
65	I	1
64	I	1
62	I	1
60	I	1

N = 29

TABLE 12.4
Test Scores Arranged by Class Intervals

Class Interval (ci)	Frequency (f)
98–100	2
95–97	2
92–94	1
89–91	1
86–88	1
83–85	6
80–82	1
77–79	4
72–76	2
69–71	1
66–68	4
63–65	2
60–62	2

N = 29

Class Intervals

Class intervals (ci) are used to organize data into groups so that they may be easily read by teachers and others. Using Data Set 1, class intervals will be developed for the twenty-nine scores on the science test. The results are illustrated in Table 12.4.

The first step is to determine the size of the class interval. To do this, subtract the lowest score in the distribution from the highest (for example, 99 − 60 = 39). Next, divide the result obtained in step one by 15 (39 ÷ 15 = 2.6) and round the answer to the nearest odd number (3). Thus, the class will contain three numbers.

Next, the lowest class interval number must be identified. This number should be a multiple of 3. For example, the size of the class interval was 3 and is a multiple of 60; therefore, the lowest number in the class interval will be 60. See Table 12.4.

Next, the lowest class interval number must be identified. This number should be a multiple of 3 (divides evenly by 3) and include the lowest score in the distribution. For example, the size of the class interval was 3, and 3 divides evenly into 60; therefore, the lowest interval for the data will begin with the number 60. (See Table 12.4.)

MEASURES OF CENTRAL TENDENCY

Measures of central tendency—the mean, median, and mode—are used to describe a group of scores by using a single score to represent the group. The purpose of this section is to acquaint teachers with the three measures of central tendency, not to provide them with the skills necessary for computing them. However, in describing the measures of central tendency, the computing mechanisms will be utilized in order to show how the measures are derived. Because standardized test results often are reported for one or more measures of central tendency, the user needs to understand them.

Mode

The mode identifies the most frequently occurring score in the distribution. A distribution may have no mode, one mode (unimodal), two modes (bimodal), or three or more modes (multi-modal). The mode is very easy to identify. For example, determine the mode for the following data sets:

Data Set 2		Data Set 3	
Scores (X)	**Frequency (f)**	**Scores (X)**	**Frequency (f)**
92	3	92	4
90	6	90	4
88	4	88	4
85	2	85	4
81	6	81	6
78	1	78	4
74	2	74	4
N = 24		N = 30	

For Data Set 2, 90 and 81 are the modes because both scores were obtained by six students. This distribution would be described as bi-modal. For Data Set 3, 81 is the mode because it is the most frequently occurring score, and the distribution of scores is unimodal.

Median

The median is the middle score in a distribution. It divides the distribution in half and is a useful measure in understanding percentiles (median = 50th percentile). Determine the median for the following data sets:

Data Set 4		Data Set 5	
Scores (X)	**Frequency (f)**	**Scores (X)**	**Frequency (f)**
10	1	10	1
8	1	8	1
7	1	7	1
5	1	5	1
4	1	4	1
	2		
N = 5		N = 6	

For Data Set 4, the median is equal to 7 because the numeral 7 is the middle score of the distribution. For Data Set 5, the median is between the numerals 5 and 7. To find the median, average the numerals as follows: (5 + 7)/2 = 6. The median for Data Set 5 is 6.

Mean

Most teachers have calculated the mean when computing the average grade for students. The mean is equal to the arithmetic average. The formula for determining the mean is:

$$\bar{X} = \frac{\Sigma X}{N}$$

The above equation states that the mean (X) is equal to the sum of the scores (ΣX) divided by the total number of cases (N). To illustrate the use of the formula the following data sets will be used:

Data Set 6		Data Set 7	
Student A		**Student B**	
Scores (X)	**Frequency (f)**	**Scores (X)**	**Frequency (f)**
81	1	81	1
78	1	78	2
92	1	92	3
84	1	84	2
95	1	95	2
N = 5		N = 10	

To find the mean, add all the scores for each student. The sum of scores (ΣX) in Data Set 6 for Student A is 430; the sum for Student B in Data Set 7 is 871. Next, divide the sum of scores (ΣX) by the total number of scores (N) for each student. For Student A, N = 5 and for Student B, N = 10; therefore:

$$\text{Student A} \quad \text{Mean} = 430/5 = 86$$

$$\text{Student B} \quad \text{Mean} = 871/10 = 87.1$$

In the next section, on measures of variability, the measures of central tendency will be used to determine the spread or variability of scores in a distribution. Measures of variability enable one to further describe the data.

MEASURES OF VARIABILITY

Measures of variability indicate the spread of scores for a group of students. The larger the spread of scores, the more heterogeneous (different) the population. Likewise, the smaller the spread of scores, the more homogenous (same) the population. Three of the basic measures of variability are the range (R), the quartile deviation (Q), and the standard deviation (SD).

Each of the measures of central tendency has a corresponding measure of variability. For example, the mode corresponds with the range, the median with the quartile deviation, and the mean with the standard deviation. For example, when the mean is reported, the standard deviation is also reported.

Range

The range (R) is very simple to find; simply compute the difference between the highest and lowest scores. For example, suppose we wanted to determine the range for the following set of scores:

Data Set 8

A	B	C	D
94	99	94	99
90	90	90	90
88	88	88	88
74	74	84	84

$$\text{Range of A} = 94 - 74 = 20$$
$$\text{Range of B} = 99 - 74 = 25$$
$$\text{Range of C} = 94 - 84 = 10$$
$$\text{Range of D} = 99 - 84 = 15$$

Notice in the example that if the highest, lowest, or both scores change, the range also may change. Thus, the range is not a stable measure of variability.

Quartile Deviation

The quartile deviation (Q) describes the scores in the middle 50% of the population and is reported with the median. A quartile deviation is found by (1) locating the 25th percentile and the 75th percentile for the data, (2) subtracting the 25th percentile from the 75th percentile, and (3) dividing the result by 2. Note that the quartile deviation does not include the scores below the 25th percentile or above the 75th percentile. The quartile deviation is the measure of variability to use when the distribution is skewed.

For example:

Example 1: $Q3 = $ 75th percentile $= 83$
$Q2 = $ 50th percentile $= 73 = $ (median)
$Q1 = $ 25th percentile $= 63$

Quartile deviation $= (Q3 - Q1)/2 = (83 - 63)/2 = 20/2 = 10$

Example 2: $Q3 = $ 75th percentile $= 80$
$Q2 = $ 50th percentile $= 75 = $ (median)
$Q1 = $ 25th percentile $= 70$

Quartile deviation $= (Q3 - Q1)/2 = (80 - 70)/2 = 10/2 = 5$

In the first example, Q is 10 and in the second example it is 5. The smaller the Q, the closer the scores are between the 25th and the 75th percentile. The spread of scores in the second example is less than the spread of scores in the first example.

Standard Deviation

The most widely used measure of variability is the standard deviation (SD). It is usually reported with the mean and is computed using the following formula:

$$SD = \sqrt{\frac{\sum X^2}{N}}$$

Using the following data set, find the standard deviation.

Data Set 9

Student	Score	Student	Score
A	95	K	79
B	93	L	78
C	92	M	77
D	92	N	77
E	87	O	74
F	85	P	72
G	84	Q	71
H	82	R	70
I	81	S	65
J	81	T	65

N = 20

The first step is to find the mean for the twenty scores. To find the mean, total the twenty scores and divide the sum by twenty. The sum of scores for Data Set 9 is 1600; dividing by 20, the resulting mean is 80.

Next, subtract the mean from each test score to obtain the deviate score (x). The deviate score indicates how far each score differs from the mean. The results for the example can be found in the 3rd column of Table 12.5. Be careful to indicate negative numbers.

Notice that the sum of the deviate scores equals 0. We therefore need to eliminate the negative numbers. To eliminate the negative numbers, square the deviate scores. The squared deviate scores for the example are found in Column 4 of Table 12.5. Next, find the sum of the squared scores ($\Sigma x2 = 1532$).

Finally, substitute the values for the sum of the deviate scores (1532) and the number of cases (20) into the formula for the standard deviation as follows:

$$SD = \sqrt{\frac{1532}{20}}$$

TABLE 12.5
Process for Calculating the Standard Deviation

Student	Score	Test Score – Mean = Deviate Score	Squared Deviate Score
A	95	95 – 80 = 15	225
B	93	93 – 80 = 13	169
C	92	92 – 80 = 12	144
D	92	92 – 80 = 12	144
E	87	87 – 80 = 7	49
F	85	85 – 80 = 5	25
G	84	84 – 80 = 4	16
H	82	82 – 80 = 2	4
I	81	81 – 80 = 1	1
J	81	81 – 80 = 1	1
K	79	79 – 80 = –1	1
L	78	78 – 80 = –2	4
M	77	77 – 80 = –3	9
N	77	77 – 80 = –3	9
O	74	74 – 80 = –6	36
P	72	72 – 80 = –8	64
Q	71	71 – 80 = –9	81
R	70	70 – 80 = –10	100
S	65	65 – 80 = –15	225
T	65	65 – 80 = –15	225
N = 20	$\Sigma X = 1600$	$\Sigma x = 0$	$\Sigma x2 = 1532$

$$SD = \sqrt{76.6}$$

$$SD = 8.7$$

To understand the standard deviation, refer to Figure 12.1. Notice that one standard deviation above and below the mean includes approximately 68% of the population, two standard deviations above and below the mean includes approximately 95% of the population, and three standard deviations above and below the mean includes approximately 99% of the population.

Using the standard deviation of 8.7 and a mean of 80 in the above example, the following conclusions may be drawn:

1. One standard deviation above and below the mean (68% of the population) would include the following scores:

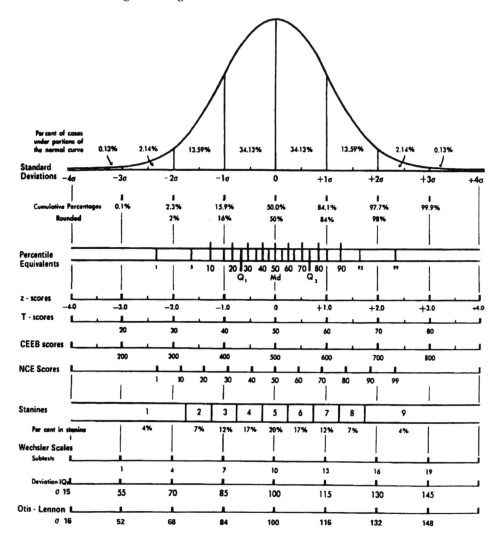

Figure 12.1. The Normal Curve, Percentiles, and Selected Standard Scores. *Note.* From *Test Service Notebook No. 148.* Copyright © 1980 by The Psychological Corporation. Reproduced by permission. All rights reserved.

1 SD – MEAN; MEAN + 1 SD

8.7 – 80; 80 + 8.7

71.3; 88.7

2. Two standard deviations above and below the mean (95% of the population) would include the following scores:

   $(2 \times SD)$ – MEAN; MEAN + $(2 \times SD)$

   17.4 – 80; 80 + 17.4

   62.6; 97.7

3. Three standard deviations above and below the mean (99% of the population) would include the following scores:

   $(3 \times SD)$ – MEAN; MEAN + $(3 \times SD)$

   26.1 – 80; 80 + 26.1

   53.9; 106.1

INTERPRETING STANDARDIZED TESTS

The school counselor or school psychologist is usually responsible for interpreting standardized test results. He or she has received specialized training in this area. However, teachers also need to understand the interpretation. The purpose of this section, therefore, is to describe some commonly used testing terms and concepts.

Standardized Tests

Standardized tests are the procedures used for administering professionally prepared instruments. Regardless of where the test is administered, the test administrator reads the standardized directions and adheres to the time limit given in the test manual. Students taking the test in Ohio, California, or any other state will be tested under the same conditions.

Norms

Standardized tests are normed. This means that the test was administered to a population of students within a given age or grade level. The results of this norming become a frame of reference by which to compare students. Norms may be reported in percentiles, grade-equivalents, stanines, or T-scores.

Raw Scores

Raw scores are the number of items answered correctly by a student. Raw scores by themselves are meaningless. On standardized tests, raw scores are usually transformed into percentiles or standard scores in order to give them meaning.

Percentiles

Percentiles are a popular method of reporting standardized test results. They describe a student's position within the established norming group. Percentiles range from a low of 1 to a high of 99. Refer to Figure 12.1 and note that percentiles 16 to 84 are found one standard deviation below and above the mean. Also note from Figure 12.1 that percentile units are not equal. The distance at the extreme ends of the normal curve are greater than at the middle of the curve.

Data Set 10 presents the results of a standardized math test for 4th grade students and will be used to illustrate the use of percentiles.

Data Set 10

Student	National Percentile
A	67
B	50
C	8

Using the information in Data Set 10, we will interpret the percentile results of students A, B, and C. The percentile score of 67 means that Student A equaled or did better than 67% of the students in the norming group, and 33% of the students in the norming group did better than Student A. For Student B, the percentile of 50 means that Student B did as well or better than 50% of the norming sample and that 50% did better than B. Likewise, for Student C, the percentile of

8 means that Student C equaled or did better than 8% of the students in the norming group and that 92% of the norming group did better than C. Remember that percentiles refer to the percent of the norming population that a student has equaled or surpassed and not to the number of items that the student answered correctly.

Grade Equivalents

Grade-equivalent scores are presented in terms of grade and month based on a 10-month school year. Grade-equivalents are often misused and misinterpreted. For example, a standardized reading test is administered in October to a third-grade student. The student obtained a grade-equivalent score of 7.5. This does not mean that the student is doing seventh grade math. It does mean that this student did above average in math.

Using information in Data Set 11, interpret the results of Students A, B, and C based on their grade-equivalent scores in math. The test was administered during the seventh month of the school year. A grade-equivalent score of 4.7 is expected.

Data Set 11

Student	Grade Equivalent
A	4.8
B	6.4
C	3.2

Student A obtained a grade-equivalent score of 4.8, an average score on the math test. Student B obtained a score of 6.4, which is considered to be above average. For Student C, the grade-equivalent score of 3.2 indicates that this student is below average in math compared to the norming group.

STANDARD SCORES

Standard scores are often reported for standardized tests. For example, the Scholastic Aptitude Test (SAT) and the Graduate Record Examination (GRE) report standard scores. Unlike percentiles, standard scores may be added, subtracted, multiplied and divided. In addition, they may be averaged. To gain a better understanding of standard scores, the reader should refer to Figure 12.1 while reading the following sections.

Z-Scores

The basic unit for all standard scores is the z-score. Z-scores are computed by using the raw score (number of correct items), the mean, and the standard deviation of the norming population. Note in Figure 12.1 that z-scores have a mean of 0 and a standard deviation of 1. The formula used to compute the z-score is as follows:

$$z = \frac{X - \bar{X}}{SD}$$

Data Set 12

Student	Raw Score
A	91
B	82
C	60

Data Set 12 illustrates three students who obtained raw scores of 91, 82, and 60 on a standardized test. The mean and standard deviation was 82 and 6 respectively for the norming group. Find the z-scores for Students A, B, and C using the formula provided:

For Student A: $z = (91 - 82)/6 = 1.5$.

For Student B: $z = (82 - 82)/6 = 0$

For Student C: $z = (60 - 82)/6 = -2.00$.

Using Figure 12.1, locate the positions for the above z-scores. For Student A, the z-score of 1.5 is a unit and a half above the mean. Likewise, for Student B, the z-score of 0 is located at the mean, while the z-score of –2.00 is two units below the mean for Student C.

When interpreting standardized test results to students or parents, it is important to note the location of a particular score using the norming group as the reference point. For example, using the z-score results and Figure 12.1 we may conclude that Student A ($z = 1.5$) did very well on the test because he or she equaled or did better than approximately 94% of the norming population. On the other hand, Student C ($z = -2$) did not do as well; student C equaled or did better than only 2% of the norming population.

Although most standardized tests use z-scores, z-scores are not reported. Z-scores would be difficult for students or parents to understand because of the zero, negative numbers, and decimal fractions scores that may result. For example, imagine reporting a z-score of 0 to parents and trying to explain that this score means that their son or daughter obtained an average score. Z-scores are therefore transformed into standard scores in order to eliminate negative numbers, decimal fractions, and the zero so that the results will be more meaningful.

Transforming Z-Scores into Standard Scores

The general formula for transforming z-scores into standard scores is

$$\text{Standard Score} = (\text{Z-Score} \times \text{Standard Deviation}) + \text{MEAN}$$

Note that the z-score was found using the actual standard deviation and mean of the tested population. In the standard deviation formula, the z-score is multiplied by a predetermined standard deviation and added to a predetermined mean. This will be explained in more detail as examples of standard scores are derived in the following sections.

GRE and SAT Scores

For GRE and SAT scores, a standard deviation of 100 and a mean of 500 are used. To illustrate GRE & SAT scores, three examples using z's of 1.5, 0, and –2.0 will be used.

$$\text{GRE \& SAT} = (Z \times 100) + 500$$

$$
\begin{aligned}
\text{For z of 1.5: \quad GRE \& SAT} &= (1.5 \times 100) + 500 \\
&= 150 + 500 \\
&= 650
\end{aligned}
$$

$$
\begin{aligned}
\text{For z of 0: \quad GRE \& SAT} &= (0 \times 100) + 500 \\
&= 0 + 500 \\
&= 500
\end{aligned}
$$

$$
\begin{aligned}
\text{For z of –2.0: \quad GRE \& SAT} &= (-2.0 \times 100) + 500 \\
&= -200 + 500 \\
&= 300
\end{aligned}
$$

T-Scores

For T-scores, a standard deviation of 10 and a mean of 50 are used. To illustrate T-scores, three examples using z's of 1.5, 0, and –2.0 will be used in the computation. Refer to Figure 12.1 after each computation and locate the position of the three T-scores on the normal curve.

$$\text{T-scores} = (Z \times 10) + 50$$

$$
\begin{aligned}
\text{For z of 1.5:}\quad \text{T-score} &= (1.5 \times 10) + 50 \\
&= (15) + 50 \\
&= 65
\end{aligned}
$$

$$
\begin{aligned}
\text{For z of 0:}\quad \text{T-score} &= (0 \times 10) + 50 \\
&= 0 + 50 \\
&= 50
\end{aligned}
$$

$$
\begin{aligned}
\text{For z of } {-2.0}\text{:}\quad \text{T-score} &= (-2.0 \times 10) + 50 \\
&= -20 + 50 \\
&= 30
\end{aligned}
$$

Deviation IQ Scores

For deviation IQ scores, a standard deviation of 15 or 16 may be used, depending on the instrument. For example, on the Stanford Binet a standard deviation of 16 is used, and 15 is used on the Wechsler Scales. The mean for both instruments is 100. To illustrate the deviation IQ, three examples using a standard deviation of 16, a mean of 100, and z-scores of 1.5, 0, and –2.0 are used. Refer to Figure 12.1 after each computation and locate the three deviation IQ scores on the normal curve.

$$\text{Deviation IQ} = (Z \times 16) + 100$$

$$
\begin{aligned}
\text{For z of 1.5: deviation IQ} &= (1.5 \times 16) + 100 \\
&= 24 + 100 \\
&= 124
\end{aligned}
$$

$$
\begin{aligned}
\text{For z of 0:}\quad \text{deviation IQ} &= (0 \times 16) + 100 \\
&= 0 + 100 \\
&= 100
\end{aligned}
$$

$$
\begin{aligned}
\text{For z of } {-2.0}\text{: deviation IQ} &= (-2.0 \times 16) + 100 \\
&= -32 + 100 \\
&= 68
\end{aligned}
$$

Stanines

For stanine scores, a standard deviation of 2 and a mean of 5 are used. Stanines are reported in whole numbers and may range from a low of 1 to a high of 9. Stanines 2 through 8 are .5 standard deviation points wide. To illustrate stanines, three examples using z's of 1.5, 0, and –2.0 will be used. Refer to Figure 12.1 after each computation and locate the three positions of the three stanines on the normal curve.

$$\text{Stanine} = (Z \times 2) + 5$$

$$
\begin{aligned}
\text{For z of 1.5:}\quad \text{stanine} &= (1.5 \times 2) + 5 \\
&= 3 + 5 \\
&= 8
\end{aligned}
$$

$$
\begin{aligned}
\text{For z of 0:}\quad \text{stanine} &= (0 \times 2) + 5 \\
&= 0 + 5 \\
&= 5
\end{aligned}
$$

$$
\begin{aligned}
\text{For z of –2.0:}\quad \text{stanine} &= (-2.0 \times 2) + 5 \\
&= -4 + 5
\end{aligned}
$$

STANDARD ERROR OF MEASUREMENT

To understand the standard error of measurement (SEmeas), one needs to have some understanding about reliability. Reliability means the consistency, dependability, stability, or trustworthiness of test results. Reliability is reported as a coefficient (r). A reliability coefficient may range from a –1.00 to +1.00. Coefficients of –1.00 and +1.00 indicate perfect reliability. Unfortunately, no test is 100% reliable. All standardized tests contain some degree of error. Therefore, in reporting test results to students or parents, the teacher should report the scores using banded scores. Banded scores are intervals built around a student's obtained score using the standard error of measurement. An explanation of this process follows.

The standard error of measurement answers the question, What are the chances that a student's obtained score would be the same if the test were administered for a second, third, or fourth time? The standard error of measurement is usually found in the test manual, or one can easily compute it using the following formula:

$$SEmeas = SD\sqrt{1 - r}$$

The above formula states that the standard error of measurement is equal to the standard deviation times the square root of 1 minus the reliability coefficient (r). Using the standard error of measurement, certain predictions can be made. For example, suppose a student obtained a score of 42 on a standardized test. The standard deviation and reliability coefficient of the test are 6 and .91 respectively. What is the standard error of measurement? How is it used?

To find the standard error of measurement, we substitute the values of the standard deviation (6) and the reliability (.91) in the formula; the resulting SEmeas for this example is 1.8.

Using the obtained score of 42 and the SEmeas of 1.8, the following predictions may be made:

1. For two out of three times (1 SEmeas above & below the score), or approximately 68% of the time, the students's true score would be:

Score = SEmeas. – Obtained Score + SEmeas. = Score

40.2 = 1.8 – 42 + 1.8 = 43.8

Using the above, a banded score of (40.2–43.8) is reported. This means that if the student were to take the test three times, two out of the three times the student's score would fall somewhere between the scores of 40.2 and 43.8. Only one out of three times would the student's score be outside of the banded score (40.2–43.8) range.

2. For 19 out of 20 times (2 SEmeas above & below the score) or approximately 95% of the time, the student's true score would be:

Score = 2 × SEmeas - Obtained Score + 2 × SEmeas. = Score

= (2 × 1.8) - 42 + (2 × 1.8) =

38.4 = 3.6 – 42 + 3.6 = 45.6

Using the above, a banded score of (38.4–45.6) is reported. This means that if the student were to take the test one-hundred times, ninety-five times out of one-hundred times the student's score would fall somewhere between the scores of 38.4 and 45.6. Only five times out of one-hundred times would the student's score be outside of the banded score (38.4–45.6) range.

3. For 99 out of 100 times (3 SEmeas above & below the score) or approximately 99% of the time, the student's true score would be:

Score = 3 × SEmeas. - Obtained score + 3 × SEmeas. = Score

= (3 × 1.8) – 42 + (3 × 1.8) =

36.6 = 5.4 – 42 + 5.4 = 47.4

Using the above, a banded score of (36.6–47.4) is reported. This means that if the student were to take the test one-hundred times, ninety-nine times out of one-hundred times the student's score would fall somewhere between the scores of 36.6 and 47.1. Only one time out of a hundred-times would the student's score be outside of the banded score (36.6–47.4) range.

Standardized tests prepare profiles to indicate students' scores. Banded scores are computed using 1 SEmeas. above and below the obtained score. To indicate the banded scores, lines are drawn from the lower banded score to the upper band. On the profile, lines that overlap each other are not significantly different; lines that do not overlap are significantly different. Teachers may use this information to present test results to parents and students. An example of a profile is illustrated in Figure 12.2.

The profile was prepared using one standard error of measurement above and below the obtained score of Student A. Note the length of each line. The narrower the line, the smaller the standard error of measurement. Likewise, the wider the line, the larger the standard error of measurement.

Name John Doe   Grade 4th Grade

                                SCORES

SUBJECT	10	20	30	40	50	60	70	80
Reading							___	
Spelling							___	
Language							_____	
Math	_____							
Science					_____			
Social Studies			_____					
Study Skills		_____						

Figure 12.2.   Profile of Standardized Achievement Test Scores.

Using Figure 12.2, note that the lines (banded scores formed by using 1 SEmeas) of the reading, spelling, and language subtests overlap. These results indicate that for Student A, the three scores are not significantly different from each other. On the other hand, the scores obtained on the math, science, social studies, and study skills subtests do not overlap with each other or with the reading, spelling, and language subtests. These scores are significantly different from each other.

Activity

1 *Define and explain the following terms:*
   a *Frequency*
   b *Mean*
   c *Median*
   d *Mode*
   e *Class Interval*
   f *Range*
   g *Quartile Deviation*
   h *Standard Deviation*
   i *Z-Score*
   j *Stanine*
   k *T-Score*
   l *Percentile*
   m *SEmeas*
2 *Given the following scores: 90, 80, 70, 60, 50*
   a *Rank the scores.*
   b *Find the mean, median, and mode.*
   c *Find the standard deviation, quartile deviation, & range.*
3 *Given the following scores:*

69	69	40	53	88
69	88	88	53	88
40	69	88	28	53
88	69	88	72	63

   a *Rank the scores.*
   b *Find the mean, median, and mode.*
   c *Find the standard deviation, quartile deviation, & range.*
4 *The results of a standardized achievement test for a third grade class are reported in Table 12.6 using grade equivalents and percentiles.*
   a *Parents of students A, E, and J have come to you for an explanation of their children's scores. How would you explain the results?*

TABLE 12.6
Third Grade (3.8) Standardized Achievement Test Results

Student	Reading G.E.	Reading Percentile	Language G.E.	Language Percentile	Math G.E.	Math Percentile
A	2.6	22	3.7	50	3.9	57
B	3.4	39	4.3	63	3.8	53
C	2.4	17	3.3	39	3.7	49
D	3.3	37	3.7	50	4.8	85
E	3.4	41	3.4	42	3.4	34
F	5.9	90	7.9	94	5.3	93
G	4.8	77	6.2	85	3.5	40
H	3.0	31	4.1	59	4.2	66
I	3.2	34	2.6	22	3.6	44
J	7.0	97	6.8	90	5.1	89

    b Which students scored at the median on the language test?

    c Which students may need additional help in reading, language, and mathematics?

  5 Obtain a copy of a standardized achievement test manual from your school or instructor.

    a How are the test scores reported?

    b How many students were used to develop the norming population?

    c What are the mean and standard deviation for the norming population?

    d What is the standard error of measurement?

REFERENCE

Test Service Notebook 148—Methods of expressing test scores. (1980). New York: The Psychological Corporation.

Chapter 13

UTILIZING TEST INFORMATION

What is a standardized test? What role does the teacher play in the testing process? What is the meaning of testing terms such as norm-referenced, reliability, and validity? Answers to these questions as well as general information about tests are presented in this chapter.

Teachers should be somewhat familiar with standardized tests. Most teachers have been exposed to these tests since they were students in elementary, middle, and high school. For example, prior to placement in kindergarten or first grade, many students take reading readiness tests to determine developmental skills needed to learn to read.

Exposure to standardized tests does not end when one graduates from high school. College students may take standardized tests at the end of courses. Some teachers are required to take a standardized test such as the National Teachers Examination prior to becoming certified to teach.

The purpose of this chapter is to survey some of the basic testing terms applicable to standardized tests. Because teachers are involved in the school's testing program, it is important to understand key testing terms and to be able to identify different kinds of standardized tests. The chapter also contains a discussions of the competency movement and truth-in-testing laws. For those desiring a more thorough understanding, sources of additional information and selected references on standardized tests are included.

This chapter does not include information on the selection of standardized tests or on the construction of teacher-made tests. These topics are omitted because most standardized tests used by schools have been preselected either by a testing committee, school board, testing director, administrator, or counselor. Also, teachers have been trained in the development of classroom tests during their teacher preparation classes.

TESTING TERMINOLOGY

Standardized Tests

Standardized tests are administered, scored, and interpreted under standard or uniform conditions. Students taking the same test in Ohio, North Carolina, and Texas will follow standard directions and uniform time limits. The directions are read to the students directly from the testing manual. A section in this chapter on sources of test information will describe the test manual further.

Elementary, middle, and senior high school teachers may be required to administer standardized tests or end-of-year tests to their students. During the first, third, fifth, and eighth grades, students may take an achievement test battery to determine what they have learned in reading, language, and math. In addition, prior to being admitted to college, students may take either the Scholastic Aptitude Test (SAT) or the American College Test (ACT).

The items on a standardized test are carefully planned and prepared. It is then field-tested on a population of students who are similar in age, sex, grade, locality, economic status, and curriculum to the students who will be tested. Based on the results of the field test, an analysis is made. Those items that proved to be too difficult, easy, or ambiguous are rewritten or eliminated.

Prior to publication, standardized tests are normed. This means that a student's test results are compared to the average or typical performance of other students for a given age, sex or grade. Norms may be reported as grade or age equivalents, percentiles, and standard scores (stanines, deviation IQ's, T-scores, and so forth). Descriptions of these terms and how they are used in the interpretation of scores are included in Chapter 12.

Nonstandardized Tests

Nonstandardized tests, as referred to in this book, are classroom tests, usually developed by the teacher to assess the amount of material students have learned. The conditions described under standardized tests may or may or may not apply to classroom tests. Classroom tests assess the achievement attained by students over a given period of time. Teachers may develop and administer a test at the conclusion of a chapter or unit. For example, a teacher may administer a spelling test containing 20 words. A student who correctly spelled 18 of the 20 words would obtain a score of 90%. A percentage score is not a standard score because it does not tell us how the student compared to other students in his or her grade.

Pencil-and-Paper-Tests

A pencil-and-paper-test requires students to respond to a test item by either writing the answer immediately after the question or using a separate answer sheet. Most standardized tests are of the pencil-and-paper variety.

Performance Tests

Unlike pencil-and-paper tests, performance tests require students to perform some sort of task. For example, on an individual intelligence test, students may be required to solve a maze or to complete a design using blocks. Additionally, performance tests are used on the General Aptitude Test Battery (GATB) to test motor coordination, manual dexterity, and finger dexterity. Likewise, classroom tests may be of the performance type. In a woodworking class, for example, students may be evaluated on their final product, such as the completion of a lamp or stool, while in a typing class, students may be evaluated on the number of words accurately typed.

Verbal Tests

Most of the standardized tests available today are verbal. A verbal test uses words in the test item. Students may be required to read the directions or to read the question and indicate the answer in the test booklet or on a separate answer sheet.

Nonverbal Tests

Nonverbal tests do not use written words in the test items. These tests often require students to respond to pictorial materials. The directions are administered orally. An example of a nonverbal test is the Nonverbal Battery of Cognitive Abilities test, Multi-Level Edition, published by Houghton-Mifflin, 1972 and 1978.

Speed Tests

A speed test usually requires students to answer as many questions as possible during a given time limit. Speed tests contain items of equal difficulty. For example, the clerical speed and accuracy test on the Differential Aptitude Test (DAT), is a speed test because it determines how quickly and accurately one can identify same and different number and name combinations.

Power Tests

Power tests contain items arranged according to degree of difficulty. Because speed is not a factor, power tests give students an ample amount of time to complete the test. Most standardized and teacher-made tests are power tests.

Objective Tests

The objectivity of a test refers to the scoring of the test. The results of an objective test will be consistent, regardless of who is scoring it. The correct answer is determined when the test item is created. The scorer uses a template or answer key to score each answer as either correct or incorrect. Objective tests may be in the form of true-false, matching, multiple-choice, or completion items. In addition, most objective tests may be machined scored.

Subjective Tests

As for objective tests, the subjectivity of a test refers to the scoring of the test. Unlike objective tests, the results of subjective tests may differ depending on the scorer. Subjective test items may or may not have one correct answer. Therefore, the correct answers may need to be determined after the items have been answered. Essays are subjective items because different scorers may assign different scores to the same essay.

Norm-Referenced Tests

Norm-referenced tests are useful in interpreting test scores. A test that is normed-referenced compares students to others (the norming population) who have taken the same tests. The norming population matches the students as much as possible with respect to age, grade, sex, and time of year that the test was administered. Norms may be developed nationally, regionally, or locally. It is therefore important that proper norms are used when interpreting test results.

For example, suppose Form C of the DAT was administered in the spring to eleventh grade students and we wanted the results in percentiles. In interpreting John's score, we would need to find the equivalent percentile score using the percentile norm tables for Form C, grade 11, boys, and spring semester. If a student scored at the 92nd percentile on the Verbal section of the DAT, the results would be interpreted as better than or equal to 92 percent of the norming population (grade 11, boys, spring semester). Most standardized tests are norm referenced.

Criterion-Referenced Tests

Unlike norm-referenced tests, which compare students to a given population, criterion-reference tests interpret results based on the performance of individual students. Criterion-referenced means that, for a given objective or goal, a certain number of items must be answered correctly for the objective or goal to be considered mastered. For example, an objective may require students to divide a four-digit number by a one-digit number with remainder of zero. On a test, ten questions are sampled to test this objective. To satisfy the, objective students may be required to answer seven out of ten questions correctly (70%). Students who obtained 70% or better would pass the objective or criterion. Competency and mastery tests often indicate results using criterion referencing.

Group Tests

Group tests are administered to more than one individual at a time. These tests require students to use paper and a pencil when answering the questions.

Individual Tests

Individual tests are administered to one student at a time. These tests usually require students to respond orally to a question read by the examiner or to perform a given task such as solving a maze, describing an ink blot, or completing a design using blocks. Unlike group tests, individually administered tests permit the examiner to observe the behavior of the examinee.

Raw Scores

Raw scores are the total number of items answered correctly on a test. For example, on a 20-word spelling test, a student who spells 16 words correctly earns a raw score of 16. Used alone, the raw score of 16 yields very little information.

However, converting a raw score of 16 into a percent or standard score gives the teacher more information about how well a student did in spelling.

Standard Scores

On standardized tests, raw scores are often converted into standard scores. Standard scores are used to determine a student's position or rank in relation to the norming group. Using the standard deviation and mean, a raw score can be transformed into a standard score using a relatively simple formula. Transforming raw scores into standard scores are explained in Chapter 12. Fortunately, one does not need to use the formula because a conversion table of raw scores to standard scores is usually provided in the test manual. Using the conversion table, one may locate a particular standard score (stanine, T-score, etc.) for each raw score. However, one must be careful to use the correct conversion table.

Validity

Validity refers to the degree to which a test measures what it was designed to measure. Validity is divided into content, construct, and criterion-related validity. Content validity refers to the extent to which the contents of the test sample a behavior, skill, or course of study. Construct validity is the degree to which a test measures a hypothetical quantity, such as self-concept, personality, or intelligence. Criterion-related validity is divided into concurrent and predictive validity. Concurrent validity compares one test with another test that has a reputation of validity. For example, a newly developed mental abilities test may be compared to the Stanford-Binet in order to establish concurrent validity. Predictive validity is the ability of a test to foretell performance on a specific criterion such as end-of-year course grades, or job performance.

Reliability

Reliability refers to the consistency, dependability, stability, or trustworthiness of test results. There are four approaches that may be used to determine test reliability. Test-retest reliability is determined by administering the same test to same students after some period of time. Split-half reliability is determined by dividing the test into halves, usually with all even numbered items in one test and all odd numbered items in another test. The scores obtained on the two halves are compared to determine the degree of internal consistency of the test. Alternate form reliability involves administering different forms of a test to the same people and comparing their performance on each form. Kuder-Richardson reliability involves determining how consistently all the items on a single test measure the same domain.

Reliability is reported as a correlation coefficient, "r," which ranges from −1.0 (perfect negative relationship) to 0 (no relationship) to 1.0 (perfect positive relationship). It is important to note that if a test is valid, it is also reliable. However, if a test is reliable, it may or may not be valid.

Test Battery

A test battery contains a number of subtests that have been standardized using the same population. Achievement test batteries may contain several subtests—such as reading, language, math, science, and social studies—in one booklet. The norms reported for each subtest have been normed using the same population. Therefore, the results of each subtest may be compared to each other.

Activities

> 1 *Select a standardized achievement test and determine whether the instrument is*
> a *Pencil-and-Paper or Performance*
> b *Verbal or Nonverbal*
> c *Speed or Power*
> d *Objective or Subjective*
> e *Group or individual*
> 2 *Give reasons for your choice.*

Kinds of Standardized Tests

This section describes some of the different kinds of standardized tests currently in use in schools. The survey begins with a description of achievement tests, because most teachers are involved with administering them. Interpretation of results of any of the standardized tests described in this section should not be attempted, however, without the help of the school counselor or school psychologist.

Achievement Tests

Achievement tests are designed to measure students' knowledge or skill in a specific area. Most teachers are familiar with achievement tests. Classroom tests are achievement tests because they assess the amount of information that has been learned by the students during a particular time. Teachers prepare classroom tests to measure a unit of instruction, or final exams to test a year's worth of learning. These tests measure the outcomes of the school's curriculum and, for the most part, are criterion-referenced.

Standardized achievement tests are developed by experts in testing and are available from commercial publishers. These tests may be designed to assess one subject or a group of subjects (test battery) and to sample learning outcomes common to the general population. Unlike classroom tests, standardized achievement tests provide the user with a manual, norms, and interpretive aids. Standardized achievement tests may be norm-referenced, criterion-referenced, or both.

Readiness Tests

Readiness tests are usually used to predict success when a child enters school. For example, children about to enter school may be required to take a reading readiness test to determine whether they have the skills necessary to successfully learn to read. The reading readiness test is the most commonly used readiness test. While readiness tests are often used in the early grades, they also may be used in the upper grades to predict whether a student is ready to take a specific subject; for example, a student may be required to take an algebra readiness (prognosis) test before enrolling in an algebra class, to determine the probability of his or her successfully completing the course. Readiness tests may also reveal weaknesses that may require special attention and remedial work; the student who does not do well on a readiness test may be delayed in entering school or taking algebra.

Intelligence Tests

Sometimes referred to as ability tests, intelligence tests are frequently used to assess learning ability and success in school. An intelligence test may contain verbal, numerical problem-solving, and nonverbal sections. In addition, intelligence tests may be group or individually administered. Group intelligence tests may be administered by teachers; however, individually administered intelligence tests are administered by a specially trained professional such as the school psychologist. For example, a school psychologist may administer an individual intelligence test to students to determine whether placement in a special class (specific learning disability, gifted and talented, or mentally handicapped) may help them achieve their maximum potential.

Caution should be used when interpreting scores on intelligence tests. Teachers must seek the help of the school psychologist to insure that intelligence test results are completely understood. To illustrate this point, suppose a student with a reading deficiency was given a verbal intelligence test. The score that he or she received would reflect the reading deficiency and not intelligence. In addition, intelligence tests may not reflect the intelligence of a student who comes from an environment that differs from that of the norming population.

Aptitude Tests

Aptitude tests are designed to measure students' present status in order to predict their ability to learn or succeed in a future task. For example, students desiring to enroll for vocational training, take a special class, or major in a special field in college may be given an aptitude test to determine their chance for success.

Aptitude test results, together with achievement test results and other data, may help students obtain information about themselves to help them plan their future. For example, students may be better able to plan their educational and occupational goals using the results of these tests. On the basis of their indicated strengths and weaknesses, students may be able to decide whether they should take a particular subject, major in a particular field, or pursue a certain career objective.

Aptitude tests should not be used as the sole criterion for making decisions. It would be wiser for teachers to use additional criteria such as grades, interests, motivation, or achievement test results in helping their students make decisions.

Teachers should seek the help of the school counselor before discussing results of aptitude tests with the class. In fact, it would be wiser for teachers to invite a counselor into the classroom to present and explain results of aptitude tests to the students.

Many standardized aptitude tests are available. Three of the most popular are the General Aptitude Test Battery, the Differential Aptitude Test, and the Armed Services Vocational Aptitude Battery.

The General Aptitude Test Battery (GATB) is administered by the local state employment service. In some areas, high school counselors may request a special administration of the GATB at their school for students desiring to take the test. This test measures nine areas including intelligence, verbal, numerical, spatial, form perception, clerical perception, motor coordination, finger dexterity, and manual dexterity.

Published by the Psychological Corporation, the Differential Aptitude Test (DAT) is a battery of eight tests: verbal reasoning, numerical ability, abstract reasoning, clerical speed and accuracy, mechanical reasoning, space relations, and language usage (spelling and grammar). Unlike the GATB, the DAT is entirely a paper and pencil test.

The Armed Services Vocational Aptitude Battery (ASVAB) is published by the United States Enlistment Processing Command, and schools may request a special administration from their local military recruiter. The ASVAB yields three academic composite scores: academic ability, verbal, and math. In addition, the ASVAB yields four occupational component scores: mechanical and crafts; business and clerical; electronics and electrical; and health, social, and technology. The recently revised ASVAB also contains an interest inventory.

Diagnostic Tests

Diagnostic tests are used to determine an individual's specific subject area deficiency. The results may be used to individualize instruction by focusing on the particular area of weakness. For example, a third grade teacher discovers, based on the results of a reading achievement test, that a student is reading more than two grade levels below expectancy. However, the teacher does not know where the specific difficulty lies. Administering a reading diagnostic test such as the Stanford Diagnostic Reading Test may reveal that the difficulty is in one or more of the following areas: reading comprehension, vocabulary, auditory discrimination, syllabication, beginning and ending sounds, blending, and/or sound discrimination. Using the diagnostic test results, the teacher may determine that the student needs remedial help in resolving the particular deficiency.

Interest Inventories

Interest inventories are used to assess an individual's likes and dislikes. These inventories usually require students to indicate whether they like, dislike, or are indifferent to a list of interest areas, hobbies, occupations, school subjects, and activities. Results yield general interest patterns which may correspond to an occupation or broad interest group. Two of the most commonly used interest inventories are the Kuder Occupational Interest Survey and the Strong Interest Inventory (SII).

Projective Tests

Projective tests require extensive training in administration and interpretation. Therefore, while teachers should become familiar with projective tests, they will never administer one. These tests are commonly included among those called personality tests. Examples of some of the commonly used projective tests are the 16PF Questionnaire, the Minnesota Multiphasic Personality Inventory (MMPI), the Rorschach Inkblot, and the Thematic Apperception Test (TAT).

Suppose a student exhibits behavior that appears to be atypical. The teacher refers the student to the counselor who, with the permission of the parent, may determine that the student needs a referral to the school psychologist for further exploration. The school psychologist may administer one or more projective tests to determine whether the student has a special problem. Based on the results of the projective test and other measures, a decision may be made to place the student in a special class or to seek professional counseling.

Table 13.1 lists and categorizes some standardized tests. It is important to note that some tests listed under one category may also apply to another category.

Summary

The descriptions of the standardized tests reviewed in this section were brief because the purpose of the section was to familiarize teachers with a variety of tests. While several types of tests were discussed, the achievement, diagnostic, and readiness tests are the most important for teachers to understand, because these are the tests with which they will have the most contact. Teachers desiring additional information about tests may find the references at the end of this chapter useful.

USES OF STANDARDIZED TESTS

Grouping Students

Results of standardized tests may be used by teachers to group students with similar talents or deficiencies. Grouping may reduce the number of students in a class to a more manageable, smaller number, enabling teachers to focus on each individual's needs. For example, in a third grade class, a teacher

TABLE 13.1
Examples of Standardized Tests

Type of Test	Name of Test
Achievement	California Achievement Test
	Comprehensive Tests of Basic Skills
	Metropolitan Achievement Test
	Stanford Achievement Test
	National Teacher Examination
	Iowa Tests of Basic Skills
	Wide Range Achievement Test
Aptitude	Armed Services Vocational Aptitude Battery
	Differential Aptitude Test
	General Aptitude Test Battery
Radiness/Prognostic	Boehm Test of Basic Concepts
	Durrell Analysis of Reading Difficulty
	Metropolitan Readiness Test
	Stanford Diagnostic Tests
Interest	Kuder General Interest Survey
	Ohio Vocational Interest Survey
	Position Classification Inventory
	Self-Directed Search
	Strong Interest Inventory
Cognitive Ability — Group	Culture Fair Intelligence Test
	Henmon-Nelson Test of Mental Ability
	Short Form Test of Academic Aptitude Test
	Kaufman Assessment Battery for Children
	Slosson Intelligence Test
Cognitive Ability — Individual	Stanford-Binet Intelligence Test
	Wechsler Intelligence Scales
Projective/Personality	16 PF Questionnaire
	Minnesota Multiphasic Personality Inventory
	Rorschach Inkblot Test
	Thematic Apperception Test

may have four separate reading groups. These reading groups may have been developed to help students who have similar deficiencies in auditory discrimination, vocabulary levels, comprehension, or sound discrimination. Each of the four groups may now focus their attention on eliminating one or more of these deficiencies.

Identifying Students with Specific Needs

With the passage of PL94-142, many school systems throughout the country have developed programs specifically designed to meet the needs of exceptional students. For example, results of standardized tests such as intelligence and achievement tests may indicate that a particular student needs special help. Teachers may use the results of these tests, together with nontest information, as a basis for referral to the counselor, school psychologist, or special education teacher.

Modifying the Curriculum

A teacher may use the results of standardized tests to modify the curriculum. For example, results of a standardized achievement test in arithmetic may indicate that several students are having difficulty with multiplication. Based on these results, the teacher may determine that more emphasis needs to be placed on this concept. The teacher may therefore may need to change the method of presentation, assign more problems, or increase the amount of time spent in developing mastery of this concept.

Determining Readiness

A standardized test may help a teacher determine whether students are ready to enroll in a particular class. For example, using an algebra prognosis or readiness test, a teacher may find that several students do not have the necessary skills to succeed in algebra. Therefore, the teacher may need to provide remedial work for these students.

Helping in the Decision-Making Process

Students may need assistance in making academic or career decisions. The results of standardized tests (aptitude, interest, intelligence, and/or achievement) may help students decide whether to pursue a particular major in college, train for a particular occupation, or enter a vocational training program. Teachers aware of students who are having difficulty making decisions are urged to obtain assistance from their school counselor.

MISUSES OF STANDARDIZED TESTS

Assigning Grades

Standardized tests should not be used as the sole criterion for assigning grades in a course. Grades should be assigned based on both test and nontest data. Assigning grades based on results of one standardized test assumes that the test is infallible. Every standardized test has some degree of error which is expressed by the standard error of measurement. Remember that the objectives for which standardized test items were developed may not adequately reflect the curriculum in a particular school. Therefore, in assigning grades to students, teachers need to use other instruments and devices (classroom tests, rating scales, checklists, etc.) in addition to standardized tests.

Evaluating Teachers

Because of the strong emphasis placed on the results of standardized tests in some school districts, teachers may find that their principals are using the results to assess their teachers' effectiveness. In fact, principals have been known to inform their teachers that their evaluations will be based, in part, on how well their students perform on the standardized tests. Teachers as well as administrators need to understand that standardized test results indicate whether objectives are being achieved. If objectives are not being achieved, then teachers and administrators need to modify the curriculum or place more emphasis on the objective. The results of standardized tests should be used to help students achieve learning outcomes; they should not be used to evaluate teachers.

Teaching the Test

If school systems place a great amount of emphasis on the results of a standardized test, teachers may decide to teach the test. This practice is unethical. It compromises the test, which results in scores that are not valid. If the school system decides to change the test, or if the publisher revises the test, or if new norms are developed, the scores obtained by the students who were taught the test will fall dramatically. A better practice is to teach to the objectives that will be assessed.

Labeling Students

Test results should not be used to label students. A conversation overheard in a faculty lounge illustrates this point. One teacher was telling another that this year is going to be an impossible one. The teacher said, "I don't know how I will be able to teach them. Not one of my students has an I.Q. over 95." This comment was made after reviewing the results of group intelligence tests scores from the previous year. Avoid labeling students.

Evaluating the School

Standardized test results should not be used to evaluate a school or school system. A newspaper reported the results of a countywide achievement testing program. The article listed the schools in order of how well each scored on the standardized achievement test. Schools that fell short of the national norms were identified by placing an asterisk next to the school's name. The article placed undue emphasis on the results of a single achievement test. This practice may result in the community making faulty judgments about the effectiveness and quality of their schools.

SOURCES OF INFORMATION ABOUT TESTS

The purpose of this section is to provide teachers with some of the basic sources of information about standardized tests. This section should be used as a guide to locating information on the uses, purposes, validity, reliability, cost, and directions for administering, scoring, and interpreting standardized tests.

The School Counselor

School counselors have training and experience in the administration and interpretation of standardized tests. Teachers should seek the help of the counselor if they believe they will have difficulty with the administration of the standardized test. Prior to the administration, these teachers may request from the counselor an in-service training program. The in-service training received by the teachers may prevent problems from arising during the actual administration of the test.

The Test Manual

Prior to administering any standardized test, teachers need to have a copy or know where they may obtain a copy of the test manual. A test manual contains directions for administering the test. Usually, the directions, which must be read aloud to the students, are printed in boldface type. Teachers need to strictly adhere to the directions in the manual to insure that the test is being administered under standardized conditions.

In addition to providing teachers with detailed directions, test manuals should provide information on the development of the test. For example, using the manual, the examiner should be able to determine the purpose and use of the test. The test manual also provides information on the norming population, scoring and interpreting the results, and evidence of validity, reliability, and intercorrelations of subtests.

Test manuals may include a "table of specifications" (test blueprint) which includes, in chart form, the contents as well as the objectives of the test. Some test manuals also include a list of objectives along with sample items that are similar to those on the actual test. These sample items may be useful in preparing students for the actual standardized test. Teaching to the test is acceptable, but teaching the test is not.

An excellent source of information on the use and development of manuals and standardized tests is the *Standards for Educational and Psychological Tests* (1985), published by the American Psychological Association. This publication was a collaborative effort of three professional associations: the American Psychological Association, the American Educational Research Association, and the National Council on Measurement in Education. Each standard is categorized into three levels: primary, secondary, and conditional.

Activity

Select a standardized test manual appropriate to your educational setting and answer the following questions:

1. *What are the stated purposes and uses for the test?*
2. *What are some, if any, of the special qualifications needed to administer the test?*
3. *Are directions for administering the test stated clearly?*
4. *How is the test scored?*

5. *Does the test require the use of special answer sheets?*
6. *Describe the norming sample. Are separate norms provided for minority and special groups (gifted, learning disabled, etc.)?*
7. *How are scores reported (percentiles, grade equivalents, stanines, etc.)?*
8. *Are sample questions given in the manual? If so, are they similar to the items in the test?*
9. *Which validity coefficients are reported?*
10. *Which reliability coefficients are reported?*

Test Publishers

Most publishers provide catalogues of their tests. These catalogues are free, they list tests by area (intelligence, achievement, aptitude, etc.), and they describe each test. In addition, catalogues give the cost, number of tests per package, and ordering information.

Table 13.2 lists some of the publishers of standardized tests.

TABLE 13.2
Publishers of Standardized Tests

American College Testing Program P.O. Box 168 Iowa City, IA 52243	Psychological Assessment Resources, Inc. P.O. Box 998 Odessa, FL 33556
American Guidance Services, Inc. Publishers Building Circle Pines, MN 55014	The Psychological Corporation 555 Academic Court San Antonio, Texas 78204
The College Board 45 Columbus Avenue New York, NY 10023	Riverside Publishing Company 8420 Bryn Mawr Avenue Chicago, IL 60631
Consulting Psychologists Press, Inc. 3803 East Bayshore Road Palo Alto, CA 94303	Scholastic Testing Services, Inc. 480 Meyer Road Bensenville, IL 60106
CTB/McGraw-Hill Del Monte Research Park Monterey, CA 93940	Science Research Associates, Inc. 155 North Wacker Drive Chicago, IL 60606
Pro-Ed 8700 Shoal Creek Boulevard Austin, TX 78758	Western Psychological Services 12031 Wilshire Boulevard Los Angeles, CA 90025

Buros' Mental Measurements Yearbooks (MMY)

The MMY is a valuable source of information about tests. It is an excellent resource for selecting standardized tests. The MMY contains reviews of tests prepared by experts in the field. In addition, it includes a directory of tests and publishers, and an index by title and author of tests. Previous editions of the MMY are cross-referenced in the current edition.

Textbooks

Measurement and evaluation textbooks provide useful information about tests. Teachers desiring to learn more about classroom and standardized tests are urged to refer to one or more of the textbooks listed at the end of this chapter.

Professional Journals

Some professional journals provide technical articles and test reviews on standardized tests. Two of the most popular journals are *Measurement and Evaluation in Counseling and Development* and the *Journal of Educational Measurement.* These journals are published quarterly.

STATEWIDE ASSESSMENT PROGRAMS

Statewide assessment programs developed in response to a public cry for accountability in schools. Payne (1992) defined minimum competency tests as "measures of basic skill competencies in subject areas (and writing) used to make graduation, certification, and promotion decisions" (p. 551). Today, most states have mandated some form of minimum competency testing. Due to space limitations, it is impossible to report on all statewide assessment programs. Therefore, a description of the Florida Assessment Program will serve as example. Teachers interested in learning more about the testing program in their state are advised to write for information from their state's department of education.

The Florida State Assessment Program is designed to test students in grades 3, 5, 8, and 11 in the basic skills. In grade 11, students take two parts of the test. Part one tests the students in the areas of mathematics, reading, and writing. Test items in part two require students to apply the basic skills to real situations. For example, some of the skills in part two include determining the solution to problems involving comparison shopping, distinguishing between facts and opinions, and correctly completing a check with its stub. Students in grade 11 must pass part two of the test. Students who do not pass part two will have two additional chances in grade 11 and two chances in grade 12 to pass the test. Students who fail part two in grade 12 may elect to continue high school for another year.

When results are returned to the school, teachers receive a computer print-out for each student indicating which skills were assessed and whether the skills tests were passed. This information is indicated on the print-out by a yes or no under the "skill achieved" column.

An example of a report for a hypothetical student, John, is presented in Table 13.3. Using this report, a teacher has a list of skills that were tested in third grade mathematics. For each skill, a teacher can determine the correct answers needed to achieve the particular skill (column 1). A teacher can then determine the number of correct answers that John obtained for each skill (column 2). A list of item numbers on the test that correspond to each skill can be observed (columns 3 to 7). The letter next to the item number indicates the incorrect response made by the student. A teacher may check the test booklet to find out what response was selected by the student. In the "skills achieved" column, a teacher can easily find those skills that were not achieved by looking for the word "no." For those skills not achieved, a teacher may provide John with remediation. Once the skill has been remediated and assessed, the teacher can document this by initialing and dating the space provided on the report. The report is then placed in John's folder.

Uses of Statewide Assessment Tests

Uses of standardized tests included in a previous section of this chapter are applicable to statewide assessment tests. The *Guide to 1980–81 Statewide Assessment Results* (1980) published by the Florida State Department of Education provides teachers with questions that may enhance the use of the test results. These questions include:

1. In what instructional areas are students strongest?
2. In what areas are they weakest?
3. Did students perform well on skills that are local priorities?
4. Are there any surprise areas of weakness?
5. On which skills do students appear to need further assistance and in what order should they be considered?
6. How do these results compare with previous results? (p. 15).

TABLE 13.3
Example of Student Report from State Assessment Program

MATHEMATICS SKILLS   1980–81 STUDENT REPORT   FLORIDA STATEWIDE
NAME: John Smith   BIRTHDATE: 2/25/70   ASSESSMENT PROGRAM
STUDENT I.D. 4001   DIST. DATA

Grade 3

	Mathematics Skills	Correct Answers Needed	# of Items Answered Correctly	Item Nos. and Responses					Skill Achieved	Remediation Initial	Remediation Date
	A. 1. Count up to 100 objects	4/5	4	81	82B	83	84	85	YES		
	B. 2. Read and write numbers less than 100	4/5	5	140	141	142	143	144	YES		
M	E. 7. Identify halves, thirds, or fourths	4/5	3	131D	132	133C	134	135	NO		
A	F. 9. Add three 1-digit numbers (sum less than 19)	4/5	5	86	987	88	89	90	YES		
T	F. 10. Add two 2-digit numbers (no carrying)	4/5	4	91C	92	93	94	95	YES		
H	C. 12. Subtract basic combinations (subtraction facts)	4/5	3	101C	102	103C	104	105	NO		
E	C. 13. Subtract 1-digit from 2-digit numbers (no borrowing)	4/5	5	106	107	108	109	110	YES		
M	C. 14. Subtract 2-digit numbers without borrowing	4/5	5	111	112	113	114	115	YES		
A	O. 17. Tell time on the hour and half-hour	4/5	4	121	122B	123	124	125	YES		
T	O. 18. Determine the length of an object	3/4	4	145	146	147	148		YES		
I	Q. 20. Identify sets of coins equal in value	4/5	5	116	117	118	119	120	YES		
C	T. 21. Solve word problems involving addition	4/5	4	126A	127	128	129	130	YES		
S	T. 22. Solve word problems involving subtraction	3/4	4	136	137	138	139		YES		
	V. 24. Subtract to solve practical money problems under .50	4/5	2	96C	97B	98A	99	100	NO		

Note. From *A Guide to 1980–81 Statewide Results* (p. 4), 1980, Tallahassee, FL: Department of Education.

Pros and Cons

The controversy that has developed over the minimum competency movement is widespread. This controversy has even extended to the courts.

Supporters of minimum competency testing believe that it can help to eliminate weaknesses and enhance learning. Students who do not pass particular skills tests may need remediation. The information provided by the results of these tests may help teachers identify learning problems. These problems may be remediated before additional problems develop. Students may receive the individual help they need. The supporters of this movement believe that through accountability the public may support education.

Nonsupporters of minimum competency tests believe that these tests are biased. Students in Florida who failed the test have brought the issue into the courts (Debra P. v. Turlington). Pullin (1981) reported that the court ruled it to be unfair and unlawful to deny a diploma because a student failed a test that measured skills he or she had not been taught.

Nonsupporters also believe that the importance placed on minimum competency tests will force teachers to teach the test. This may result in some areas of the curriculum receiving little or no coverage.

Finally, some people believe that schools administer too many tests to students. For example, in one school district, students tested with the minimum competency test in the fall were also administered an achievement test battery in the spring. It is interesting to note that the results of neither test were used to modify the curriculum nor address student weaknesses.

Teacher Competency

The competency testing movement has extended into the area of teacher certification. Many states currently require teacher candidates to take a competency test prior to awarding them a teaching certificate. These tests may be developed by a commercial testing corporation or by the state department of education. Teacher certification examinations may test teacher candidates in the following areas: mathematics, English, writing ability, and general education methods. Like minimum competency tests for students, teacher competency tests also assess basic skills that teachers are expected to have before entering a classroom.

Truth-in-Testing Laws

In addition to the competency testing movement, the work of Ralph Nader and his associates deserves special attention. Nader and his staff have attacked some of the standardized tests used to regulate admissions to college, graduate, and professional schools. In Nairn's (1980) report on the Nader investigation, *The Reign of ETS: The Corporation That Makes Up Minds,* Nader reported that SAT scores are no better than gambling with dice in predicting college success. This report proposed that ETS permit students to obtain the test questions and answers for the SAT that was administered to them and to provide them with enough information about the test to help them understand their results. As a result of their work, truth-in-testing laws have been enacted in New York and California.

BIBLIOGRAPHY

Textbooks on Testing

Anastasi, A. (1988). *Psychological testing.* (6th ed.). New York: Macmillan.

Cronbach, L. J. (1990). *Essentials of Psychological Testing.* (5th ed.). New York: Harper & Row.

Drummond, R. J. (1992). *Appraisal procedures for counselors and   helping professionals.* (2nd ed.). New York: Merrill.

Gronlund, N. E., & Linn, R. L. (1990). *Measurement and evaluation in teaching.* (6th ed.). New York: Macmillan.

Mehrens, W. A., & Lehmann, I. J. (1991). *Measurement and evaluation in education and teaching.* (4th ed.). Fort Worth, TX: Holt, Rinehart & Winston.

Oosterof, A. (1990). *Classroom applications of educational measurement.* Columbus, OH: Merrill.

Payne, D. A. (1992). *Measuring and evaluating educational outcomes.* Columbus, OH: Merrill.

Thorndike, R. M., Cunningham, G. K., Thorndike, R. L., & Hagen, E. P. (1991). *Measurement and evaluation in psychology and education.* (5th ed.). New York: Macmillan.

Test Bulletins

The following test bulletins are available from the Psychological Corporation, 757 Third Avenue, New York, NY 10017, for a nominal charge.

Burrell, L. E. *How a standardized achievement test is built.* Test Service Notebook, No. 125.

Burrell, L. E., & Wilson, R. *Fairness and the matter of bias.* Test Service Notebook, No. 36.

Lennon, R. T. *Testing: Bond or barrier between pupil and teacher?* Test Service Notebook, No. 82.

Mitchell, B. C. *A glossary of measurement terms.* Test Service Notebook, No. 13.

On telling parents about test results. Test Service Notebook, No. 154.

Ricks, J. H. *Local norms—when and why.* Test Service Notebook, No. 148.

Seashore, H. C. *Methods of expressing test scores.* Test Service Notebook, No. 148.

Some things parents should know about testing. Test Service Notebook, No. 34.

Westman, A. G. *Aptitude, intelligence, and achievement.* Test Service Notebook, No. 151.

Wilson, R. *Criterion-referenced testing.* Test Service Notebook, No. 37.

Wrightstone, J. W., Hogan, J. P., & Abbott, M. M. *Accountability in education and associated measurement problems.* Test Service Notebook, No. 33.

REFERENCES

Nairn, A. (1980). *The reign of ETS: The corporation that makes up minds.* Washington, DC: Ralph Nader.

Payne, D. A. (1992). *Measuring and evaluating educational outcomes.* New York: Macmillan.

Pullin, D. (1981). Minimum competency testing and the demand for account-ability. *Phi Delta Kappan, 63,* 20–22.

Standards for educational and psychological testing. (1985). Washington, DC: American Psychological Association.

Chapter 14

INTERRELATING NONSTANDARDIZED INFORMATION WITH OTHER DATA

Chapter 13 examined the use of test data as one source of information about students. Used alone, tests give only a partial picture of the student. Tests, particularly standardized tests, provide the user with objective data. Teachers who have not been trained in interpreting test results should consult with their school counselor.

Other sources of information about students include cumulative records, observational techniques, rating scales, sociometric techniques, autobiographies, anecdotal records, and case studies. These will be described in the following sections. Teachers may use these sources to obtain additional information about their students.

CUMULATIVE RECORDS

Suppose a teacher needs to obtain some information about a student. The teacher may check the student's cumulative record folder. This folder is usually found in a file in or near the main office. Depending on the school's policy, the teacher may need to sign a check-out form or obtain permission from the principal or school counselor to review a cumulative folder.

A cumulative folder is a large file folder designed to organize and collect essential information about students. As students progress from elementary to middle to high school, the cumulative folder accompanies them.

Cumulative records usually contain a section on personal and family background. Here teachers will find a student's address, date and place of birth, and telephone number. Also included are the names of the student's parents with information about whether they are living or deceased, married, divorced, or separated. In addition, a record of enrollment, race, and primary language spoken at home may also be included. An example of a personal information record is illustrated in Table 14.1.

A record of a student's standardized tests and grades (Table 14.2) may be found either on the front cover of the cumulative folder or on a permanent record card inserted in the folder. Using this information, teachers may determine the academic strengths and weaknesses of each student, and design a course of study geared to all student levels.

With the competency test movement underway, teachers may also find student progression folders for mathematics, reading, and writing within the cumulative folders. These individualized folders contain work samples and a checklist of competencies that must be mastered for each grade. Classroom teachers are responsible for maintaining student progression folders. When a student withdraws from a school, teachers must include the student's progression folders with the cumulative folder.

The cumulative record usually contains a health record. The health record usually includes a list of diseases and illnesses a student has had and a record of immunizations and medications. The information provided by the cumulative health record may be vital. For example, a teacher may find that a student is having difficulty staying awake in class. An examination of the student's health record may uncover clues to the student's problem. If the teacher fails to determine the reasons for the difficulty, he or she may talk to the student or schedule a parent conference.

Cumulative folders may contain comments made by former teachers. Teachers must use care when inserting information about a student in the cumulative record. They should not include information that would be injurious to a student. To protect the student from such practices, the *Family Educational Rights and Privacy Act* was enacted by Congress in 1974. A student and his or her parents now have the right to examine the contents of the cumulative record and to remove information deemed to be overly negative or injurious. Unfortu-

TABLE 14.1
Cumulative Record: Personal Information

PERSONAL:

STUDENT'S NAME _____

               Last   First   Middle

ADDRESS _____

CITY _____ STATE _____ TELEPHONE _____

DATE OF BIRTH _____ PLACE OF BIRTH _____

SEX M or F _____ RACIAL or ETHNIC GROUP _____ LANGUAGE SPOKEN AT HOME _____

PARENT(S) NAME(S) _____ IS FATHER LIVING Y or N? MOTHER LIVING Y or N?

STUDENT IS LIVING WITH: BOTH PARENTS MOTHER or FATHER GUARDIAN

OTHER (SPECIFY) _____

RECORD OF ENROLLMENT

SCHOOL	ADDRESS	DATE ENTERED	DATE WITHDRAWN	GRADUATION DATE

TABLE 14.2
Cumulative Record: Academic Grades and Standardized Tests

ACADEMIC

SCHOOL ———————————— GRADE —————— YEAR ————

IS THE STUDENT IN A SPECIAL PROGRAM YES OR NO. IF YES, SPECIFY

———————————————————————————————

TOTAL DAYS ABSENT ———————————— PRESENT ——————

ACHIEVEMENT

Subject	Grade
ENGLISH	
MATH	
SCIENCE	
SOCIAL STUDIES	
PE	
MUSIC	
HEALTH	

TEACHER'S COMMENTS:

PROMOTED: YES or NO

TEACHER'S COMMENTS ————————————————————

———————————————————————————————

nately, this has resulted in teachers refraining from making comments on the cumulative record. Teachers should, however, continue to write comments, being careful to include only information that may be useful to other school professionals in helping the student succeed.

A teacher must remain objective when reviewing the information contained in the cumulative folder. Teachers must avoid using isolated, negative data and making judgments based solely on this information. It is also important that the information contained in the folder be current. Remember, the purpose of reviewing the cumulative record is to use the information to help a student achieve his or her maximum potential.

Used over a period of time, the cumulative record provides a student's teachers, counselors, administrators, and school psychologists with important information. Information contained in the cumulative record is confidential and may be shared with other agencies only if written permission is obtained from the student or from the parent if the student is under eighteen years of age.

Many school systems are using computers for data storage. A computer can store all the information needed by a school or by an entire school system. Some schools have included the information usually contained in the conventional cumulative folder on their computer. This practice permits school personnel to easily access information about a particular student. However, because of the confidential nature of student files, only authorized school personnel with a need to know should have access to them.

OBSERVATIONAL TECHNIQUES

During the first few weeks of school, a teacher discovers that one student is having difficulty sitting in his or her seat. The teacher has reviewed the cumulative record and is unable to determine the cause of the behavior. Additional data is needed. What can the teacher do?

The teacher may decide to use one of the observational techniques discussed in this section. Observational techniques are non-test methods used to gather information about students. We will limit our discussion to the commonly used observational techniques: observation, rating scale, sociogram, autobiography, anecdotal record, and the case study.

Observations

An observation is a record of a particular behavior. Using the previous example, the behavior we are interested in observing is how often and under what conditions the student leaves his or her seat. A description of the step-by-step process follows.

First, a teacher must determine what behavior will be observed. Before beginning the actual observation, the teacher is advised to consult with the school counselor. The counselor should be able to help the teacher define as well as determine the best means for recording the particular behavior. In our example, the teacher decided to record the number of times the student left his or her seat over a specified time period.

Second, a teacher should determine whether the observation will be recorded in narrative form or coded. In our example, the teacher decided to tally the number of times the student left his or her seat during a thirty minute time period using a code. The code for leaving his or her seat without permission was "S". When the behavior was observed, the teacher placed a tally mark next to "S." Tallying is not only quicker but also insures that other behaviors are not overlooked.

Third, a teacher should observe only one student during a given time period. If a teacher observes more than one student at a time, chances are that he or she will miss observing the behavior or record one student's behavior in place of another.

Fourth, a teacher should observe a student on at least three different days and during different time periods. This practice reduces sampling errors. For example, a teacher may find that a student left his or her seat more in the afternoon than in the morning. Upon further investigation, the teacher found that the student ate three candy bars for lunch. This fact was communicated to the student's parents during a conference. The student was restricted from eating candy during lunch time and the unwanted behavior was eliminated.

Fifth, a teacher needs to know how to record inferences. Although observations should record behavior as objectively and accurately as possible, certain circumstances may require inferences. An easy way to indicate an inference in the observation is to place it in parentheses. This procedure will enable the reader to determine that the statement is an inference, or an observer's opinion. As a rule, inferences should be used sparingly because the primary function of the observer is to record the behavior of a student.

Finally, a teacher should record the behavior when it occurs. Recording the behavior at a later time may result in an inaccurate assessment of the student.

Advantages of Observations

1. Observations focus on a particular behavior and student.
2. Observations record the behavior as it occurs.

Disadvantages of Observations

1. Observations are time consuming. A teacher may discover that recording behaviors is taking time away from teaching.
2. Observations may be biased. Some teachers may find it difficult to record a student's behavior objectively when the student manifests unwanted behavior.

The disadvantages may be eliminated by selecting someone other than the student's teacher to act as observer. This observer may be a counselor or another teacher. To avoid bias, the counselor or teacher should be someone who does not know the student.

Concluding Remarks

An observation is only as good as the observer. The observer needs to be trained in observational techniques. Teachers can request the counselor to conduct an in-service training program on observational techniques. During the in-service training sessions, the counselor may include instruction on how to determine what is to be observed, bias in observation, how to record observations, and how to record inferences.

Observations should provide the school personnel with information to help students. Used in conjunction with other data, observations may help the teacher and counselor determine ways to eliminate unwanted behavior. Before concluding this discussion on observation, an additional point must be made. An observer is not an invisible person. The presence of an observer may cause students to show their best behavior. In this case, the observer may need to sit in the back of the room or increase the number of observations.

RATING SCALES

A rating scale is usually more structured than the observational technique. While the observational technique typically requires an observer to either write descriptive behaviors or tally the frequency of selected behaviors, the rating scale requires a rater to read a statement and place a check mark or an X under the appropriate category. The categories may be "outstanding", "satisfactory", "unsatisfactory", or other similar categories.

Direct observations are completed when the observation is made. Rating scales may be completed during an observation or at a later time. Rating scales completed at a later time are usually referred to as remembered behavior. For example, a teacher, administrator, or counselor may be asked to complete a rating scale for a former student who has applied to a college or for a job.

Unlike direct observations, rating scales are easy to complete. The rater is required to read only a few statements and check "below average", "average", "good", "outstanding", or "did not observe".

Uses of Rating Scales

School personnel may use rating scales for end-of-the-year comments; as recommendations to schools, jobs, and exceptional and scholarship programs; to evaluate social and work habits; and to make referrals to outside agencies.

Report cards have utilized rating scales to indicate conduct, work habits, cooperation, and effort on the part of the student. A teacher may mark "+" or "–" next to the statements describing the behavior, or use letter designations such as "O," "S," or "U" for "Outstanding," "Satisfactory," or "Unsatisfactory" (see Table 14.3). The type of designation and form used is determined by school system policies.

Additionally, teachers and administrators frequently receive requests for recommendations from former students who have applied to colleges or technical schools, or for jobs. These recommendations usually consist of a rating scale with space provided at the bottom for additional comments. The statements or words on a college rating scale, for example, may include academic potential, emotional stability, cooperation, motivation, and an ability to work independently. After considering each of the statements or words, the rater may be directed to place a mark under one of the following categories: "low," "average," "high," or "not observed."

TABLE 14.3
Example of One Part of a Report Card

IN MARKING, USE THE FOLLOWING DIRECTIONS:

O = OUTSTANDING   S = SATISFACTORY   U = UNSATISFACTORY

	1st Quarter	2nd Quarter	3rd Quarter	4th Quarter
1. Completes Assignments				
2. Class Participation				
3. Effort				
4. Work Habits				
5. Works Well With Others				
6. Cooperation				
7. Citizenship				
8. Conduct				

Kinds of Rating Scales

Kerlinger (1986) listed five kinds of rating scales: numerical, graphic, checklist, category, and forced-choice.

Numerical Rating Scales. These rating scales include statements that describe various traits or personal attributes such as "works well with others," "completes work," and "shows initiative." A rater would be required to place a number next to each statement. These numbers would correspond to selected words or comments. For example, 1 = Always, 2 = Sometimes, and 3 = Never.

Numerical rating scales may be self-rated or they may be completed by someone else. Self-rating scales provide a teacher or counselor with information about a student as recorded by the student. It indicates how a student views himself or herself. The rating scale that is completed by another person indicates how this person views the student.

Graphic Rating Scales. These rating scales may list several traits on a continuum and they require a rater to place a check or "X" at a point along the continuum that best describes the student. For example:

——————————   ——————————   ———————————————————   ——————————————
Very Cooperative   Cooperative   Sometimes Cooperative   Never Cooperative

Checklists. Checklists (Table 14.4) may be used by school personnel as screening devices. They may be used prior to placement in an exceptional pro-

TABLE 14.4
Example of a Check List

STUDENT _____ GRADE _____ DATE _____

FOR EACH STATEMENT, PLACE A CHECK OR "X" UNDER THE CATEGORY WHICH BEST DESCRIBES THE STUDENT.

	OUTSTANDING	AVERAGE	BELOW AVERAGE	NOT OBSERVED
1. Completes Assignments on Time				
2. Use of Time				
3. Shows Initiative				
4. Resourceful				
5. Follows Directions				
6. Works Well With Others				
7. Works to Full Capacity				
8. Seeks Additional Tasks				
9. Shows Effort				
10. Is Responsible				

ADDITIONAL COMMENTS: _____

_____

_____

_____
TEACHER'S SIGNATURE

gram, such as for the gifted and talented, the emotionally handicapped, the specific learning disabled, or the mentally handicapped. Checklists may be completed by the student's classroom teacher, counselor, or administrator.

Category Rating Scales.　A category rating scale lists a number of statements related to a particular category followed by choices. The rater is required to place a check or "X" next to the choice that applies. For example, one might find the following rating scale under the category sociable:

How sociable is the student? (Check one.)

_____Very sociable
_____Sociable
_____Sometimes sociable
_____Seldom sociable
_____Unsociable

Forced Choice Rating Scales.　These scales enable the rater to check one or more choices under a particular trait or category. For example:

Check all the words that best describe the student:
_____Reliable
_____Likeable
_____Resourceful
_____Alert
_____Cooperative
_____Creative
_____Intelligent
_____Sociable

Constructing a Rating Scale

Almost any teacher, counselor, or administrator can construct a rating scale with practice. In constructing a rating scale, one must know and define the purpose(s) and objective(s) of the scale. For example, will the rating scale be used as a screening or an evaluative device? Second, the individual must decide which kind or type of rating scale to construct. For example, will it be a numerical, graphic, checklist, category, or forced-choice type?

Many school systems have constructed their own rating scales suitable for most situations. These rating scales are available to school personnel. If a teacher needs a rating scale that is not available locally, one may be purchased commercially. Teachers and other school personnel may locate a suitable rating scale by referring to the latest edition of the *Mental Measurements Yearbook* or to test publishers' catalogues. A selected list of published rating scales are included in Table 14.5.

Strengths of the Rating Scale

1. A rating scale is easy to construct. Any teacher, counselor, or administrator can construct a rating scale with some practice.
2. A rating scale is easy to complete. Usually, a rater is simply required to place a check or "X" in a box or space following the statement or word.
3. A rating scale may be adapted to different situations. Rating scales may be used by the classroom teacher as an evaluative, screening, or self-rating device.

Weaknesses of the Rating Scale

1. A rating scale may be biased. The teacher's impressions of a student may influence the ratings. For example, a teacher who likes a particular student may rate the student more highly than he or she rates a student he or she dislikes.
2. Some raters are too easy or too strict in rating students. The easy rater may check all statements high, while another may check all statements low.
3. Some raters may consistently rate students in the middle of the scale. This often occurs when the rater does not understand the terminology used for a trait or term. Therefore, raters must seek understanding of the terminology before rating any student.
4. Rating scales are subjective. Two or more raters may rate the same individual differently. Therefore, raters may need training in completing rating scales prior to rating an individual.

Concluding Remarks

A rating scale should never be used alone. To obtain a complete picture of a student, the teacher should collect as much information as possible about a student using various instruments and sources. Rating scales alone give only a partial picture of a student as perceived by raters.

TABLE 14.5
Commercially Prepared Rating Scales

Names of Scale	Grade	Author(s)	Publisher
Academic Advising Inventory	Undergraduate Students	Roger Winston Janet Sander	Student Development Association
College Student Experiences Questionnaire	College Students	Robert Pace	Center for the Study of Evaluation
The Instructional Environment Scale	Elementary Students	James E. Ysseldyke	PRO-ED
School Environment Preference Survey	Grades 4–12	Leonard V. Gordon	EDITS
School Subjects Attitude Scales	Grades 5–12	V. R. Nyberg S. C. T. Clarke	Learning Resources Distribution Center
Our Class and Its Works	Grades 3–12	Maurice Eash Hersholt C. Waxman	Maurice Eash
Statements About Schools Inventory	High School	Gerald R. Smith Thomas B. Gregory Richard Pugh	Richard Pugh
Teacher Role Survey	Elementary, Secondary, Technical	Darrell E. Anderson Wayne R. Maes	Wayne R. Maes
Thinking About My School	Grades 4–6	Joanne Whitmore	United Educational Services

Note. Table based on information in *The Tenth Mental Measurements Yearbook* (1989) (p. 946) by Conoley, J. C., & Kramer, J. J. (Eds.). Lincoln, NE: The Buros Institute of Mental Measurements.

SOCIOMETRIC TECHNIQUES

In order to determine the internal social structure in a class, a teacher may construct a sociogram. A sociogram is simple to construct and may provide teachers with valuable information about the relationships among the students. For example, a sociogram would be helpful to teachers who want to determine friendship patterns and class leaders when forming groups. A sociogram may be used for any grade level. Sociograms are commonly referred to as nominating techniques, because students are usually asked to choose people with whom they prefer to work. Table 14.6 contains sociometric terms, definitions, representative symbols.

Procedures and Methods in Constructing Sociograms

In constructing a sociogram, a teacher may say, "We are going to form groups to work on a project for our unit on fractions. On a sheet of paper, I would like you to write your name in the upper right-hand corner and list three people with whom you want to work on this project."

The teacher collects the papers and begins to construct the sociogram. Choices are indicated by an arrow pointing to each choice. An arrow pointing in both directions indicates a mutual choice. Squares may be used for boys and circles for girls. Figure 14.1 illustrates a sociogram constructed from choices made by students in an elementary school class. The students' choices were as follows:

Student	Choices
Timothy	Michael, Jeff, Kenneth
Kenneth	Michael, Timothy, Joan
Joan	Michael, Karl, Timothy
Michael	Kenneth, Lynn, Thomas
Lynn	Michael, Faye, Timothy
Thomas	Michael, Joan, Lynn
Jeff	Anne, Joseph, Ginger
Anne	Jeff, Joseph, Susan
Joseph	Anne, Ginger, Jeff
Patricia	Anne, Joseph, Susan
Karl	Ginger, Susan, Fred
Ginger	Susan, Anne, Faye
Susan	Ginger, Fred, Anne
Fred	Ginger, Susan, Karl
Anne B.	Ginger, Susan, Faye
Faye	Ginger, Anne, Fred

TABLE 14.6
Sociometric Terms, Definitions, and Representations

Term	Definition	Representation
Star	A student who receives a large number of choices, or a number larger than chance	
Mutual Choice	Students who choose each other	
Isolate	A student who receives no positive choices (e.g., student C)	
Rejectee	A student who is actively rejected by group members (if rejection data are gathered)	
Neglectee	A student who receives very few positive choices (e.g., student C)	
Sociometric Clique	A number of individuals who make very few choices outside the group	
Sociometric Cleavage	A lack of sociometric choices between two or more subgroups (e.g., boys and girls)	

Results

Michael, Susan, and Ginger would be the "stars" of the class because they received the largest number of choices. They are popular students and may prove to be good group leaders.

A number of "mutual" choices were made. For example, Timothy and Kenneth, Kenneth and Michael, Michael and Thomas, Michael and Lynn, Jeff and

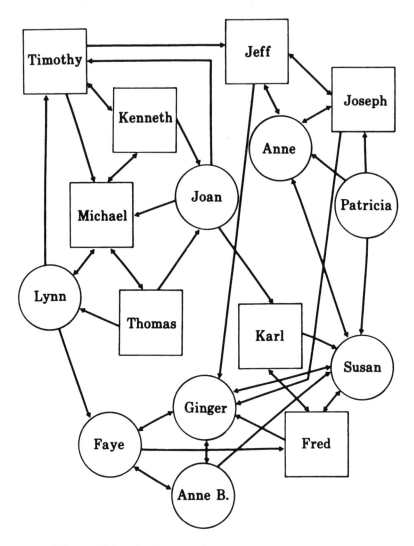

Figure 14.1. Sociogram of an Elementary School Class.

Joseph, Jeff and Anne, Anne and Joseph, Anne and Susan, Karl and Fred, Susan and Fred, Ginger and Susan, Anne B. and Ginger, Anne B. and Faye, and Ginger and Faye selected each other. These students often sit at the same table at lunch and socialize with each other after school.

Patricia is the "isolate"; she did not receive any choices. She was a transfer student and was in the class for only a few days prior to constructing the sociogram.

Except for Patricia, most of the students have known each other for several years. The students get along well together and appear to enjoy one another's company. The teacher had the opportunity to form a number of groups, using various combinations, with favorable results. In addition, Patricia, shortly thereafter, became an active group member.

Uses

Using sociometric techniques, teachers may identify class leaders, followers, and isolates. Teachers who desire to develop better classroom relationships will find the sociogram to be a valuable measurement tool.

While many commercially prepared scales of social acceptance and relationships exist, the teacher-made instrument is favored. The sociogram is easy to construct, use, and interpret. It provides the teacher with a pictorial representation of classroom relationships.

Sociograms may also be used by teachers and counselors to improve relationships and to identify students needing additional help in making friends and developing positive relationships. A sociogram helps a teacher identify which students have been accepted, rejected, or isolated. However, it does not provide information about the reasons students were selected. To obtain this information, teachers may need to explore the situation further by using direct observation.

Teachers should use the results derived from a sociogram for the purpose intended. For example, if the purpose was to form groups to study fractions, then the information obtained from the sociogram should be used for that purpose.

AUTOBIOGRAPHIES

The autobiography may be used to obtain additional information about students. Depending upon the structure and design of the autobiography, a teacher may gather information about students' interests, goals, feelings about self, and other general and specific concerns. An autobiography may be used in most class settings, but it is most adaptable in English or social studies classes.

An autobiography may reveal information about students that may enable a teacher to help students understand themselves better. For example, an autobiography may describe a student's family structure in such a way that a teacher may be able to determine whether the student has a happy or unhappy home life. In addition, a student may be helped with making career decisions by writing an autobiography that focuses on his or her interests, hobbies, and vocational aspirations.

Sometimes an autobiography may indicate that an individual is having personal problems coping with self or family. A teacher may wish to discuss these concerns with the student and, with the permission of the student, refer him or her to the counselor for additional help and assistance.

Types of Autobiographies

There are two basic types of autobiographies. The first type is the unstructured autobiography. The student is simply asked to write his or her autobiography. Because it is unstructured, the student is free to choose the areas of his or her life to include and exclude.

In an unstructured autobiography, students may include when and where they were born, what they like to do, and information about their family. Because the unstructured autobiography allows students to focus on any area of interest, they may avoid writing about sensitive areas. To help eliminate this tendency, a teacher may choose to assign a structured autobiography.

A structured autobiography usually is written according to guidelines prepared by a teacher. These guidelines may be in the form of open-ended questions or a list of subtopics. For example, a teacher may include the following subtopics: my family, my goals, my friends and what they mean to me. Within these subtopics, a teacher may ask the students to respond to structured subareas such as the following: "Things I like to do with my family," "Reasons I want to enter this profession," and "What my friends and I do for fun." In addition, a teacher may wish to limit the length and breadth of the autobiography. For example, a student may be assigned a 500-word essay on one of the following topics: "My family and friends," "My best vacation," "What I want to be when I grow up," and "My Biggest Problem."

Lastly, the autobiography can provide a teacher and counselor with information that may be used to help students with their problems or with adjustment to their environment. Students who reveal problem areas in their autobiography may be referred to the school counselor.

ANECDOTAL RECORDS

The anecdotal record is an observational technique commonly used by teachers to collect information about their students. Collected over time, the anecdotal record may provide useful information about students. An anecdotal record is especially useful with students who exhibit behavioral problems.

An anecdotal record (Table 14.7) is easy to make and use. Comments made by the recorder may be placed on an index card or on a sheet of paper. It is suggested that index cards be used for anecdotal records because they are easier to handle and file.

An anecdotal record should include the student's name, class or teacher's name, and date, and it should provide ample space for comments. Then all a teacher needs to do is write a comment and date it. A comment may be a word, a sentence, or any number of words and sentences deemed necessary by a teacher.

TABLE 14.7
Example of an Anecdotal Record

STUDENT'S NAME _____ CLASS _____

DATE	COMMENT

TEACHER'S SIGNATURE

Mehrens and Lehmann (1991) list four characteristics of good anecdotal records:

1. They should contain a factual description of what happened, when it happened, and under what circumstances the behavior occurred.
2. The interpretation and recommended action should be noted separately from the description.
3. Each anecdotal record should contain a record of a single incident.
4. The incident recorded should be one that is considered to be significant to the pupil's growth and development."(p. 193–194)

An anecdotal record is an objective record of student behavior(s). If an observed behavior is atypical or unusual for a student, then it should be noted by the recorder. The recorder may include interpretative comments about atypical or unusual behaviors on the anecdotal record by enclosing them in parentheses. Separating the comments may provide professionals with vital information to help a student resolve a problem area.

CRITICAL INCIDENT TECHNIQUE

Developed by Flanagan (1950), the critical incident technique is a special type of anecdotal record. The critical incident describes a situation in narrative form. We asked a graduate class in counseling to write a critical incident. The class was instructed to think of a significant past event that involved them in a helping role. They were asked to describe the situation, what they did in the situation, how they felt about the situation, and how they feel about the situation now. The anonymous responses were collected. An example of a critical incident obtained from the graduate class follows:

> One day during the Spring Semester, one of the students came to my office very upset about a problem she was having at home. She was in tears and wanted to talk to me. She told me that her father and mother were getting a divorce, and she was afraid about what was going to happen to her and her sister.
>
> I talked to her and told her that getting a divorce was not the end of the world and that because both parents had decided that this was the best thing for all concerned, then perhaps it was for her welfare as well. I also told her that it did not mean that her parents loved her any less and she must not blame herself.
>
> I felt very concerned and very sorry for this child. I recommended professional help for her and her family.

> I feel at this time that I did the proper thing. The situation was worked out completely with the family and all is well and happy. The student has adjusted nicely.

Unlike the anecdotal record, the critical incident technique is a complete description of a situation from the writer's perspective. With training and practice, the critical incident technique may provide a teacher or counselor with useful information about a student. Although both techniques are used by school personnel, schools continue to use the anecdotal record more often.

THE CASE STUDY

Shertzer and Stone (1981) defined the case study as "the collection and report of all available evidence social, psychological, environmental, and vocational that explains the individual, including an analysis of the interrelationships among the various data" (p. 294).

From the definition, one may conclude that the case study is comprehensive and time consuming. Many sources are used to gather the information contained in the case study. Some of the major sources used are the student's cumulative folder, rating scales, checklists, anecdotal records, observations, test results, health records, sociometric methods, parents, and teachers.

A case study is initiated when a teacher, counselor, administrator, or parent believes that a student may need to be placed in an exceptional class, is not motivated, or is constantly fighting with other students. In such instances the student may be referred to the counselor. A teacher may indicate the reasons for the referral either in writing or orally to the counselor. If the counselor believes that the student needs additional help, he or she may refer the student to the school psychologist.

The counselor working with the school psychologist begins the case study by collecting data. Before a student meets with the school psychologist, a counselor may send a Permission to Test Form and a Student History Form home to the parents. The parents are requested to sign the forms as soon as possible. Any questions or concerns that a parent may have are referred to the school counselor.

As soon as permission and history forms are returned, a counselor may continue to collect additional information from the student's teachers. In addition, test and non-test techniques may be used to gather information about the student.

Prior to writing the case study, a psychological folder is prepared. This folder contains spaces reserved for standardized test scores; vision, hearing, and speech tests results; interventions attempted (e.g., moving seat or special tutoring); anecdotals; information gathered from parent conferences; and reasons for the referral. In addition, the folder may contain work samples, observations, rating scales, and checklists.

When all the information is gathered, the psychological folder is sent to the school psychologist. The school psychologist determines whether additional data are needed. If additional information is needed, the school psychologist meets with the student and may administer a standardized intelligence test such as the Stanford Binet or Wechsler Intelligence Scale for Children (WISC) and/or projective tests such as the Bender Gestalt or the Thematic Apperception Test (TAT). After all data are gathered, the school psychologist completes the case study.

The purpose for writing a case study is to organize, summarize, and analyze this enormous amount of data. Once the case study is completed, the school psychologist can determine whether placement in a special education class or remedial work is needed. When making placement decisions, the welfare of the student must be given top priority. An example of a case study is provided in Table 14.8.

Case Conference or Staffing

Once the case study is written, a case conference or staffing is called to determine the best course of action to take.

The school counselor is often responsible for scheduling the case conference. A form is sent to the student's parents informing them of the date, time, and place, and identifying who will be attending the staffing. Parents are requested to sign the form and indicate whether or not they will be able to attend the conference. If the date selected is not convenient, then the parent is requested to indicate a convenient date. Next, the counselor informs the school psychologist, principal, and teachers of the date, time, and place of the conference.

During the case conference, all relevant data are explained by the school psychologist to all in attendance. Any questions and concerns are answered and discussed.

After the results of the case study are explained, the school psychologist, together with the other participants, plan a course of action. This action may

TABLE 14.8
Illustration of a Case Study

Report No. P-3853   Name of Student: John Doe
Date: 4/7/92   Birthdate: 3/6/85
Psychologist: J. D. Smith   Age: 7-1   Sex: Male   Grade: 2
                                     Address: 739 Any Street
                                                New York, NY
                                     Phone: 387-4127
                                     Parent: James & Dora Doe

Submitted to Eligibility and Placement Committee

REASON FOR REPORT:
John was referred due to restless behavior. He cannot complete his work, constantly asks to go to the restroom, and states that he does not like school.

BACKGROUND INFORMATION:
John is a seven-year, one-month-old boy, who resides with his father and mother. The parents reported the following information: John display's lack of self-esteem, concentration, and appears to dislike school. The problem manifested itself when John could not relate to his peers in kindergarten. Mr. & Mrs. Doe discipline John with reprimands and spanking. These measures do not appear to work.

PSYCHOLOGICAL DATA:
ASSESSMENT: The following tests were administered:

Name of Test	Date
Bender Gestalt	3/15/92
Weschler Intelligence Scale for Children	3/15/92
Detroit Tests of Learning Aptitude	3/16/92
Wepman Auditory Discrimination Tests	3/16/92
Thematic Apperception Test	3/16/92
Wide Range Achievement Test	3/17/92
Sentence Completion	3/17/92

TEST RESULTS:
Weschsler Intelligence Scale for Children-Revised
>   Verbal I.Q.   107
>   Performance I.Q.   97
>   Full Scale I.Q.   103
Wide Range Achievement Test

	Grade Equivalent	Standard Score	Percentile
Reading Recognition	2.8	100	50
Spelling	1.4	84	15
Arithmetic	1.7	98	44

(*Continued on next page*)

TABLE 14.8 (*Continued*)
Illustration of a Case Study

Test	Age	Interpretation
Bender Gestalt	4–8	Below 70%
· Detroit		
Test 4 (Association)	6–3	
Test 6 (Memory)	3–6	Below 70%
Test 9 (Memory)	7–0	
Test 13 (Memory)	5–0	Below 70%
Test 16 (Memory)	11–0	
Wepman (Auditory)	6–9	

Interpretation of Results
Intellectual Test Results
John's level of intellectual potential falls within the normal range. Sub-Test scores revealed little scatter. However, there was significant strength in comprehension with a score of 15 to an apparent weakness on Object Assembly.

Academic Test Results
John scored below the 20th percentile on spelling. He does not appear to have mastered the basic sound/symbol relationships for spelling on his grade level. Reading and arithmetic were at grade level.

Auditory and Visual Discrimination
On the visual discrimination (Bender Gestalt), John is performing below the 70th percentile. His ability to visually discriminate and motorically reproduce shapes and forms appears poorly developed for his age.

Social/Emotional Development
Projectives (TAT) suggest that John is a sad child who views his environment as threatening. He seems to see authority figures as punitive and thus seeks recognition and approval from anyone who will give him the attention he seems to desperately need. His struggle to create compatible interpersonal relationships may result in emotional tendencies.

Summary
This report suggests that John is functioning in the normal range of intelligence, but is evidencing significant academic deficits. His performance indicates that John is a sad child who seeks nurturance, recognition, and acceptance.

John is a learning disabled child and his case is referred to the Eligibility and Placement Committee for an appropriate educational program.

Note. Format based on outline in *Psychological Report Writing* (1979), pp. 127–128, by J. Hollis and P. Dunn. Muncie, IN: Accelerated Development. Copyright 1979 by Accelerated Development.

include placing the student in a special education class, referring the student to an outside agency, or keeping the student in his or her present class. Additional suggestions for helping the student are also discussed at this time.

At the conclusion of the case conference, all members present sign a form indicating whether they agree to the placement or findings. If additional follow-up is needed, it is discussed at this time. For example, a child who is placed in a special education class must have his or her records reviewed every year and must be reevaluated every three years. A student who is to remain in his or her class may need to meet with the school psychologist, counselor, and/or teacher to determine whether he or she has improved academically. Chapter 7 includes a more detailed discussion of conference procedures associated with "special students."

SUMMARY

Used in conjunction with tests, non-test techniques provide teachers with additional information about a student. They may be used to assist students with personal, social, or academic problems and concerns, and thus help them to become more fully functioning members of society.

REFERENCES

Conoley, J. C., & Kramer, J. J. (Eds.). (1989). *The tenth mental measurements yearbook.* Lincoln, NE: The Buros Institute of Mental Measurement.

Family Educational Rights and Privacy Act, PL 93-380. (1974, Aug. 21).

Flanagan, J. C. (1950). The critical incident technique. *Psychological Bulletin, 51,* 327–357.

Hollis, J. W., & Donn, P. A. (1979). *Psychological report writing: Theory and practice.* Muncie, IN: Accelerated Development.

Kerlinger, F. N. (1986). *Foundations of behavioral research* (3rd. ed.). New York: Holt, Rinehart & Winston.

Mehrens, W. A., & Lehmann, I. J. (1991). *Measurement and evaluation in education and psychology* (4th ed.). New York: Holt, Rinehart & Winston.

Shertzer, B., & Linden, J. D. (1979). *Fundamentals of individual appraisal.* Boston: Houghton Mifflin.

Shertzer, B., & Stone, S. C. (1981). *Fundamentals of guidance* (4th ed.). Boston: Houghton Mifflin.

INDEX

Italic letters after numbers denote tables (*t*), figures (*f*), and footnotes (*n*).

ABOUT THE AUTHORS

Don C. Locke is Director of the North Carolina State University doctoral program in Adult and Community College Education at the Asheville Graduate Center. Immediately prior to assuming his present position in July 1993, he was Professor and Head of the Department of Counselor Education at North Carolina State University in Raleigh. He began his career as a high school so-cial studies teacher in Fort Wayne, Indiana where he also worked as a high school counselor for two years. He earned his doctorate at Ball State University in 1974. He has been active in state, regional and national counseling organiza-tions. Prior professional service includes President of the North Carolina Coun-seling Assocaition, Chair of the Southern Region Branch of American Counsel-ing Association, President of the Southern Association of Counselor Educators and Supervisors, and a member of the ACA Governing Council. He is 1994–95

Chair of the Counseling and Human Development Foundation, Associate Editor of *Mental Health Counselors Journal*, and Parliamentarian for the American School Counselor Association. He is the author or co-author of more than 60 publications, with a current focus on multicultural issues. His 1992 book, *Increasing Multicultural Understanding*, is in its sixth printing.

Joseph C. Ciechalski, counselor educator, writes with a feel for the psychological componenents of effective teaching.

At present he is an Associate Professor in the Department of Counselor and Adult Education at East Carolina University in Greenville, North Carolina. Dr. Ciechalski earned an Ed.D. in Counselor Education at North Carolina State University. He co-edited the book, *Elementary School Counseling in a Changing World*, published by the American Counseling Association. He has written numerous articles and reviews. He currently is test review editor for the *Measurement and Evaluation in Counseling and Development* journal and a member of the National Career Development Media Committee. He formerly was editor of the Assocaition for Assessment in Counseling newsletter (*NEWSNOTES*) and was an editorial board member of the *Elementary School Guidance and Counseling* journal.

Dr. Ciechalski has had extensive public school counseling and teacher experience. His licensures include teacher and professional counselor in North Carolina. He holds memberships in several professional organizations including the American Counseling Assocaition, American School Counselor Association, American Educational Research Association, and the American Psychological Association.